Zinkov Memorial Book (Zinkiv, Ukraine)

Translation of
Pinkas Zinkov: Gedenkbukh

Original Book edited by: Shmuel Aizenshtadt

Published in Tel Aviv and New York, 1966

Published by JewishGen

An Affiliate of the Museum of Jewish Heritage—A Living Memorial to the Holocaust
New York

Zinkov Memorial Book
(Zinkiv, Ukraine)

Translation of *Pinkas Zinkov: Gedenkbukh*

First Printing: April 2021, Iyyar 5781
Second Printing: April 2022, Nissan 5782
Third Printing: August 2023, Elul 5783

Editor of Original Yizkor Book: Shmuel Aizenshtadt
Project Coordinators: Susan and Shawn Dilles
Layout and Name Indexing: Jonathan Wind
Cover Design: Rachel Kolokoff-Hopper

Published by JewishGen, Inc.
An Affiliate of the Museum of Jewish Heritage
A Living Memorial to the Holocaust
36 Battery Place, New York, NY 10280

JewishGen, Inc. is not responsible for inaccuracies or omissions in the original work and makes no representations regarding the accuracy of this translation. Digital images of the original book's contents can be seen online at the New York Public Library website.

The mission of the JewishGen organization is to produce a translation of the original work, and we cannot verify the accuracy of statements or alter facts cited.

Printed in the United States of America by Lightning Source, Inc.

Library of Congress Control Number (LCCN): 202193651

ISBN: 978-1-954176-11-9 (hard cover: 276 pages, alk. paper)

Cover Credits

Front Cover Illustration: *The synagogue*, drawn by Nochem Yoshpeh, page 49

Front Cover Background Photo and Texture: Rachel Kolokoff Hopper

Illustration on Spine: Original cover, page 2

Back Cover Photo: *Shapse Zalas's father, his sister Itta and her husband, Leyzer Palatnik, with their two daughters, who later graduated. All were murdered*, page 180.
Back Cover Background Map: *Hand–drawn map of Zinkov and its immediate surroundings*, page 16 (26)

JewishGen and the Yizkor Books in Print Project

This book has been published by the **Yizkor Books in Print Project**, as part of the **Yizkor Book Project** of JewishGen, Inc.

JewishGen, Inc. is a non-profit organization founded in 1987 as a resource for Jewish genealogy. Its website [www.jewishgen.org] serves as an international clearinghouse and resource center to assist individuals who are researching the history of their Jewish families and the places where they lived. JewishGen provides databases, facilitates discussion groups, and coordinates projects relating to Jewish genealogy and the history of the Jewish people. In 2003, JewishGen became an affiliate of the **Museum of Jewish Heritage — A Living Memorial to the Holocaust** in New York.

The **JewishGen Yizkor Book Project** was organized to make more widely known the existence of Yizkor (Memorial) Books written by survivors and former residents of various Jewish communities throughout the world. Later, volunteers connected to the different destroyed communities began cooperating to have these books translated from the original language — usually Hebrew or Yiddish — into English, thus enabling a wider audience to have access to the valuable information contained within them. As each chapter of these books was translated, it was posted on the JewishGen website and made available to the general public.

The **Yizkor Books in Print Project** began in 2011 as an initiative to print and publish Yizkor Books that had been fully translated, so that hard copies would be available for purchase by the descendants of these communities and also by scholars, universities, synagogues, libraries, and museums.

These Yizkor books have been produced almost entirely through the volunteer effort of researchers from around the world, assisted by donations from private individuals. The books are printed and sold at near cost, so as to make them as affordable as possible. Our goal is to make this important genre of Jewish literature and history available in English in book form, so that people can have the personal histories of their ancestral towns on their bookshelves for themselves and for their children and grandchildren.

A list of all published translated Yizkor Books in the project with prices and ordering information can be found at:
http://www.jewishgen.org/Yizkor/ybip.html

Lance Ackerfeld, Yizkor Book Project Manager
Joel Alpert, Yizkor-Book-in-Print Project Coordinator
Susan Rosin, Yizkor-Book-in-Print Project Associate Coordinator

JewishGen
Yizkor Book Project

This book is presented by the
Yizkor-Books-In-Print Project
Project Coordinator: Joel Alpert

Part of the Yizkor Books Project of JewishGen. Inc.
Project Manager: Lance Ackerfeld

These books have been produced solely through efforts of volunteers
from around the world. The books are printed using the Print-on-Demand technology and sold at
near cost, to make them as affordable as possible.

Our goal is to make this intimate history of the destroyed Jewish shtetls
of Eastern Europe available in book form in English, so that people can
experience the near-personal histories of their ancestral town on their
bookshelves and those of their children and grandchildren.

All donations to the Yizkor Books Project, which translated the books,
are sincerely appreciated.

Please send donations to:

Yizkor Book Project
JewishGen, Inc.
36 Battery Place
New York, NY, 10280

JewishGen, Inc. is an affiliate of the
Museum of Jewish Heritage
A Living Memorial to the Holocaust

Project Coordinator Introduction

I first heard of the place called Zinkov over 50 years ago from my grandmother Celia nee Greenberg z"l. As she showed me her cherished Yizkor book of the town that she described her early years in vivid detail, recalling the active town and a variety of people. She often told of the time when her father left for America to seek a better life for his family, and just a short while later when her mother and her youngest sister succumbed to illness. This remarkable child of 9 and her 4 surviving younger siblings endured immense hardships in Zinkov before making the perilous overland trip with some older cousins to reach a port and eventually be reunited with their father in America. I was – and remain – in awe of this woman who with remarkable strength and perseverance started a new life and raised what has become a thriving family. During one the last visits, Grandma Celia allowed my husband and me to take notes on her 'family story', and at the end of our 'interview' she entrusted us with her beloved copy of the Zinkov Yizkor Book. The book has a short introduction in English, but the bulk of it is written in Yiddish and Hebrew – languages that we are far from fluent in.

The Yizkor Book captures the history of Zinkov in good times and bad, of vibrant life in the town, and of the efforts by some to make aliyah to Israel or to depart for the west. Describing the living town of Zinkov – however briefly – brings into focus what was lost during the nightmare years when the Jews in Zinkov were systematically murdered, bringing over 300 years of history to an end. The Zinkov Committee understood that it is imperative for personal accounts of this dark period be documented, remembered and recounted, and this is why the book was written - and why we undertook to translate it.

It has been a privilege to help unlock the story of Zinkov for new generations of readers. The process brought us into contact with distant relatives and other descendants of Zinkov residents who all have remarkable stories. One relayed that her grandmother perished in a fire in the women's section of the Zinkov Synagogue during a high holiday service. This account was identical to one that we heard from Celia – who lost a relative in the same fire. The two women perished within feet of each other during that tragedy over 100 years ago, half way around the world.

Zinkov was a small town - and remains so even today. Few if any Jews live in the town today. The surviving landsmen of Zinkov and their descendants have built lives in Israel, America, France, the Latin America and elsewhere. This translation is for them, their children and their children's children.

Susan Dilles
Vienna, Virginia, U.S.A.

Acknowledgments

This project was made possible by JewishGen, an organization dedicated to (among other aims) translating more than 800 Yizkor Books from their native languages into English, and making the translations widely available over the internet and through print on demand editions like this one. We thank Mr. Avraham Groll for his strategic vision and oversight of the organization. Mr. Binny Lewis provided us with valuable assistance in the first stage of the project, and Mr. Lance Ackerfield provided expert support and advice for the core effort that resulted in the online version of the text. We also want to thank Mr. Joel Alpert, who oversees the group of volunteers that produce the Yizkor Book print-on-demand editions, including this one. Joel provided important guidance early in the project that saved significant effort later.

The network of JewishGen volunteers helped us to find expert translators fluent in Yiddish, Hebrew, and English. We owe the translation itself mainly to Yael Chaver, and extraordinarily learned and talented translator, who did much of the work during the COVID pandemic. Yael not only translated the words from Yiddish and Hebrew but also the Ukrainian and Russian words transliterated into those languages. Yael 'rescued' the meaning of many words and idiomatic phrases, which may otherwise have been lost. For example, the words 'verst' and 'parsings' are archaic measures of distance. Yael's footnotes provide context for current-day readers on historic events, organizations, personalities and Jewish religious terms for readers not familiar with them. I also thank Yocheved Klausner for translating the Table of Contents, and to Aryeh Sklar for translating a short section of the book.

The translation was funded by the many donors who contributed to the JewishGen Yizkor Book Project:
(https://www.jewishgen.org/yizkor/Translations/).

Donors may contribute to the general Yizkor Book fund or directly toward specific translation projects. We are extremely grateful to the donors who helped make the Zinkov translation possible!

Finally, we would like to extend our heartfelt appreciation to all of the volunteers that work behind the scenes at JewishGen to help preserve Jewish family history and heritage for future generations.

Susan Dilles
Vienna, Virginia, U.S.A.

Notes to the Reader:

We apologize ahead of time for the poor quality of images in the book. Often these images had been scanned from the original Yizkor books which were of poor quality to begin with, being copies of old photographs. Each transfer results in loss of quality. We have done the best we could, given the original material and the resources and technology at hand. Even though images often appear of higher quality on computer screens, that does not transfer to high quality images in print. A reader can view the original scans on the web sites listed below.

Within the text the reader will note "{34}" standing ahead of a paragraph. This indicates that the material translated below was on page 34 of the original book. However, when a paragraph was split between two pages in the original book, the marker is placed in this book after the end of the paragraph for ease of reading.

Also please note that all references within the text of the book to page numbers, refer to the page numbers of the original Yizkor Book.

The original book can be seen online at the New York Public Library site:

https://digitalcollections.nypl.org/search/index?utf8=%E2%9C%93&keywords=zinkov

or at the Yiddish Book Center web site:

https://www.yiddishbookcenter.org/search/collection/%22NYPL-Yid-dish%2520Book%2520Center%2520Yizkor%2520Book%2520Collection%22?search_api_views_fulltext=zinkov&Submit+search=&restrict=

In order to obtain a list of all Shoah victims from Zinkov, the reader should access the Yad Vashem web site listed below; one can also search for specific family names using family name option. These lists are continually updated by Yad Vashem, so it is worthwhile to periodically search these lists.

There is much valuable information available on this web site, including the Pages of Testimony, etc.
http://yvng.yadvashem.org

A list of this book and all books available in the Yizkor-Book-In-Print Project along with prices is available at:
http://www.jewishgen.org/Yizkor/ybip.html

Geopolitical Information:

Zinkov (Zinkiv), Ukraine is located at 49°05' N, 27°04' E and 180 miles WSW of Kyyiv

	Town	District	Province	Country
Before WWI (c. 1900):	Zinkov	Letichev	Podolia	Russian Empire
Between the wars (c. 1930):	Zinkov	Kamenets-Podolski	Ukraine SSR	Soviet Union
After WWII (c. 1950):	Zin'kov			Soviet Union
Today (c. 2000):	Zin'kiv			Ukraine

Alternate names for the town:
Zin'kiv [Ukr], Zin'kov [Rus], Zinkov [Yid], Zińków [Pol], Zinkev

Nearby Jewish Communities:

- Solobkovtsy 7 miles W
- Vinkivtsi 8 miles ESE
- Sharovka 10 miles NNW
- Yarmolyntsi 13 miles NW
- Kosohirka 14 miles W
- Myn'kivtsi 16 miles S
- Dunayivtsi 17 miles SW
- Nova Ushytsya 20 miles SSE
- Zamikhiv 20 miles SE
- Yaltushkiv 21 miles ESE
- Derazhnya 21 miles NE
- Kupyn 22 miles W
- Velikiy Zhvanchik 22 miles S
- Hvardis'ke 23 miles NW
- Balin 23 miles SW
-
- Sokilets 23 miles S
- Khmelnytskyy 23 miles N
- Horodok 23 miles WNW
- Kudryntsi 25 miles NW
- Smotrych 25 miles WSW
- Makiv 25 miles SW
- Staryi Zakrevskiy Maydan 27 miles ENE
- Shatava 27 miles SW
- Bar 27 miles E
- Snitivka 27 miles NE
- Kuz'myn 27 miles WNW
- Volkovintsy 28 miles ENE
- Medzhybizh 29 miles NNE
- Verbovets 29 miles SE
- Verkhivka 30 miles ESE
- Vil'khovets' 30 miles SSE

Jewish Population: 3,719 (in 1897), 2,248 (in 1939)

MAP OF UKRAINE IN 2014

Map of Ukraine with Zinkov

Title Page of Original Yizkor Book

פנקס
זינקוב

מעדענקבוך

הוצאת ועד זינקוב תל־אביב—ניו־יורק
אויסגאבע פון זינקאװער קאמיטעט תל־אביב—ניו־יארק
תשכ״ו—1966

Translation of Previous Page

PINKAS ZINKOV

NOTEBOOK

Published by the Zinkov Committee Tel Aviv – New York
5726 - 1966

TABLE OF CONTENTS

Natives of Zinkov in America

The Erection of the Monument

English Section

Surname Index

Zinkov Memorial Book
(Zinkiv, Ukraine)

49°05' / 27°04'

Translation of:
Pinkas Zinkov: Gedenkbukh

Editor: Shmuel Aizenshtadt
Published in Tel Aviv, New York 1966

———

Acknowledgments
Project Coordinator:
Susan and Shawn Dilles

———

This is a translation of:
Pinkas Zinkov: Gedenkbukh (Zinkov memorial book)

Editor: Shmuel Aizenshtadt
Joint Committee of Zinkover Landsleit in the United States and Israel
Published: Tel Aviv, New York 1966 (H,Y,E 255 pages)

Note: The original book can be seen online at the NY Public Library site: Zinkov

———————————

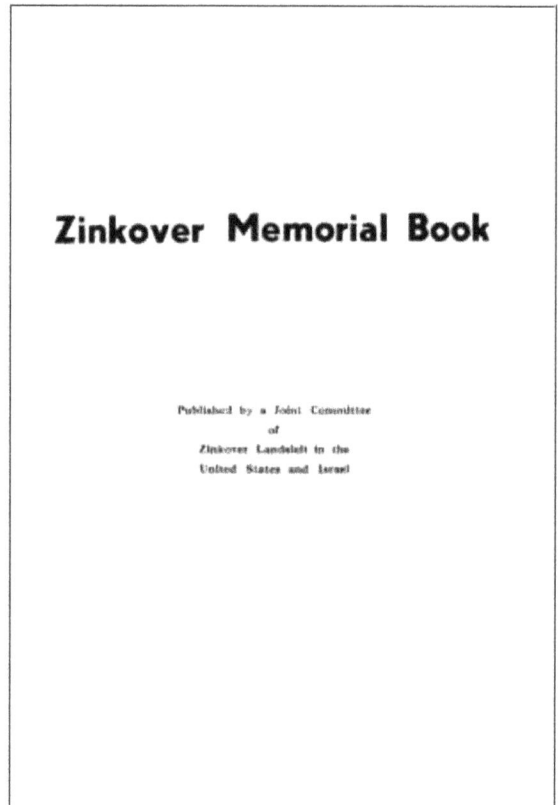

[Page 10]

Paintings and Photographs
Translated by Yocheved Klausner

The page numbers below are the page numbers of the original Yizkor book, not this translation.

[Page 11]

Editor's Foreword
Translated by Aryeh Sklar

My beloved friends have thrust upon me the role and responsibility to speak for and edit for modest and precious people. These are people who come from a town of the slaughtered, who have come to recall what happened to them and to eulogize the families of the dead, those who have been felled by the depravity of man and the genocidal murderers, alongside millions of our brothers and sisters.

A precious storehouse of Jewish existence and normal life, serene and honest, has been revealed herein, accompanying love of the Jewish people and love of the national tradition – a love that unites all the scattered people of Zinkov with their brethren in Israel.

This treasure of the Zinkov Book elevates and glorifies its image, and adds to it splendor and worth. It breaks away from the enclosure of modesty, its initial character, and through this force joins the literature of the nation, the literature of the destruction and the Holocaust. It adds waves of tears to the flood of tears of our generation.

Not just that – it creates an opening toward the hope of nation and humanity. The remnants of Zinkov in Israel, though not significant in number, are mighty, and together with their fellow townspeople in the Diaspora, they cling to the belief in the prosperity of the State of Israel, and in its thriving future for our people, and in its international integration with nations of redemption and peace.

Prof. Shmuel Aizenshtadt
Tel Aviv, Tammuz, 5726 (July, 1966)

[Page 12]

A Word from the Editor
by Professor Shmuel Eizenstadt
Translated by Yael Chaver

It is at once my privilege and my weighty and painful task to gather, organize (thematically and stylistically), and combine into a single work of remembrance, individual accounts of human experience, and memories of a quiet and comfortable youth spent in the Ukrainian countryside. I have been entrusted with collecting into a single spiritual vessel the hot tears shed for destroyed homes, beloved parents, brothers, and sisters, who were ruthlessly murdered by tyrannical and eternally cursed Nazism.

Behind the flow of bloody tears, the slaughtered world of Jewish life in all its splendor, customs, and folklore becomes revealed to us, the readers. Kind and sincere people have written chapters of Jewish history in Podolia during the first half of the twentieth century. These chapters are collected into an entire memorial book that will, like other memorial books of the era of murder, be useful as documentary sources for Jewish historians.

While editing this memorial book, I was particularly intrigued, and challenged, by the linguistic differences in the material (Hebrew, Yiddish, English) and the geographical variety of the individual writers. It is gratifying to point out that the writers of the Yiddish sections, though they have lived in America for many years, nevertheless retain a warm connection with their home of their youth as well as to the rich folk language of their personal homes. They also remain deeply attached to the Hebrew language that they learned in the *cheder* and *talmud–toyre* schools during early childhood, and the aroma of Torah is often felt in their Yiddish usage. [1]

[Page 12]

Just as colloquial are the Hebrew sections of the memorial book that were written by Zinkov natives living in Israel, who came to the country many years ago. Most of them were Zionist pioneers, who personally participated in building the country and defending it. Their memoirs are written in the language that became the natural language of their thoughts and experiences.

A small part of the material was written in English, by writers living in America. They did so in order to make the memorial book at least partially accessible to the grandchildren and great–grandchildren of Zinkov Jews in the United States and Canada who, unfortunately, do not read Yiddish or Hebrew. This will evoke the memory of the mass murders perpetrated by the Nazis on their people, on their ancestors in general, and in Zinkov in particular.

None of the writers of this memorial book is a professional author, and I did not try to turn them into professionals. While editing the materials, I made only the changes necessary to eliminate linguistic, grammatical, and stylistic errors, to avoid redundancies, and to render a few articles more readable.

This memorial book is published thanks to the generous and strenuous efforts of Zinkov natives in Israel and in America, in the hope that it would function as a family history in the homes of Zinkov natives throughout the world. The book therefore includes as many images as possible of Zinkov residents (besides the photographs of the murdered martyrs and their families). This was done so that everyone would be able to find the unforgettable images of relatives, friends, and those near and dear.

However, in spite of the local character of this memorial book, this volume – as a page of modern Jewish history – will be just as interesting to broader circles of readers, and will certainly join the growing ranks of Holocaust literature that can be found in community archives and libraries in Israel and in Jewish cultural centers throughout the world.

Translator's footnote:

1. The *cheder/cheider/heder/kheyder* and the *talmud–toyre* were traditional elementary religious schools for boys.

[Page 14]

[Page 15]

Introduction

[Page 16]

———

[Page 17]

A Word of the People of Zinkov in Israel
Translated by Aryeh Sklar

On behalf of the citizens of Israel who fled Zinkov, we extend our hand to any of our townspeople across the seas. Through the power of a great love of our land, which has beat within us from the beginning of our youth, we have become pioneers in building the land during the times of harsh national birth pangs. We stand here as well on the defensive line for the peace of our land, fighting for its independence, yet we have never forgotten, nor shall we ever forget, what was wrought by the genocidal murderers, murderers of our nation, toward our precious town, of those who ruined our families and our precious friends, within whose boundaries we were raised.

Together with all our fellow townspeople scattered in the Diaspora, we today establish this memorial monument, joining flesh and spirit in producing this memorial collection, which will tell for generations the pleasant and modest life, steeped in Jewish tradition, friendship and good community, which reigned in our town before the Holocaust, bearing a lament for our town which was destroyed, its sons and daughters, its elderly, its women and children, who were wiped out, killed, murdered, dying the sacred death of martyrs.

May it be so that their memories stay in our hearts and be blessed forever.

The Action Committee in Israel:

Yosef Yishpa

Yitzchak Frankel

Yisrael Ben–Shachar (Shwartzman)

———

[Page 17 – Hebrew] [Page 18 – Yiddish]

A Word to the Readers of this Memorial Book
Translated by Yael Chaver

Dear friends and Zinkov natives,

We present to you the work of a small group of Zinkov natives, who for years have been greatly affected by the fate of their murdered home–town people and are unable to find peace. We could not let the dreams of our young people also be buried under the ruins of destruction, or prevent our burning sorrow for all the Jewish men, women, and children from being properly expressed, and be totally forgotten with the cruel passage of time. We could not accept the fact that each small house and alley, each sacred spot, each marketplace and meadow, so well known to us and in which we spent so much time, should not be memorialized, as a commemoration of ruin. [1]

With our simple Yiddish language and our meager artistic talent, we started sketching out events, figures, and occasionally even laughing at certain characters. We collected images, and presented as best we could a gallery of familiar and beloved faces of bygone times and of today. Our possibilities were limited. There were many historical facts that we could not collect or establish. However, we have here set out for you all that we had; we have made available for future historians a glimpse of the life, and murder, of a Jewish community that was deeply rooted in Ukrainian soil.

Above all, we present you with faithful documentary evidence by living witnesses who survived the terrible destruction, and can recount the terrible chronicle of our destroyed home for history and for future generations.

May the Zinkov Memorial Book stand before the court of world conscience, as the greatest accuser of the barbaric Nazi people–murderers.

The American Committee to Commemorate the Town of Zinkov

Moyshe Garber, Moyshe Grinman, Borekh Laskin, Dovid Fuks, Avrom Rapoport, Yisro'el (Sanis) Roytbord

Translator's footnote:

1. The term 'commemoration of ruin' refers to the traditional practice of leaving an unpainted patch inside a home, as a reminder of the destruction of the Jewish Temple by the Roman Empire in 70 CE.

———

[Page 19]

Congratulations

by Dovid Fuks, President of the Zinkov Society

Translated by Yael Chaver

I congratulate all brothers, sisters, and friends, as well as the Book Committee, on the publication of our memorial book, the *Zinkov Pinkes*. [1] In the name of our Society, I express my heartfelt thanks and acknowledgment to the small group of faithful and devoted sons of Zinkov for their tireless work, which they put into these two sacred projects in order to preserve forever the memory of our martyrs.

Dovid Fuks

It is quite amazing that such a small group of members found the courage and vision to undertake the creation of these two huge and symbolic memorials as the imposing monument in our cemetery, and now the *Zinkov Pinkes* memorial volume. Organizations that are richer and much larger than ours did not have the courage or the slightest initiative to carry out even one such project. We know that this achievement did not come easily. The road was difficult, with many obstacles. Our faithful activists devoted long hours to this work. They spent their weekends at the Book Committee meetings, as well as time after work. The Committee, which consisted of our brothers Moyshe Grinman, Yisro'el Roytburd, Moyshe Garber, Borekh Laskin as well as some help from myself, therefore deserves a comradely "well–done!"

We now have two symbolic memorials for our brothers, monuments which are also an eternal flame burning in their memory. These are two pillars of light that will illuminate our future lives, and warn us that every possible measure must be taken to make sure that the bitter, gloomy past with the terrible, barbaric deeds of the brown–and–black Nazi epidemic shall gradually be forgotten and totally vanish into the darkness of distant days.

[Page 20]

And, last but not least, special thanks and praise are due to our Zinkov natives and friends in Israel and America, for their generous material support, without which we would never have been able to complete these two great and sacred achievements.

We also extend heartfelt thanks to our distinguished editor, Professor Shmuel Eisenstadt in Tel Aviv, his esteemed wife, and the entire staff of workers who made possible the high intellectual standard of the book. Thanks to his devoted work with us, Professor Eisenstadt joined our circle, as though he too was a member of our family circle.

Translator's footnote:

1. Shtetls typically had a *pinkes*, a record book in which the noteworthy events of the Jewish community, good as well as bad, would be documented. The term *pinkes* in this title thus refers to a longstanding tradition in Jewish culture. The Hebrew title of Holocaust memorial books usually starts with *Pinkes*, followed by the name of the town in which the community lived.

———

[Page 21]

Our Memorial Book

by Avrom Rapoport

Translated by Yael Chaver

Avrom Rapoport

We have before us a rare book, created by rare writers. Both book and writers are unique. Most importantly, the writers are all natives of Zinkov, whose thematics breathe the social climate of their home town. Like all artists, they are suffused by their immediate surroundings. The cruelty of the lawless bands during the Second World War, when the bloodthirsty Nazis rampaged through Europe, particularly Europe's Jewish community, is especially deeply graven in their vulnerable souls.

The mission of this memorial book is clear. First, to present (as far as possible) the horrifying, catastrophic murders that took place in Zinkov. Second, to create a book that would serve as a document narrating the life of Jews in Zinkov from its earliest days to the tragic hours of its annihilation. The chapters in Hebrew, Yiddish, and

English are arranged according to topic and order. Especially remarkable are the descriptions of human characters and of the landscape. The unique manner of speech, with all its special features, nuances, and local quirks, is also presented here to a certain degree. Our writers had, if not their own style, their own manner of expression – the Zinkov mode. In fact, they drew on their Ukrainian Yiddish folk vocabulary.

Considering this memorial book as a collective work, it is clear that it expresses the deep cry of pain and longing for those murdered and for their home, in which each of us was profoundly integrated.

[Page 22]

Thinking that such an important documentary work could have remained in manuscript form and not been published, never to be seen by the eyes of a reader, we are deeply grateful to our brothers, natives of Zinkov, Moyshe Garber, Yisro'el Roytburd, Moyshe Grinman, Dovid Fuks and Borekh Laskin, for their tireless efforts to facilitate the compilation of the manuscripts and images and the publication of this remarkable book.

[Page 23]

Members of the Memorial Book publishing committee of the Zinkov society in New York
Seated (from right): Moyshe Grinman and Moyshe Garber
Standing (from right): Yisroel Roytburd, Benny Laskin, Dovid Fuks

[Page 24]

Committee of Zinkov women activists in New York, who assisted in publication of the Memorial Book:Standing: Itta Grinman, Sonya Fuks, Polya Garber Seated: Beyle Laskin, Khane Roytburd

[Page 25]

The Geographic Situation of Zinkov and its Public Life

[Page 26]

Translated by Aryeh Sklar

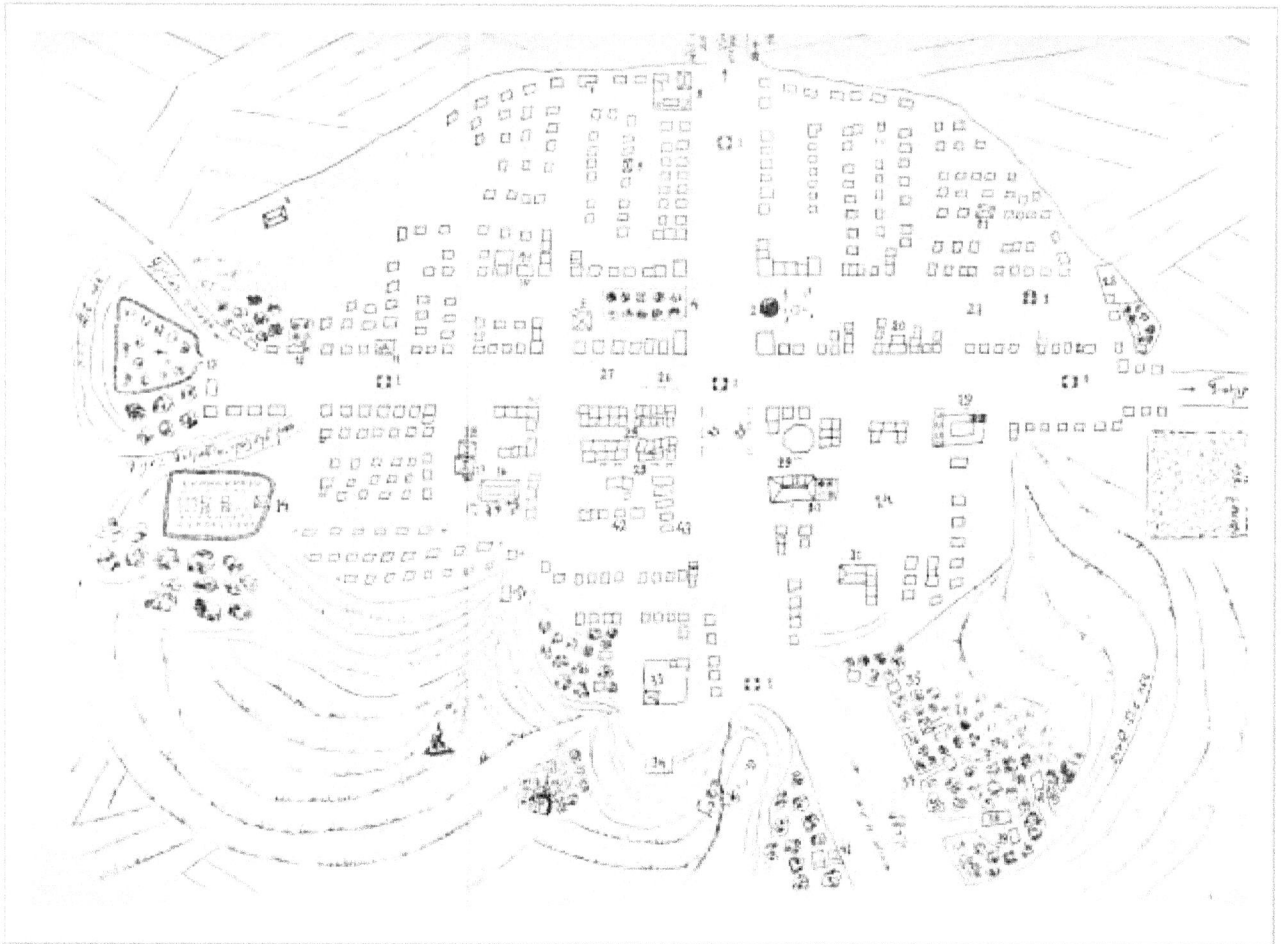

[***Translator's note:*** Hand–drawn map of Zinkov and its immediate surroundings]

Legend: [translated from Hebrew]

1 – Gas streetlights
2 – Well

3 – Manual pumps

4 – Public park

5 – Fire brigade

6 – Slaughterhouse

7 – *Talmud Toyre*

8 – Court of the *admor Pinches*[1]

9 – Old–age home (*hekdesh*)[2]

10 – Pharmacy

11 – Zemstvi hospital[3]

12 – Dr. Gorbatovski

13 – Christian cemetery

14 – Cemetery

15 – Graves of *admors*

16 – Great synagogue

17 – *Bes Medresh*[4]

18 – The old *kloyz*[5]

19 – Court of the *admor Moyshele*

20 – Alter Katzenelbogen's *kloyz*

21 – Artisans' synagogue

22 – The house of Yaakov–Moyshe and the *hachshara* garden[6]

23 – Domestic animal market (*torhobitse*)[7]

24 – Pork market

25 – Stalls selling bread and fruit

26 – Hatters

27 – Potters…[8]

28 – Commercial center

29 – Butchers' alley

30 – Yosl Shayes

31 – Markovsky house (history)[9]

32 – Public toilets

33 – Post office

34 – Ruins of fortress (the schloss)[10]

35 – Courthouse

36 – School (*uchilishtsa*)[11]

37 – *Bistitske*[12]

38 – The *vlost/ vlust*[13]

39 – Jail

40 – Police station 41 – Notary

42 – Moyshele the folk–healer[14]

43 – Yechiel the folk–healer 44 – Shmuel the folk–healer

45 – Azi Zecherman (the office)[15]

Note: the *ubshivka* (slum)

[**Translator's note:** The map includes Hebrew notations that indicate roads leading to/from other locations, as well as geographical features; they are listed in counter–clockwise order, starting at the Legend.]

Center right: To Vinkivtsy

Center top:
– Arrow indicating N.
– To Derazhnya and Proskurov
– Area of Saturday walks

Center left:
– To Adamovka and Yarmolintsy
– Area of Saturday walks
– To Kalinovka, Solovkovets, Kamenets[16]

Bottom right:
– *krevuly*[17]
– Wells
– The *yar*[18]
– The path
– Area of Saturday walks

Translator's footnotes:

1. *Admor* is the honorific title for the leader of a Hasidic group. The *admor* receives his followers in his "court."

2. *Hekdesh* signifies a service supported by the community.

3. The Russian *zemstvo* indicates "government"; this may have been a government–run hospital.

4. The *bes medresh* (House of Study) is a voluntary, public institute for Torah learning, functioning for generations within Jewish communities alongside the synagogue.

5. *Kloyz* is a term for a smaller synagogue.

6. *Hachshara* is the Hebrew term is used for training programs and agricultural centers in Europe and elsewhere. At these centers Zionist youth would learn technical skills necessary for their emigration to Palestine/Israel and subsequent life as members of *kibbutzim* (communal settlements).

7. *Torhobitse* is the Ukrainian term for animal market.

8. The ellipsis is in the original text.

9. The reference to "history" is unclear.

10. The use of the German *schloss* is not explained.

11. *Uchilishtsa* is the Ukrainian term for 'school.'

12. I could not translate this non–Yiddish term.

13. I could not translate this non–Yiddish term.

14. The hebraic term *rofeh* is usually used for a folk healer. An accredited medical physician is usually termed *dokter*.

15. It is not clear what this refers to.

16. I could not identify the town of Solovkovetz

17. I could not translate *krevuly*

18. Ukrainian yar means "ravine".

——

[Page 27]

The Town of Zinkov
A Geographical–Historical Survey
by Chana
Translated by Aryeh Sklar

Zinkov is a town in the Letichev district, in the province of Podolia. We have no clear and precise information regarding when the city was founded. There are remains of an ancient fortress there, and tradition has it that it is an [archeological] witness to the times of Turkish rule in that region in the years 1672–1699, which went as far as Kamenets–Podolski, which is near Zinkov. Based on this, one can surmise that the town of Zinkov existed for 300 years before its destruction by the Nazis.

Zinkov is situated a distance of 60 parasangs from Kamenets–Podolski, and a distance of 40 parasangs from Proskurov. It sprawls over a wide hill which encompasses meadows and valleys, and at the foot of it passes the River Ushitsa, which intersects with the Dniester.

The soil of the area is the fertile black earth of Ukraine, and its fields grow rich crops. There are 13 villages surrounding Zinkov, its inhabitants farmers of small fields. Nearby are great plots of land belonging to Polish owners, who built factories for sugar, paper, and beer.

Zinkov's populace was entirely Jewish, with the exception of a small number of Ukrainians and Russians. In 1847, the population of Jewish inhabitants was 2150. In 1897, according to the official census which took place that year, there were 3719 Jews, and in the 1920s and 1930s, there were an estimated 5000 people.

The Jews of Zinkov, for the most part, made their livings among one another, even standing up to the economic revolution with the landowners in neighboring areas. They mostly dealt with wheat and fruits, which Ukraine was blessed with, and they supplied bread and fruit tree products to the world at large. There were also honeycomb sellers and those who leased out flour mills.

There were no especially wealthy people in the town, but there were many average, working–class people, making a living however they could. There were also unemployed, who lived hard and meager lives.

Judaism in Ukraine, especially in Podolia, was not exceptional in its erudition and academics, yet the people were also far from boorishness and ignorance. Every Jew, regardless of wealth, taught their children Torah. Study began in children's classrooms (heder), or in a "Talmud Torah" [traditional school], and culminated with the study of the Talmud. There were some special individuals in Zinkov who studied Torah when they were free from their jobs. Among the teachers of Torah were Torah scholars, well–versed in Torah. 7 study halls and "*kloyzim*" existed in the town, within which they would study at night the Mishna and *Ein Yaakov* (Legends of the Talmud).

[Page 28]

Once the Enlightenment movement (*Haskala*) started to make inroads in Russian Jewry, it came to Zinkov as well. Parents began to send their children to learn general studies in Russian schools that [taught] both areas [of study], which were operating nearby. Already at the start of the 20th century, many sought a high school education, and young students with those aspirations left to the bigger cities.

From the start of the emergence of political Zionism, the Zionist idea spread throughout Zinkov as well, and many parents educated their sons and daughters in the spirit of this movement, arousing in them a love for the land of Israel. This caused, after some time, a youth pioneer movement, with many from Zinkov immigrating to Israel to work and participate in building it up.

The [General Jewish Labour] "Bund" movement also gained members and supporters in Zinkov, even though the working–class Jews were, to put it mildly, not relevant [to the movement]. They were not in the factories of production, nor did they have the background of the political debates. But a feeling of rebellion was stirred in those workers against their masters [to sympathize].

R.Moyshele,
May the righteous' memory be a blessing

Zinkov was close to the cradle of Hasidut, that of Medzibush, which continued the Hasidic dynasty of Apt. Jewish holidays allowed for their spirit to be felt in the area, for they would come from all the surrounding areas, to sing Hasidic melodies. In particular, there was tremendous enthusiasm with song and dance during the festival of Simhat Torah. The court of the Rebbes were always open for anyone seeking counsel, for anyone down- trodden. There they would lead passionate public prayer, there they would judge cases of Torah law, filled with truth, justice, and righteousness.

[Page 29]

Among the personalities, a few noteworthy individuals should be mentioned:

Rabbi Moshe Barsuk, may his memory be a blessing, secretary of the [Hasidic] Rebbe Rabbi Moyshele, may the righteous' memory be a blessing – or, as he was called then, "the Gabbai" [the sexton]. He was an exceptionally studious man, and the sacred teachings never ceased from his mouth, day or night. He would trade questions and answers of Jewish law with many famous rabbis from the surrounding areas, and he recorded his notes in the margins of his Talmud that he was studying.

Rabbi Mordechai Nachmanes, an exceptional teacher of Talmud – [he was] studious, wise, and an extremist.

Rabbi Chaim Ravizes, may God avenge his blood, a popular and engaging Jew, good–hearted, studious, noted for his collection of stories and especially his sayings, which were abundant with folk wisdom. One of them was: "As bad as it gets in this world, be happy you're not dead where it's worse. Az es iz nit gut aoyf der velt, zal men zikh aoyf yener velt nit veyzn." "Ikh farshtey – areyngeyn lebedikerheyt in himl vi alihu ader eyngezunken vern in der erd vi krkh, aber nit bleybn heyngen vi abshlum tsvishn himl aun erd – I understand going to heaven like Elijah, or being swallowed up by the earth like Korah, but not Absalom, remaining between heaven and earth." He was murdered by soldiers of Hitler, may his name be erased. His son, Yitzhak Isaacson, may he rest in peace, was a scribe; he died after a short time in Argentina.

Mordechai Vartzman, an honorable man, with a large and illustrious family, a "Shlomo Nagid"–type.

Herschel Moshe Hayses, with his wife, a "woman of valor," Rachel. [Rachel] selflessly managed their large family, giving her husband the ability preoccupy himself with Torah.

After the pogroms perpetrated by [Symon] Petliura's men [as part of the Ukrainian People's Republic], and after the massive pogroms in Proskuriv and in Felestyn, places close to Zinkov, many young people abandoned Zinkov, which was close to eastern Galicia, and they were able to cross the border. Some immigrated [to Israel] as pioneers, and others settled in America, and some time later their parents followed them.

[Page 30]

Zinkov, Our Town
(A Historical–Geographical Survey)
by Chana
Translated by Yael Chaver

Zinkov is a town in the Letychiv district, Podolia province.

We have no clear, accurate information about the time it was founded. There are remnants of an old fort in the town, known as "the castle"; and, as passed down the generations, it is evidence of the Turkish occupation of the region, in 1672–1699; Turkish rule extended as far as the nearby city of Kamenetz–Podolsk. Thus, Zinkov apparently existed for about 300 years before it was destroyed by the Nazis.

Zinkov is 60 *versts*[1] from Kamenetz–Podolsk, and 40 *versts* from Proskurow. It lies across a broad hill, and is surrounded by valleys and meadows. The Ushitsa River flows at its foot, en route to the Dniester. The soil in the region is the blessed black soil of Ukraine, and the choicest crops flourish and ripen in its fields.[2]

Thirteen villages lie around Zinkov, inhabited at that time by peasants. There were large estates nearby, owned by Polish nobles. Adjoining these estates were factories that produced sugar and paper, as well as breweries.

All the town's inhabitants were Jews, with only a few Ukrainians and Russians. In 1847 the Jewish population of Zinkov numbered 2150. In 1897, when the official census was carried out, the population of Zinkov numbered 3719. During the 1920s and 1930s, it rose to 5000.

The Jews of Zinkov made their living, for the most part, by trading with each other. Until the revolution, they had trading connections with the landowners of the region as well. They were mostly occupied with trading in grain and fruit, with which Ukraine is blessed. They exported bread and various fruits all over the world. The residents included lumber merchants and mill leasers. No one in the town was very rich; but there were many average householders and craftsmen, who lived by their trade. There was also no shortage of people who had no occupation and lived in want and poverty.

[Page 31]

The Jews of Ukraine – especially in Podolia – were not famous for their education and scholarship, but the Jews of Zinkov were far from ignorant and uncultured. Every Jew, whether rich or poor, sent his child to study Torah, starting with the *Talmud–Toyre* and ending with Talmud study.

Images of Zinkov

There were also a few in town who spent their free time studying. The local teachers included some scholars and experts. The town numbered seven *bes-medresh* institutions and small synagogues, where people studied Mishna and *Ein Ya'akov* in the evenings.[3]

When the Enlightenment movement expanded among Russian Jews, Zinkov was included. Parents started sending their children to secular schools, sending them increasingly to middle schools as well. The young people of Zinkov were attracted to large cities for this reason.

[Page 32]

Once political Zionism began, that idea became popular in Zinkov as well.

Many parents raised their children in this spirit, and awakened a love of *Eretz-Yisra'el* in them. Eventually, a Zionist youth movement was established in the town, and young people of Zinkov immigrated to Palestine, worked there, and participated in the development of a Zionist community.

The Bund also started a youth movement in town, which attracted many members and sympathizers, although there was no Jewish proletariat in the full sense of the word, as there were no factories. Thus, there were no grounds for class warfare.[4] However, manual workers developed a sense of protest against their bosses.

Geographically, Zinkov was close to Medzhybizh, the cradle of Hasidism, and carried on the chain of Hasidic tradition.[5]

The Jewish holidays would imbue the town with spirituality. The Hasidim, who would gather from all over the region, would sing their melodies. The major musical event was at *Simkhas–Toyre*, accompanied by an ecstatic Hasidic dance. The courts of the rabbis were always open to all, anyone who was depressed or sought advice. People would pray whole–heartedly with the congregation. Rabbinical legal cases were heard there, inspired by truth, justice, and decency.

The following personalities, which distinguished Zinkov, included the following:

Rabbi Moyshe Barsuk (may his memory be for a blessing), secretary to Rabbi Moyshele (may his righteous memory be for a blessing), was usually called "the manager." He was an extraordinary scholar, and was constantly studying. He would exchange learned opinions with famous rabbis in the region, and would note his comments in the margins of Talmud volumes as he studied.[6]

Rabbi Mordkhe (Nachmen's son) (may his memory be for a blessing) was one of the best *melameds* in Zinkov. He was smart, pious and a scholar.

Rabbi Yankev Altanir (may his memory be for a blessing) was a typical scholar, modest, and unassuming.

Rabbi Khayim Royzis (may God avenge his blood) was a pithy, kind, decent person, as well as a scholar.[7] He was known for his tales, and especially for his proverbs, which were suffused with folk wisdom, such as, "If life here is not good, don't show up in the next world," and "I understand ascending to heaven while alive, like the prophet Elijah, or sinking into the ground like Korach, but not hanging between heaven and earth, like Absalom."[8] He was murdered by Hitler's monsters, may their names be blotted out.*[9] His son, Yitzchok Itzikzon (may be rest in peace) was a writer. He died in Argentina not long ago.**[10]

[Page 33]

Mordkhe Vertsman (may his memory be for a blessing). He was an outstanding person, the father of a large, honorable family, a *Shloyme Nogid*.[11]

Hershl (Moyshe Khayim's son) (may his memory be for a blessing) and his wife, the "woman of valor" Rokhl, who supported the family by her work and enabled her husband to devote his entire life to study.[12]

After the pogroms carried out by the Petlyurists, especially the major pogroms of Proskurow and Felstin (near Zinkov), many young people crossed the nearby border to eastern Galitzia. Some continued on to *Eretz–Yisra'el* and others emigrated to America; they were eventually followed by their parents.

(Translated from Hebrew)

[Page 34]

Remnant of the Turkish fort, and the path to the spring.[13]
"The Castle," remnant of a Turkish fort, and the path to the spring.[14]

Translator's footnotes:

1. Versts (also called parsings) is an obsolete Russian unit of measurement equal to 0.663 miles (3,500 feet) or 1.067 km.

2. "Black soil" is a literal translation of the Russian term for this type of soil (Russian *chernozem*), which is a fertile black soil typical of temperate grasslands such as the Russian steppes and the American prairies.

3. *Ein Ya'akov* is a very popular 16th–century compilation, by Jacob ben–Habib, of all the Aggadic material in the Talmud together with commentaries. It is still in print.

4. Inevitable class war between proletarian factory workers and capitalist factory owners was an important part of Marxist thought.

5. Rabbi Israel ben Eliezer Baal Shem Tov (1698–1760), the founder of Hasidism, lived in Medzhybizh from about 1742 until his death. His grave is still pointed out in the old Jewish cemetery.

6. Such exchanges of opinions, known as Responsa, form a body of written decisions and rulings given by Jewish legal scholars in response to questions addressed to them.

7. This honorific for the dead is generally used for Jews who were martyred or killed by anti–Semites.

8. These biblical references are, respectively, to II Kings, 2, 10; Numbers 26, 11; and II Samuel 18, 10.

9. Original note:* See "The Destruction of Zinkov" by Y. R.

10. Original note: **See: "Zinkov Figures."

11. This alludes to a character in an early story with this title by Sholem Asch.

12. "Woman of valor" are the opening words of Chapter 31 in Proverbs.

13. Translated from Hebrew.

14. Translated from Yiddish.

———

[Page 35]

The Zionist Pioneering Movement in Zinkov[1]

by Nakhum Yoshpeh

Translated by Yael Chaver

I remember well the day Dr. Theodor Herzl died; I was then seven years old.[2] This event had a strong effect on the town. His deeds might not have been widely known, but everyone knew his name. There were two Hasidic rabbis in town, most of whose followers opposed political Zionism, but on that day everyone felt the strong connection between Dr. Theodor Herzl and the phrase "May our eyes see Your return to Zion, with mercy" in daily prayers. The news of Herzl's death shocked the nation. The children came to *kheyder* that day (I was studying with the *melamed* Yoel Khodanchik) and said that a great Jewish man had died, one similar to Moshe Rabeinu.[3] The *melamed* scolded them, but one of the children added, "That's what my father said." The Zionists in our town were very depressed because their leader had died.

Over time, interest in Zionism increased in our town. Whenever a Zionist congress was in session, my father would bring a copy of the *HaTsfira* newspaper from

Proskurow, with a detailed account of the deliberations; the newspaper would be passed from hand to hand, even reaching Rabbi Moyshele.[4] The rabbi opposed secular Zionism on principle, for religious reasons, but made his peace with those who were unwilling to wait passively for the Messiah, and believed that they should emigrate to *Eretz Yisra'el* and settle there. He did not consider it a sin. My older brother, Menachem, once asked the rabbi, "Why shouldn't we accept Herzl as our savior, as the Messiah? Should we really describe the Messiah as the legends depict him, as an angel who will appear and sound a great *shofar*?" The rabbi answered him, saying, "It is difficult to imagine the Messiah as a physical creature. He may appear in the form of a prophet, too. But the Bible says that when Messiah will come 'the earth will be full of knowledge,' meaning that everyone will recognize the Messiah when he is revealed.[5] Previously, the Messiahs who appeared were recognized only by part of the nation; the end result was that not only did they not bring salvation, but caused much harm through their failure." One must observe all the commandments and lead a righteous life, until the entire nation is in a condition that justifies salvation or, God forbid, damnation.

[Page 36]

The emissaries from *Eretz Yisra'el* would tell the Hasidim about Hebrew–speaking Jewish workers in the country who were becoming organized.[6]

The years passed, and my brother Menachem went away to study in Husyatin, near the Austrian border. He stayed with my uncle, David Blinder, who was a Zionist activist. On his visits home he would spread the word about Zionism among our young people. He would also bring copies of the monthly magazine *Moledet*, which was published in Jaffa.[7] My uncle was preparing to go to *Eretz–Israel* to inquire about settling there. I was a good artist, and planned to join him in order to enter the Bezalel Art School in Jerusalem.[8] However, World War I broke out, and the entire plan was dropped.

At the outset of the war, all Jews were expelled from the areas adjoining the Austrian border. Several families from Husyatin moved to Zinkov, among them my uncle David Blinder and his friend, the teacher Shmuel Fridman, both dedicated Zionist activists. As is well known, the Czarist regime prohibited Zionist activity, but this did not prevent them from quietly disseminating Zionist propaganda in the town. They were the center of a group of sympathizers, and set up Hebrew language classes.[9] Hebrew was the only language spoken in my uncle's home, and the children's names were biblical. His son Avshalom was killed during World War II, in Palestine, as a soldier in the British Army.

In 1917, after the revolution, my uncle David Blinder and his friend Shmuel Fridman openly encouraged Zionism. They founded a Zionist organization and named it *HaTechiya*, as well as a Zionist club bearing blue and white banners inscribed in Hebrew and Russian.[10] We collected books, mostly in Hebrew, and set up a library.

Quite a large group of young people coalesced around at the club. We sang Zionist and national songs.

Yekhiel Yoshpeh's family

[Page 37]

We also established a drama group, led by the teacher Yisra'el Shteynberg, the brother of the writer Yehuda Shteynberg.[11] My uncle and Shmuel Fridman led ideological meetings, increased the number of *HaTechiyah* members, and saw to it that Zionist representatives joined public institutions of the community such as the school board. These meetings aroused strong debates, mainly with members of the Bund, headed by Abramovich. The Bund group in Zinkov was quite large, and comprised more members than the Zionist organization. There were also arguments between us and Levi Stoliar (the carpenter), the "Zionist worker," who considered our Zionist organization a bourgeois group; his arguments with us and with *Tse'irei Tziyon* were as strong as those of Abramovich, the Bund member.[12]

Avraham Berenzon, Moshe Gershgorn, and I were in charge of keeping order. The fact that we were all members of the self–defense organization, which was unified regardless of political affiliation or ideological differences, was very helpful. At first, we carried out propaganda activity ourselves. In addition to Shmuel Fridman, my uncle David Blinder, and Moti Fayerman, we young people were also quite successful. I remember my brother Menachem saying, in one speech, "Our nation has preserved its existence as a nation for two thousand years, thanks to its ancient culture. It is like a stream originating in a spring of pure water. Its flow is strong and its water clear; when it joins the ocean, its distinctive flow is noticeable." Everyone applauded, and even his opponents said, "Mendl is a good speaker."[13]

*Shmuel Fridman (may his
memory be for a blessing)*

The Bundists once brought one of their famous speakers to Zinkov. He started as follows: "I'm addressing the simple Jew with a beard."[14] His pointed arguments impressed the listeners. He was followed by the teacher Shmuel Fridman, who was modest and physically weak, but was rich in culture and knowledge, and well–informed about Zionism. Speaking quietly and confidently, he analyzed the situation of the Jews in the Diaspora in general and in Russia in particular, saying, "The Zionist idea is planted in each Jew's heart, but orthodox Jews are waiting for the Messiah to come, while the others are waiting for the other nations to remind them of the vital need to return to their historic homeland. The Jew–haters do not distinguish between Zionists and Socialists. They hate us all, as Jews. A nation without a country is like a house without a foundation. Zionism strives to unite us as a nation in our historic homeland and restore us to a productive existence... A nation that speaks its own language, develops its own culture, and aims to live a normal life in its own country is accepted among the other nations. The world has already recognized this fact, and the British have given us the Balfour Declaration. Now it depends on us. We must prove that we are capable of being a nation like all other nations. If we do not make the effort now, when the door is open, it may not be opened for us if, God forbid, there is a catastrophe." People, including his opponents, listened quietly and with interest to Shmuel Fridman. When the audience left, there was much talk: the Bundist speaker had spoken to the point this time; but, after all, Fridman was right...

[Page 38]

Zionist speakers would also be sent to Zinkov from Proskurow. Ivi Zilberman, who resembled Ze'ev Jabotinsky in appearance and in speech, visited us.[15] He spoke in Yiddish, astutely and wittily. Sasha Nirenberg was a favorite speaker in Zinkov; he spoke Russian and attracted young people to his meetings.

Once, we held a week dedicated to *Eretz Yisra'el*. There were informational and entertainment events, and a display of Jewish strength. As I recall, this display consisted of a group of forty tall young men, wearing a uniform (which consisted of a blue–white cap, a shirt with blue insignia and a Star of David, and black trousers tucked inside Cossack–style striped boots). The group marched through the town like a military unit, headed by riders on decked–out horses. These riders included myself, wearing the uniform, and Avraham Berenzon, a dark–complexioned guy in oriental dress (as a symbol of the ingathering of exiles from east and west). The unit was preceded by a band, and followed by a large crowd. We held an assembly at the synagogue, and sang *HaTikvah*. Spirits were high, and faces shone... That evening, we had a party in the Firemen's Hall, with performances and recitations. The daytime parade and the evening performances provided a show of Jewish strength and the energy of the younger generation, that was to be directed towards productivity, construction, as well as defense.

Following the meetings and celebrations, we started practical preparations. We were connected with the *HeHalutz* central committee in Kharkov, headed by Eliezer Kaplan (may he rest in peace).[16] We were informed by the central committee that groups were being organized for agricultural training in the Jewish farming colonies of the Kherson area, and that people who wanted to immigrate to *Eretz Yisra'el* should register for training in those places.[17] It was clear to us all that the foundational premise of Zionism was a return to the land and to agriculture. There was much enthusiastic talk about the farming communities in *Eretz Yisra'el* and the cooperative settlement of Merhavya.[18] But of all the respected Zionists who sat at the head and passionately sang *HaTikvah* and the Yiddish song "We will reap rye there and no longer suffer from exile," only two put their names down for training.[19]One member and I were preparing to start training at the Dobraya colony, but I had to postpone it for urgent family reasons. The central *HeHalutz* committee approved the postponement; but in the meantime Denikin's forces took control of the Kherson region, the training project was cancelled, and we remained under Skoropadsky's rule.[20]

So as not to be idle, Ya'akov Moshe Vartsman gave us a plot of land in 1919, where we could practice farming. It was a fine, large plot, surrounded by a tall fence. It was not suitable for field crops, and we only planted vegetables, such as corn and sunflowers. I would occasionally bring over one of my Ukrainian peasant acquaintances to teach us the basics of agriculture and show us how to plant and hoe. It was hard work, as we used our hands, with no plow or horses. But we loved the work, and made constant progress. Meanwhile, our region changed hands. Denikin's forces took control, creating a connection between our town and Odessa, from which – according to rumor – a ship was supposed to sail for *Eretz Yisra'el*. Avraham Berenzon and I set out for Odessa to check out the rumor. It turned out that the "Ruslan" had indeed sailed some time earlier, and there was no chance that another ship would sail soon.[21] While we were in Odessa, it was rumored that Denikin's forces were leaving our region. We hurried back home, so as not to be cut off. Sure enough, we arrived in Zmerynka and found ourselves in the midst of a fierce exchange of gunfire. At its end, Denikin's units retreated and a unit commanded by Petlyura's ally Shchepel entered the town.[22] Once again, we were cut off from the world. Intercity travel was also suspended, and our lives were in just as much danger as before.

[Page 39]

HaTechiya Zionist Association, Zinkov

In order to make good use of the difficult period I had to spend in Zinkov, I strove to create a larger, more substantial group of Zionist pioneers who would join me in immigrating to *Eretz–Yisra'el* when the time was right. Many who were over twenty years old had reservations and did not put their names down. Their excuse was that the situation in Palestine was unclear and therefore immigration was not practical. I then energized and organized a group of younger people, aged 16–17.

[Page 40]

A group of young people (17 boys and 2 girls) joined. We made all the formal preparations, so that we could able to leave once the borders opened. We had some money, which we had earned with our gardening. In addition to the official problems, I had to counter the objections of the parents. Though they were Zionists, they argued that I was organizing minor children, and that I should deal with the parents. I countered by explaining that no one was forcing their children to immigrate, and that leaving the hellish situation that had come about with the changes of rule and the extreme danger to the Jewish community, was in the interests of the children. But they rejected me with various pretexts.

The group of Zionist pioneers from Zinkov, 1921

However, the political shifts and changes in our region were not over. Shortly afterwards, the Polish army entered, conquered all of Podolia, and reached Kiev. This was in 1920. Thanks to this new occupation, our links with the outside world were renewed. We had news from Warsaw that an immigration committee had been set up there; the committee organized groups of Zionist pioneers and arranged their move to Palestine. We also heard that a group of pioneers had already left from Kamenetz, and another group was being organized in Dunayevtsy. I went there, and found out that everything was now being organized from Warsaw.

At Passover, 1920, we heard the sad news about the events at Tel Chai, and the death of Yosef Trumpeldor and his companions.[23] This dampened the spirits of the local Zionists. They pounced on me, saying, "We were right in saying that hasty immigration was not a good idea, and that the situation in Palestine needed to be clearer." My response was, "All the more reason to

[Page 41]

organize Zionist immigration; as far as personal security is concerned, immigrating to Palestine is the lesser of two evils." I mustered the aid of Shimon Saliternik and his wife Mesiya (may their memories be for a blessing), who were seriously considering immigration, to pressure the local committee for funding to travel to Warsaw. I was able to travel there, and in two weeks had arranged the immigration documents and visas, and returned to Zinkov. However, the retreat of the Poles and the takeover by the Bolsheviks delayed our departure yet again.

[Page 42]

After many adventures, I reached Jaffa in five months (November 1920); the group of pioneers from Zinkov arrived only six months later, in early 1921. After that, Zinkov was closely linked with *Eretz–Yisra'el* thanks to its pioneers, builders of the country.

* * *

When we left Zinkov, the Bolsheviks were in charge, and the local Jews still enjoyed a measure of freedom in commerce and community life. Zionist activity went on, and immigration to *Eretz–Yisra'el* also continued to some degree, though there were already formal difficulties about leaving Russia. Some young people, as well as families whose children were already in Palestine, were interested in immigrating. The events of 1921 stopped preparations for immigration in our town, and families that were about to leave postponed their trip for a quieter time[24] Immigration increased a bit in 1922; several people and families immigrated to Palestine. These included the Frenkel family, two of whose sons had previously immigrated; Shimon Saliternik and his wife; David Stoliar and his family; Shmuel Fridman; the Zaltzman family; and a few other families. Please forgive me if I have forgotten anyone. My sister Fanny came with her fiancé Aharon Grabelski, and together we started seeking ways to make a living by agriculture for the whole family.

The group of pioneers from Zinkov at the grave of Dr. Theodor Herzl in Vienna

Not all those who immigrated from Zinkov at that time were satisfied. Some went back. One of the important Zionists of Zinkov, D. V., could not adjust to the work and to the living conditions that were generally harder than what he had been used to. He returned to Zinkov. When he was asked why, he did not say, God forbid, that life in *Eretz–Yisra'el* was not good. He said that the country was good for guys like Nachum Yoshpeh, who had the strength of an ox, the patience of a donkey, was satisfied with a meal of dried figs and pita bread, and could dance a hora with the guys after a day of hard work at the seaport.

Immigration from Zinkov did not yet stop completely. Shortly afterwards, the family of Zeyde Saliternik arrived, as well as my brother Moshe; and the Vartsman brothers. In 1926 my mother (may she rest in peace) and my brother Menachem with his family arrived.

In 1923, I joined the farming *moshav* of Merchavya; conditions were not too good. I lived in a small shack. We worked from dawn until late at night, hoping that conditions would improve with time and we would establish an economic basis for the whole family that would follow. I corresponded with Mother and my brothers in Zinkov, who were seriously considering immigration.

One day a "tourist from America" came and introduced himself as a former resident of Zinkov. His name was Ya'akov Halperin, and he had known my father well. He saw my meager "farm," saying, as he left, "I'll write to Zinkov and describe the lives of natives of the town whom I visited in *Eretz Yisra'el*." He did carry out his promise, and wrote a detailed letter about our townspeople in the country. When describing my poor, difficult life in Merchavya, he noted that I was living like

[Page 43]

"Vasil Buhatch." This Vasil Buhatch was well known in Zinkov: he was a short, skinny, cross–eyed Ukrainian, who owned a small, old, broken–down cart and a lame horse. He would do small deliveries around town. His wife was similar: short, twisted, and also cross–eyed. They lived in a small old hut on the way to the river; every time we children would pass by we would pluck out some thatch from his roof. He would sometimes come out and scold us, but we were not afraid of him, poor guy. He was a symbol of poverty; his nickname, Vasil Buhatch, was a kind of euphemism: Buhatch means "rich." It was this miserable, impoverished person to whom Ya'akov Halperin compared me in his letter to Zinkov. Mother was not told about this letter, to spare her suffering.

Luckily, another native of Zinkov came to visit me shortly afterwards. He viewed me and my farm quite differently. He surveyed every corner of my shack with affection, and joined me in the field. We did some plowing, and came back. As we parted, he said, "I'm so happy to have visited you." This was Urkeh Frenkel (may his memory be for a blessing). He wrote to people in Zinkov that he had visited a new Hebrew village in *Eretz Yisra'el*, or, as it was called there, a *moshav*, where our Nachum Yoshpeh is living. "What can I tell you? He is living like a real Ukrainian peasant. He has a pair of horses and a plow, chickens and ducks, and the main thing is 'he has his own bread' and they lack for nothing. True, they live in wooden shacks, but that's not terrible. After all, winter in *Eretz Yisra'el* is not like ours. He has plentiful crops and is building a house. 'This is what *Eretz Yisra'el* means!'"[25]

Translator's footnotes:

1. Translated from Hebrew.

2. Theodor Herzl (1860–1904) was the founder of modern political Zionism.

3. "Moses, our teacher" is the familiar term for the biblical Moses.

4. *HaTsfira* was a Hebrew–language newspaper published in Poland 1862 and 1874–1931. It became a daily in 1886.

5. The quote is from Isaiah 11, 9.

6. Rabbis living in Palestine would send emissaries abroad to collect donations for charitable institutions.

7. The Hebrew monthly (1911–1928), whose name means "Homeland", was a youth magazine.

8. The school, now known as the Bezalel Academy of Art and Design, was founded in 1906 by the Jewish painter and sculptor Boris Schatz

9. The revival of Hebrew as a spoken, secular language, was a principle and a hallmark of Zionism. During the pre–state period, "Hebrew" was often used as an adjective replacing "Jewish," to signify the new way of life that was developing in the Zionist community in Palestine.

10. *HaTechiya* is the Hebrew for "the revival." Blue and white were the colors of the Zionist flag, and were later used for the Israeli flag.

11. Yehuda Shteynberg (1863–1908) was a prolific writer in Yiddish and Hebrew.

12. *Tse'irei Tziyon* was a competing Zionist youth organization.

13. The last phrase is translated from Yiddish.

14. This phrase is translated from Yiddish.

15. I was unable to identify Ivi Zilberman. Ze'ev (Vladimir) Jabotinsky (1860–1940) was a charismatic Zionist leader, journalist, orator, and man of letters, who founded the militant Zionist Revisionist movement.

16. Eliezer Kaplan (1891–1952) was an important Zionist activist who became a major Israeli politician.

17. The first Jewish agricultural settlements ("colonies") in the Russian Empire were established in the Kherson region in 1806, after a decree in 1804 that for the first time allowed Jews to purchase land for farming settlements.

18. A co–operative farming settlement was established in 1911 in Merhavya, in northern Palestine.

19. I was unable to identify this song.

20. Anton Denikin (1872–1947) was a general who led the anti–Bolshevik ("White") forces on the southern front during the Russian Civil War (1918–20). Pavlo Skoropadsky (1873–1945) was a Ukrainian aristocrat, military and state leader, who became Hetman of Ukraine for a few months in 1918.

21. The arrival of the SS "Ruslan" from Russia in 1919 signaled the start of the third, significant, wave of Zionist immigration to Palestine (the Third Aliyah, 1919–1923).

22. I was not able to identify Shchepel (or Shchepel).

23. Tel Chai, in northern Galilee, was first settled in 1905, and in the wake of World War I passed under French control. On March 1, 1920, it was the site of the first armed skirmish between Arabs and Jews. Eight Jews were killed, including the admired commander Yosef Trumpeldor.

24. The "events" consisted of violent riots by Arabs against Jews (May 1–7), which began in Jaffa and spread to other parts of the country. 47 Jews and 48 Arabs were killed; most of the Arab deaths resulted from clashes with the British forces, who were attempting to restore order.

25. The phrases in single quotes are translated from Yiddish.

[Page 44]

The Underground Zionist Activity in Zinkov
by Yosef Yoshpeh
Translated by Aryeh Sklar

Following the first Russian Revolution in February, 1917, and the repealing of the Imperial restrictions on Jews, the Zionist movement in Russia was, as we know, liberated. In every Jewish city in the country, Zionist associations organized, including in our own city, where a large Zionist association named *Hatechiya* was founded. It encompassed the best of the city's youth and engaged in all of the culture and *ḥalutz* activities, as described by my brother Nachum.

However, I wish to briefly address a later period of activity, during the years 1921–1927, to whatever extent my memory has preserved it over the many years.

As the *Yevsektsiya* (the Jewish Section of the Communist Party)[1] took control in the Jewish milieu, the Zionist Movement was banned again, and forced underground, but it continued uninterrupted to spread the Zionist idea to Jewish youngsters. Come night, they would gather in cellars and by candle–light, learn Hebrew and read modern Hebrew literature, especially the poetry of Bialik, Yehuda Leib Gordon, and the stories of "Mendele the Book Peddler", which were youth favorites. To the observer, youths were enlisting with the *Komsomol* (the Communist youth organization), where they would study Marxism, but at night they were dedicating themselves to the study of Zionism, taking interest in questions regarding the building of the land of Israel, and being presented with information from a variety of sources about the situation in the land of Israel. We also had a strong chapter of *Heḥalutz*, whose members were learning trades and preparing to emigrate to Israel. In the nearby village Michampol, we organized an agricultural collective, founded on the model of the ones organized by the Soviet authorities. The members of this collective were all *Heḥalutz* people, who were engaged in agricultural training in preparation for emigrating to Israel.

At times we would smuggle friends from Galicia and Bessarabia across the nearby border, opening before them the path to emigrating to Israel. This activity was mortally dangerous and carried the risk of incarceration, but this did not prevent us from sticking to our course.

Our work was an annoyance to the *Yevsektsiya*, and they waged war against us. They would convene

[Page 45]

large assemblies and go to great lengths to present our movement to the public as a counter–revolutionary movement, detached from the people.

I have a lasting vivid memory of one such assembly, that was held late in 1925, in the prayer house of the *Rebbe*, Reb Pinchas'l. The *Yevsektsiya* had invited a guest speaker from the district, who was all set to ideologically crush us and sing the praise of our local antagonists. At our organization's committee meeting, we realized that we must acknowledge the impression this assembly could make on the public, and we decided that our members must also be noticed at the assembly. To this end, one of our members would request the floor, and present clearly and correctly our national ideology, even though such a presentation carried the risk of incarceration.

That evening, the chapel was filled to its capacity. The assembly commenced with a speech by the *Yevsektsiya* delegate, maligning Zionism, as planned. When his speech was over, one of our members arose and requested the floor. He then explained to the assembly that we are not, God forbid, opposed to the revolution but, as Jews, we wish to build our future as a free people in the land of Israel, and that it is our intention to turn those non–productive elements within our people, precluded in exile by those who hate us from choosing worthy vocations, into a nation that cultivates its own land and creates its own culture.

As he concluded his clear and persuasive remarks, impassioned applause broke out in the room, and it grew very loud. One of the *Yevsektsiya* members ran out to summon the police and have our member arrested. Pandemonium erupted, and we were able to free our friend from the clutches of the police officer who had meanwhile arrived, and he escaped and left town.

A group of Zinkov Labor Zionist Federation underground activists in 1925

– Devorah Feldman, Zeev Nissim, Eidel Feuerstein, Yitzhak Steinweiss, Yisrael Nissim, his sister, Moshe Gurnick, Noyne Reichstein, one of Leibush Kurtzman's daughters, Joseph Yoshpe, Fuchs from Dolina, one of Leibush Kurtzman's daughters

[Page 46]

The events of that assembly were the talk of the town for weeks to come, and our strong stance left a powerful impression on the public. But the *Yevsektsiya* increased the pressure on us, and launched a campaign of searches and harassment, and our work for the land of Israel and Zionism became more difficult.

Following one of our association's night activities, on July 30th, 1926, the police lay in wait. They were searching for members of the Zionist Organization committee, and arrested three of its members: Moshe Gurnick, of blessed memory, Devorah Feldman, and myself. They held us for three days at the local jail, and then transported us to the district jail of Kamenetz–Podolsk. One month later they released Devorah Feldman, and the two of us stood trial, following three months of interrogations and we were sentenced to exile in Central Asia, where we were sent via the convoy route from one prison to the next. My place of exile was Ashkhabad, Turkmenistan.

We would undergo many hardships en route to our place of exile. We carried the burden lovingly and never lost hope for a release from this torment. And indeed, at long last, we were given permission to leave the confines of Russia and make *Aliyah*. I arrived in late 1927, and Moshe Gurnick, of blessed memory, arrived in early 1928.

After we had gone into exile and gone on to the land of Israel, our comrades in Zinkov continued underground activities for a number of years under desperate conditions, until eventually being overcome by the *Yevsektsiya*.

In this manner the youth of Zinkov contributed their part in the resurrection of our people and our homeland. We will forever remember them and never forget them!

Many of them were not fortunate to arrive at the destination for which they yearned, and perished during the Nazi Holocaust.

May their cherished and sacred memory be preserved in our national remembrance, with all the holy martyrs forever and ever.

Translator's footnote:

These sections were established in fall of 1918 with consent of Vladimir Lenin to carry communist revolution to the Jewish masses. The stated mission of these sections was the *Yevsektsiya* destruction of traditional Jewish life, the Zionist movement, and Hebrew culture".

[Page 47]

The Street

by Yisroel Sanis, Roytburd
Translated by Yael Chaver

The street was my street, where I lived from infancy until I was nineteen. As a small child, I played and spent time on the street. When I grew up, I left the street; this was after World War I, when upheavals and unrest drove me away – as they did others throughout the world – because young people could not do anything or be hopeful in what used to be our quiet home.

Zinkov natives who read my description of the street will certainly recognize it, and remember the people whom I mention here. But those who have never lived in Zinkov will enjoy a colorful presentation of a street in a Jewish town where families lived in a happy and close–knit community for many years, before they were completely exterminated by the German murderers so that only a memory of the street remains. The street consisted of a few dozen buildings, possibly even less. The planners of the street and its buildings were apparently not too concerned with matters such as symmetry, architecture, and the like. However, looking back from a distance of over fifty years, our street had many fine features – even compared to the streets of the Jewish ghettos in the big cities of America.[1] True, the street was covered in deep mud during spring and fall, and lacked electric lighting and sanitation all year round; but it contained no cramped "tenement houses" in which masses of people lived crammed into dirty, stuffy, tiny rooms and slept

[Page 48]

exhausted at night, waking up very early to long days of work in the sweatshops, estranged from each other in an alien world and unfamiliar surroundings, often lacking even a common language with this world.

The people on our street also worried about making a living–very much so! They did not have it easy, yet they were in charge of their own lives and fates. As hard as their lives might be, they retained human qualities. They lived among their own kind, poor, yet free people. They lived with the tradition that they inherited from their ancestors, spoke their own language, knew each other and were friends. They shared troubles as well as joys, helped each other in time of need, danced at all the weddings, and took part in all the funerals. No one can truly appreciate the value of these features, except, perhaps, those for whom living an intimate, independent life is more valuable than other, material, privileges.

The street was very old, but no one knew how old. The town was old; anyone seeking an idea of its age had to rummage around the ancient gravestones in the cemetery. Some of the inscriptions on the gravestones, themselves sunken into the ground, were still legible; among them was one that my grandfather (may he rest in peace) once pointed out to me. The inscription told me that one of my ancestors had found his eternal rest there, over a hundred years earlier. This was the age of the Jewish community in Zinkov, and perhaps older. Who knows the identity of the founder? If anyone had documentation of births over all those years, he had been exterminated. No one had written a history of the community. Its life was not entered into any record book, unlike the case in many other Jewish towns. The only thing available was an occasional inscription found on the cover or the title page of an old book, noting the date of a birth, or a death. The date of a Bar Mitzvah, or of being conscripted into the military might occasionally be found somewhere. As is typical of a primitive tribe, nothing was known of later life, nothing at all.[2] There were even families that did not register births with the village elder. Unusual events in the town were passed around. Such, for example, was the incident of the great fire that took the lives of many women in the synagogue one year during the *Kol Nidre* prayer.[3] My grandmother was one of those who escaped. According to her, it was not really a fire, but just

[Page 49]

a panic.

The women's synagogue was very high up, and could be reached by climbing up dark and winding stairs, to a location where "eyes" (round holes) had been cut through the thick walls and it was possible to look down into the men's synagogue and hear the cantor.[4] The entrance was through doors that opened inward rather than outward, which certainly caused the disaster. One of the hundreds of candles that had been lit before *Kol Nidre* overturned; someone yelled "Fire," "*pozhar*," and a panic broke out among the women.[5] A few of them jumped down through the holes into the main synagogue.

 Most ran to the door. Some fell to the ground, tussling with each other while the doors were being opened. The others ran down the stairs in crowding so that many suffocated and died. From then on, the synagogue was especially full at *Kol Nidre*. Masses would come to observe death anniversaries, of those who died in the panic as well as of others. When the *Kaddish* was recited, the congregation would be overcome by fear.[6] I remember many older men saying *Kaddish*.

Older men in the town would still tell various legends about the "Fortress." This was the ruin of a long–gone fort. When one climbed a narrow path near a ravine, the remnant of a four–cornered building constructed of rectangular blocks, fitted against each other like bricks, came into view. There were deep openings in the walls. People said that cannonballs used to be shot through these openings from the artillery inside. Above, on the flat ground that stretched behind the post office, there were entrances into caves. People said that these caves stretched underground for miles to another fort, eighteen miles from the town. There were legends that this had been the site of battles with "the Turk." They might have meant the Tatar invasion. Who knows?[7]

Netanel, Itta, and Yisro'el Roytburd in 1914

[Page 50]

War stories were common in our town. Naturally, the storytellers were soldiers who had completed their service, and a few surviving "Cantonists."[8] The latter told tales of their experiences; they were kidnapped as children, and the snatchers swore that their age was 17. They served as soldiers–if they survived–for the entire 25–year term, in distant locations. Those who had money could be ransomed; the snatchers would kidnap other children from poor families in order to complete their quota. I knew one such old soldier. His name was Itzl Elkes, and he was married to a relative of mine. He would tell wonderful stories while chopping wood quickly and expertly with a sharp axe. He'd chop some wood, then sit down and tell his tales. Everyone admired his sharp axe–there were no others like it in the town. This was because Jews did not know how to sharpen an axe so well, or chop wood with such speed. The young folks took "classes" from Itzl Elkes, and those whom he considered "suitable" could borrow his axe for a moment; otherwise, the axe never left his hand.

Zinkov was also the cradle of leaders of a Hassidic dynasty.[9] The Hassidim, visitors as well as local, would often talk about miracles, and recount snippets of learning as well as events caused by rivalries between the various rabbinic "courts." People marveled at the lavish weddings and hospitality for large numbers of Hassidim who celebrated holidays and other occasions with great pomp. But I have strayed far from the street, and would like to return.

Our street was near three sacred locations: the synagogue, the *bes–medresh*, and the small synagogue. These formed a group of buildings separated from the street by a narrow passageway. The very fact that the three houses of prayer stood far from the street gave the synagogue courtyard a

[Page 51]

special function as a broad passageway for all those going to or coming from prayers. It was good to stand at the window at sundown on Friday or on Saturday morning and observe the street. After sunset on Friday, the voice of the snub–nosed synagogue sexton could be heard from the marketplace. He knocked at the shutters of the stores and chanted in a drawn–out rhythm "Into the synagogue!" That was a signal to the storekeepers that they needed to close their businesses, and that the Sabbath was around the corner. (Remarkably, this call to storekeepers "Into the synagogue" and its drawn–out echo has stayed in my memory for all these years.) The peasants, whose carts usually stood on the street, also understood this signal. They would attach full feed–bags to the horse's neck before going into the market to shop for necessities as well as to visit the tavern and snatch a glass of spirits. Hearing the call "Into the synagogue," they would prepare to leave, harnessing up the horses and vanishing one after the other, as though by magic. The alleys were cleared of carts. Any cart that was left on the street at twilight would have its horses hastily harnessed and drive away quickly, as though bound by an injunction against entering the town on the Sabbath.

　　　**********

Let's take a walk along the sparsely built–up street, become acquainted with the residents, and tell you our memories of life there.

Our house was close to that of Shloyme's Rivke. She was called that because of her husband, Shloyme–Avrom, Pini's son. Shloyme–Avrom had a small store where he sold lime for whitewashing walls. There was a kind of storeroom under the house, where barrels of lime chunks stood around the low walls. Among the barrels lived a cow – yes, a real–life cow – who calved every year and produced milk. How a living creature could survive in that place and, furthermore, produce good milk for selling, is really wondrous; a wonder that could happen only in our Zinkov – but that was the case. The milk sold by Shloyme's Rivke was famous throughout town. Every evening, women would come around with small pots. Rivke would measure out milk into the pots with a glass, and there were enough clients to buy up the entire "product." Rivke herself did not need much milk. She had no children; she was childless. A small pitcher of buttermilk and a piece of cheese were enough for her, especially because she raised ducks and geese in the attic, as well as cages full of chickens. Anyway, whoever in our town of Zinkov drank milk, unless it was a sick person, or a weak child who needed extra nourishment?

[Page 52]

Do you think that Shloyme's Rivke was fully occupied with selling milk? Think again. They barely made a living by selling lime, and the work involved with the cow was worth more than the income it brought in. But apparently they held on to the cow out of household habit. And after all, it was another living thing in the house.

Shloyme's Rivke and her husband, may their memory be for a blessing

Shloyme's Rivke was a short, stocky woman, with dark skin and a round moon–face. She wore a wig, parted in the center like an Indian woman. She was not a Zinkov native, and was proud of it. "Kiev," she would say, "is where I'm from." Although she came from a big city, she couldn't speak proper Ukrainian.[10] It was a pleasure to see her bargaining with the peasant women in an odd language: a part–Yiddish part–Slavic lingo. The bargaining was carried out in loud voices, because her negotiations with the peasants were mutual: she sold them the lime, and bought up everything they had: a wreath of garlic, a few onions, groats, a chicken, a goose, and anything else. Her voice carried down the street, and it was always bustling around her store.

Her husband, Shloyme, was the complete opposite. He was a fine–looking man, tall, broad–boned, with a nice beard and mustache that were always white because of the lime dust. He was quiet and withdrawn. Always busy, he'd be stirring the large lime barrels, or around the cow or the house. He would weigh out the lime for his clients. Rivke would stand at the door, negotiating or receiving money and placing it in the large purse that hung beneath her apron.

[Page 53]

As I mentioned earlier, Rivke had no children of her own, but she really loved children. The broad wooden stairs leading to the entrance of her house always had children on them, playing happily. When Rivke no longer needed to be at the store, on Shabbat or summer evenings, she would sit down on the stairs, talk with the women, and every so often go indoors and bring an apronful of treats. She had a wonderful store of sweets for the women and children: shortbread cookies, almond cookies, poppyseed cakes. She had jars of brandied sour cherries, which supplied cherry brandy. And she was famous for her tart, fermented apples. She offered samples of everything to her friends and the children she loved. When Purim came around, she started handing out all kinds of goodies to young and old, and continued until Passover: candy, fruit cakes made with honey, *homentashen* filled with plum preserves or poppyseed and honey.[11] Children flocked to her like bees and sat on the steps. She always treated everyone generously to wonderful baked goods and other sweets. The greatest fun was when Rivke handed out *matza* for Passover. Before stocking up with fresh–baked *matza*, she brought out her reserve of year–old *matza*, left over from the previous year. Though the *matza* now tasted stale and left over, it was in high demand. Folks would taste it like a delicacy, chew it up happily, and no one got sick.

Gogol's stories of demons and spirits are well known, but the tales told by Shloyme's Rivke of her own experiences with the devil would surely have surpassed Gogol's yarns.[12] Her style of narrating these bizarre stories was so artistic and persuasive that the children, and perhaps their mothers as well, were terrified. Though no one really believed her, people would stay seated through twilight and into darkness, listening to her very attentively. There were rumors that the horned demon she supposedly encountered going through the gloomy, cramped passageway was none other than the town billy–goat who hid out there.

We should also note, in Rivke's favor, that her elderly father–in–law lived with them; this was Pini, Shloyme's father. He was paralyzed and bedridden. Rivke took care of him to the end of his life, washing and caring for him, never complaining of difficulty. She did this not merely out of duty but also out of love.

I left this couple, Rivke and Shloyme, in their home in Zinkov, in 1919. Their image was sent to me when I was already living in America.

[Page 54]

The synagogue, drawn by Nochem Yoshpeh

Translator's footnotes:

1. "Ghetto" is the term used in the original text.

2. The "primitive tribe" terminology is in the original, and echoes some concepts of the Enlightenment.

3. The *Kol Nidre* prayer marks the onset of Yom Kippur, the most solemn day in the Jewish calendar.

4. The quote marks are in the original.

5. *Pozhar*, conflagration in Russian, is presented in Yiddish transliteration.

6. Yom Kippur is traditionally an occasion to pray for the deceased. The *Kaddish* is the prayer for the dead.

7. This reference would be to the Turco–Mongol invasion of Europe, in the 13th century

8. "Cantonists" were Jewish boys (some as young as 8 or 9) who were conscripted to military institutions in czarist Russia during 1827–1856, with the intention that their new conditions would force them to adopt Christianity. The term of service was 25 years. This period was extremely traumatic for the Jews under Russian rule.

9. Hassidic leadership was usually passed down in the family, forming a "dynasty." Zinkov is associated with the Apt–Mezhbizh–Zinkover Hasidic dynasty.

10. I have translated the Yiddish *goyish* –the term for a non–Jewish language – as "Ukrainian."

11. Purim is a spring holiday celebrating the deliverance of Persian Jews from the evil scheming of the king's minister, Homen. Treats are traditionally handed out to neighbors and relatives. *Homentashen* are triangular pastries with a sweet filling. Purim and Passover are exactly one month apart.

12. The Ukrainian writer Nikolai Gogol (1809–1852) is considered one of the great artists of Russian literature.

———

[Page 55]

The Synagogue and its Christian Visitors
by Yisrael Ben–Shachar (Schwarzman)
Translated by Aryeh Sklar

It would take volumes to tell all that I have seen and heard and all that I have experienced, outwardly as well as inwardly, in the first eighteen years of my life in my hometown in the Ukrainian steppes, the town on Zinkov: a town whose houses were mostly single–family, some double–family, and only a few were two stories tall. The four main streets of Zinkov were paved and surfaced, but they had no sidewalks, and at night they were illuminated by gas lamps. All other streets were nothing more than natural dirt paths, and at night they were immersed in total darkness.

Its Jewish inhabitants numbered about 4,000 in total. Non–Jews did not dwell within the town boundaries.

When all was well, a community council managed public matters and, to its best ability, it would ensure the financing of all social and cultural institutions, national funds and charity institutions, as well as a medical relief fund for the town's poor. In this respect it was a beacon among all of its neighboring towns.

[Page 56]

In the center of the town stood majestically the sprawling structure that was the Great Synagogue. Its exterior was modest in appearance, as was the practice from days of old, intended, presumably, so as to not incite envy or rage in the gentiles. But its interior was distinguished by its captivating beauty, and its attractive and tastefully artistic architecture. Especially prominent was the art of the *Mizrach*–the eastern wall–which housed the ornate Holy Ark, laden with silver–plating and gold–

plating and adorned with engravings of all manner of fauna and fowl. From bottom to top, the Holy Ark was four stories tall, it was shroud in glory and holiness, and all who beheld it were astounded by it to no end. And anyone who has not experienced the *Kol Nidre* prayer in that synagogue, has never experienced holiness and glory.

And so, the story goes: My father–Reb Shiye Avraham Moshe Manis, of blessed memory–took me, as he did every year, along with my two brothers to the Great Synagogue for the *Kol Nidre* service. He was not especially devout, but he did observe tradition as practiced in our town. In honor of the holiday, he dressed in a black suit, the coat of which reached down to his knees, tied a pure silk band around his waist, as was the Hassidic custom, and on his head, he wore a firm moderately tall top hat, in the fashion of the times. When we arrived at the synagogue, he wrapped himself in his *Talit*–prayer shawl–which was adorned with a beautiful gilt collar, and we both took our reserved seats, feeling the sanctity of the moment. Before us, light sown by hundreds of *Neshama* candles that burned in gigantic crafted copper seven–stem candelabra, in honor of *Yizkor*, instilling godly awe in the hearts of the congregants.

My mother–Itta Alter Sanis, of blessed memory–dressed my sisters on that festive night in magnificent garments, ascended with them to the Ladies section, and they all sat in their reserved seats, waiting in anticipation as we did, for the commencement of the service, set to begin exactly at sundown. Meanwhile, each of the congregants began the "Tefilla Zakka" prayer that precedes the *Kol Nidre*, and while there were those who supplicated aloud, there were others who prayed in a whisper, emphasizing each and every word uttered, and others still who moaned and sighed, recreating in their minds the image of standing before the creator on this Yom Kippur to confess their transgressions, committed knowingly as well as unknowingly, and answering for their sins. And even though I was but a child, I too deeply felt the holiness of the moment with every fiber of my being, because in the environment in which I was raised, our people knew how to deeply instill in the hearts of the children a Jewish identity, and teach them to be dedicated and loyal to their roots.

Suddenly, silence fell. A soft murmur washed through the large hall, which was packed to capacity, and the entire congregation turned their eyes towards the entrance.

Appearing there were delegates of the Catholic and Orthodox clergy from nearby villages, dress in their traditional garb. They had come, as was they did every year, to hear "Itzik Chazan", who, with his pleasant voice, his musicality, his technique, and the way he sang as though he was pouring out his soul, had become legendary, and his reputation preceded him throughout the district.

The synagogue ushers, of course, warmly welcomed the guests and led them to the eastern wall, offering them the seats reserved for visiting dignitaries, beside the Rabbi's seat, and past the cantor's dais. They took their seats and listened intently to the prayers, and some of them perused the prayer books given to them by the ushers, as they could read Hebrew and even understand the words (possibly among them were even converted Jews).

And when Reb Itizik blared his mighty voice, which rose liltingly to the heavens, the sound of his voice soaring

[Page 57]

with the accompaniment of the choir he led–a tremor ran through the hearts, those of the Christian guests as well. When the service was over, the seniors among them leading the more junior, all went to shake the hand of the cantor and to congratulate him with the Hebrew "*Yiyashar Kochacha!*" (Kudos, well done!).

Such was Zinkov, my hometown, a Jewish city, a modest cradle of Judaism to its children...

How the city sits solitary, her homes desolate, her children led like sheep to the slaughter.

And I, son of Itta Alter Sanis, a remnant of the beloved town of Zinkov, who knew at that time, as early as 1920, to accept–thanks to my Jewish and Zionist upbringing– the call of the divine providence to awaken at the age of eighteen from the dormancy of exile, to report lovingly and whole–heartedly for duty for my people, and return to Zion. Since then I partook in the revival of the land of Israel and fought like a lion in defense against the Arabs and the English who hindered us, and I was fortunate to witness the gathering of our exiled nation from the four corners of the earth, and the establishment of the State of Israel.

I knew all too well that my brethren were being led to the slaughter anywhere the foul genocidal killers entered, and even in my beloved hometown, but here I was, helpless and unable to assist. For this mine eye runneth incessantly down with tears, and I weep bitterly for the breach of the daughter of my people. May the Lord remember them all and cherish their souls in the bundle of life. Peace unto their dust and may their memory be blessed!

And you, my fellow Jews, remember and never forget that which the German Amalek did unto us, never forget, and never forgive!

[Page 58]

Our Synagogue

by Borech Laskin

Translated by Yael Chaver

Elsewhere in our Memorial Book, we have already told of the terrible event that occurred in our synagogue at *Kol Nidre*, when a panic caused by fire took the lives of thirty–three women of Zinkov. I myself was not present at this fearful disaster, which happened when I was an infant. But for years, people shuddered when they recounted the horrific event to later generations. In fact, when I was old enough to attend, I knew about the tragedy and would be afraid if I had to go by the synagogue in the dark, especially on winter evenings.[1]Going home with my friends from group study with Rabbi Yekl (Moyshe Yudel's son), who lived near the synagogue, we would clasp our lanterns tightly, cling together in pairs, and sing "On the day of your rejoicing"[2] to silence the fear that loomed over us. However, when I grew older, I became proud of our Zinkov synagogue for two reasons: first, because of the handsome building and its great size, and second, thanks to the synagogue cantor, Itzik Khazn, may his memory be for a blessing.

The synagogue was the tallest building in town. It was half a block long and a smaller half–block in width. It was built of large dressed stones, and looked like a fortress on the outside. The entrance into the synagogue led through a large, wide corridor. Smaller synagogues were built into both sides of the corridor, where different *minyans* prayed. One of these small synagogues was the "Tailors," in which the town's artisans gathered for prayers.[3] I remember them gathering on Saturday mornings. Alter Sanye (may he rest in peace), my friend's father, would come into the Tailor's Synagogue and teach the congregation *Eyn Yaakov*.[4] As one entered the synagogue, it appeared very tall and wide. At the very top, near the ceiling, the Women's Synagogue was built like a balcony. The powerful voice of Itzik Khazn, may he rest in peace, reached each corner of the synagogue, in spite of its great height and breadth. I was very proud of the synagogue and the cantor, especially when the Christian town officials would come for *Kol Nidre*. These included the regional police superintendent, the sergeant, and the chief policeman. They would come with their wives and their grown children to hear *Kol Nidre*, and would marvel at the beauty of the synagogue.

[Page 59]

The *bes medresh* was opposite the synagogue, and had its own small synagogue attached. Various householders of the town prayed there. The *bes medresh* was separated from the synagogue only by a narrow passageway, and the only thing missing was a sign with the traditional "This is the gate of the Lord, the righteous shall enter through it."[5] I remember that when a funeral procession came, the pallbearers would stop in the passageway between the synagogue and the *bes medresh*, and Itzik Khazn would chant the *El Mole Rachamim*, so loudly that any of the townspeople who wanted to participate in the funeral could immediately head to the synagogue.[6] The passageway would quickly fill with people. Once the cantor had finished the prayer, the procession made its way to the cemetery, which was at the edge of town yet not too far from the synagogue. One had to pass several small alleys of the "Abashuvka" neighborhood, where the poorer population of the town lived, in small, low buildings whose roofs were covered with straw. However, the synagogue was often a symbol of joy as well, when a wedding took place in the town. The band came marching first, followed by family members celebrating with the bride and groom, and all the guests. The band would play a *freylekhs* and the joyous procession would exit through the same narrow passageway. A wedding *chuppah* would be ready outside, between the synagogue and the *bes medresh*.[7] Many people, not all of them invited, would come to see the ceremony...

Now, as people have told me, everything has been destroyed and smashed by the Hitlerite murderers, may their name be blotted out. They murdered all the Jews of Zinkov, they destroyed our synagogue and *bes medresh*, plowed up the earth, and planted a garden where the synagogue once stood.

Let us engrave this in our hearts, to remember for all eternity!

Translator's footnotes:

1. Boys started their studies in *cheder* when they were as young as 3.

2. The verse in Numbers 10,10 ("On your days of rejoicing–your appointed festivals and New Moon feasts–you are to sound the trumpets") is set to a rousing melody that is traditionally sung at Hassidic group gatherings.

3. A *minyan* is the group of ten men required for communal prayer. Members of a certain trade would often band together for regular prayer.

4. The 16th–century *Eyn Yaakov* is a popular compilation of all the Aggadic material in the Talmud, together with commentaries.

5. This quote from Psalms 118, 20, is commonly set above entrances to synagogues.

6. *El Mole Rachamim* is a prayer for the soul of the person who has died, wishing it proper rest. Participating in a funeral is considered an important communal duty.

7. A *freylekhs* is a traditional wedding dance. The *chuppah* is the canopy under which the wedding ceremony takes place.

—

[Page 60]

The Synagogue

by Yisro'el Sanis, Roytburd

Translated by Yael Chaver

As sundown approached on Friday afternoons, the street would become empty. It was quiet, Shabbes–like. The Friday evening candles are already burning in the windows. Soon, Jews ready for Shabbes appear in the street; they're on their way to the ceremony ushering in Shabbes. They go along in the emptied silence, freshly washed, wearing their best Shabbes clothing. They walk with a measured stride, in no hurry, and their children walk alongside slowly. They vanish, one after the other, into the narrow street that leads to the synagogue, to the small synagogue, and the *bes medresh.*

The street grows calm, silent, and peaceful. Only murmurs are audible, like a rushing river, from the illuminated synagogues. Voices rise and fall: the Jews are welcoming Shabbes. You can't stand at the window any longer. The sounds of Shabbes eve make you feel guilty for being here and not there, in the synagogue. How long does it take a little boy to run over there? After thinking a bit, I run past the *Linas Tzedek* synagogue (where my father prays) and I am right by the synagogue.[1] The great massive door opens easily. Apparently, it was so designed. You run down a few broad stairs and you're standing at the *bimah*...[2] It is round and high, like a stage, carved on all sides. At its front, directly opposite the Ark of the Torah and leaning against the carved wood, is a long oak bench. Several reading stands are alongside the bench. Our family's seat was at the third reading stand from the corner. It had belonged to my great–grandfather, who according to family history had actually helped to build the synagogue. Our seat was always occupied by Uncle Yeshaya.

The synagogue is large, and mostly empty. You can stroll behind the *bimah*, and through the side rooms with their rounded ceilings. You could even have fun with your friends and no one in the front would notice. The long eastern wall on both sides of the Torah Ark was also not too occupied.[3] It was great fun to sit there and watch the cantor's face at the lectern.[4] But that's not where one sat. Each seat had its attraction, its own qualities (not properties!). Each person had his own spot. In actual fact, it was cramped, but no one minded. People pushed together a bit and were happy to make room for a child. By all means, sit down, young man. But who had the patience to sit there for long? The Shabbes evening ceremony is almost at an end. Itzik the cantor will soon say the blessing over wine for the congregation. After the blessing, he will give the guys already sitting on the steps leading to the Torah Ark, right next to the lectern, a sip from his large goblet – who could miss that? First of all, there's no wine sweeter than the raisin wine used for the blessing. And second, not everyone gets the chance to be important enough to drink from the blessing goblet... Later, other things occupied our minds; and, of course, we were occupied with everything that was happening around us. The synagogue was no longer the sole source of moral and spiritual possibilities for that generation.

[Page 61]

I have stayed in the synagogue for a long time, and will now describe only characteristic moments connected with the synagogue (as well as with the small synagogue and *bes medresh*), because at the time it was a popular center in the full sense of the term. People did not come for purposes of prayer only. Spending time in the houses of prayer was not exclusively connected with religiosity. Being there was like being at home. The traditional ritual of prayer was natural, an organic part of daily life. However, between prayers people discussed community matters, family events, livelihoods, and news of the world. When new breezes began to blow, of enlightenment and secular studies – and later, when ideals of revolution began to spread among Jews – there were heated debates within the synagogue walls and around the *bimah*. The community began to simmer between the walls of the synagogue, which now housed large gatherings. People now assembled for ceremonies as well as to hear speakers and political debates.

But even before the "new breezes" began to rouse the national and political senses of the Zinkov community, the ground was ready for all political elements. Jews did not need to be told that they were oppressed. They were well–aware of it in everyday life, at every step. If someone had to leave town and spend the night in another village, the police chief or low–ranking sergeant would drive him away. Within the town, people constantly encountered the "guardians of the law," at every business negotiation, and even when bringing their own produce to sell.

[Page 62]

There were two strong national aspirations. One was to be free of the bitter poverty and oppression. The other was to somehow be freed from exile and to return to Zion and Jerusalem, places that everyone dreamed about and mentioned in prayer three times a day. When a Jew came to the verses "If I forget thee, Jerusalem, let my right hand forget its cunning," or "May our eyes behold thy return to Zion with mercy," he felt it with all his heart.[5] It was hard to believe that revolution would bring about an overnight basic change in the attitude of the local population to the Jews, and they would then be able to live in peace. Every day, Jews witnessed the malice of the locals among which they lived. To our great sorrow, the Jews were not mistaken. It was only two decades after the revolution when the local population handed over the Jews to Hitler's evil–doers, and then proceeded to rob their meager possessions while jeering at them for their misfortune.

For this reason, the Jews of Zinkov, like Jews everywhere, celebrated their holidays with great joy and a deep longing stemming from these historical memories. At Passover, families went out of Egypt with their elders and hoped to leave slavery for freedom once again. People lived in confidence that the miracle of the Exodus would happen again. During Shevu'es, the first fruits were carried to the temple; people made do in the meantime by decorating their homes with branches from trees belonging to others.[6] They dreamed of their own fields and rich orchards, so that they would no longer have to buy a bit of fruit with the few pennies they could spare. During the High Holidays, the days of repentance, people trembled as they listened to the sound of the old, old shofar. The shofar was heard before dawn throughout the sleepy and dew–covered town, during the entire month of Elul.[7]These longings were felt during all the holidays as well as the days of mourning. And, of course, Yom Kippur. Yom Kippur is certainly a purely religious holiday, yet historical memories are woven into even this religious occasion. *Kol Nidre*, the Spanish Inquisition, and the atmosphere at Ne'ila, when prayers are said for Jerusalem "that is brought low, unto death."[8] The city of Jerusalem is also entrusted with using its ruins to beg God for mercy for the suffering souls who have not lost hope, because "we belong to God and our eyes turn to God."[9] The most beautiful and lofty aspect of these prayers is that they are always said as a collective, always speaking for the nation and not for the individual. And aren't the hymns praising God sung because He has fine Jewish qualities such as mercy and integrity?!

[Page 63]

I have digressed, while enthusiastically considering the spiritual treasures of our nation in general, and their effect on the Jews of Zinkov in particular, as part of the organic whole. We will be back to provide more details of our Zinkov street and its surroundings, including the beautiful building that has left an indelible impression on all natives of Zinkov and is forever engraved in their memories – the synagogue.

Translator's footnotes:

1. *Linas Tzedek* is a society helping to take care of the sick.
2. The stand on which the Torah rests during services.
3. The eastern wall of a synagogue has the most prestigious seats, as it abuts the Torah Ark.
4. The cantor prays facing east, with his back to the congregation.
5. The first phrase is a quote from Psalm 137, 5; the second is part of a prayer.
6. Shevu'es commemorates the offering of first fruits in the Temple.
7. It is customary to blow the shofar every weekday morning during the Jewish month of Elul, which precedes the High Holidays. The blasts are meant to inspire soul–searching. Days of mourning for historical national disasters are designated throughout the year.
8. Ne'ila is the solemn prayer that concludes Yom Kippur. The quote is from an 8th–century liturgical poem.
9. The quote is from the Mishnaic tractate of Sukkot.

[Page 64]

The Self–Defense Organization (*Samoobrona*) in Zinkov

by Nachum Yoshpeh

Translated by Aryeh Sklar

In memorializing the activity of the self–defense organization in Zinkov, I have no great revelations to offer. Fortunately, we never engaged in bloody campaigns with raiders. While we did have some difficult times, when gangs of raiders threatened to breach the town, thanks to our well–organized defensive activity and our close–knit and disciplined comradery, we evaded danger and instilled fear in those who would threaten the safety of our town.

From time immemorial, Jews in southern Russia, in the Ukraine, were never able to "lie down, and none shall make them afraid". They always expected trouble, and it fell upon the Self–Defense Organization to serve as the shield against this trouble.

The *Samoobrona* began as early as late 1905, when I was but nine years old. In the wake of the failure of the October 1905 revolution, a wave of anti–Jewish pogroms washed over Russia. Jews lived in fear everywhere, but doubly so in our town, due to a rumor that the "Katsasps" in the neighboring village of Petrashi (Petriceni) were being incited to attack the Jews of Zinkov. The "Katsaps" were Russians, from central Russia, who had escaped Russia during the times of Peter the Great and Catherine the Great, due to the religious reforms implemented by the Czarist authorities, and resettled in dedicated villages in the Ukraine. They were powerful and bold people, who made their living in a variety of trades, and more than a few of them were criminals. They intimidated not only the Jews, but ordinary Ukrainians as well.

Indeed, there were those who believed that on the merit of the two great *rebbes*, Reb Moshe'le and Reb Pinchas'l, no ill could befall our town, but when it came to the "Katsaps", everyone understood the matter was serious, and the prevailing motto was "*Du tu, un Got vett dir helfin*" – "You do, and God will help".

To this end, *Samoobrona* was established, in secrecy of course. People would gather in my parents' shop and whisper. They spoke of "*taytlach*" ("dates") [as code for manufacturing weapons]. Blacksmiths discussed the choice of iron for manufacturing cold weapons.[1] I remember one time, having returned from a trip to Proskurov (Khmelnytskyi), my father had brought back two rifles, and another time, a pistol.

Several of the wealthier families moved out of town to weather the storm. Ourselves as well, i.e. my mother and us children, were taken by my father to stay in the nearby town of Solovkovitz for a while, while he returned to Zinkov.

The night in question, when according to the rumor, the "Katsaps" planned to attack the town, was of course a night of fearful watching and preparing. But the "Katsaps" never came. Because the warnings sent by our people to the people Petrashi had the desired effect, and the "Katsaps" did not take up the call of the inciters.

[Page 65]

The local Ukrainians, almost all of whom were farmers, posed no serious threat, especially at that time when Zinkov was governed by the *Oriadnik* Bratinki, an old and wily police Sergeant Major, who knew ahead of time of any theft or crime about to be committed. The town lay protected under Bratinki, and he was of course handsomely rewarded.

Meanwhile, a time of calm arrived. Life resumed normalcy, Jewish children and Ukrainian children learning together in school. There was no longer a need for *Samoobrona*, and it was all but forgotten.

Following the October 1917 revolution, public safety crumbled. Regimes and authorities were rising and falling, a state of anarchy ensued, enabling gangs of pillagers and plunderers to undermine public safety, and first and foremost, attack the Jews.

Bedlam set in in 1918, and by then I was already among the activists.

Once, as a company of Russian soldiers returning from the frontlines, set up camp in Kalinovka (Kalynivka), a village near Zinkov, several of them robbed our neighbor, the Sadikovs, at gunpoint, and warned all who saw them that they would destroy anyone who protested their actions. We did not yet know how to react to the robbery, and to the ensuing threats, but as we were formulating our response the next day, a Ukrainian showed up and informed us that that night the company was planning to mobilize through our town, and that they will undoubtedly attempt to perpetrate further robberies.

The message was late in arriving. A number of the town politicos convened and discussed a plan of action. They decided to alert the head of the militia, and to set up an unarmed patrol, and they called in young people who were in possession of arms, just in case, to participate and stand guard.

Near midnight, while the politicos still sat there devising their plan of action, gunfire began to rain down on the town, coming from the direction of Kalinovka. Many of the Jewish residents responded by taking up arms and rushing outside. But due to a lack of organization and discipline, commotion and confusion took the streets.

At that time, I happened to be in the center of town. I immediately ran home. On my way I encountered a fifteen–year old boy, who held a rifle, but had no bullets. I took the rifle from him and rushed inside to get a supply of bullets from my father. He let me in and, at first, tried to dissuade me from running out there alone. But when I told him the guys outside had no bullets, he gave me a pouch full of bullets, and then he kissed me and sent me on my way. I ran straight to the *Obshivka*.[2] When I reached the home of the *Krupnik*(the groats maker) opposite the cemetery, I could see that the shots were being fired from that direction. I took a position beside the house and opened fire towards the source of the gunfire. I fired thirty–five rounds. Then the gunfire ceased, it became still, and after a few moments I could hear the sound of people speaking. As I approached that spot, I found Yankel Petyotis and Shlomo Zekel, who had also been firing in the direction of the cemetery.

On the following morning, we found in the cemetery many shell casings. headstones that had been hit by our gunfire, and even traces of blood. It became apparent that we had, with three rifles, held off an entire company. More importantly, the company that had departed Kalinovka did not pass through our town, and the rounds they shot near the town as they passed it, had wounded one Jewish resident in the arm as he sat in his home, killed a horse, and shattered a hanging lamp.

[Page 66]

That same evening, a youth meeting was convened, and *Samoobrona* was reestablished, under the command of Avraham Gusakov. The group was organized such that each member selected a secure and suitable partner who would not leave their side in an emergency. And each pair was charged with patrolling the streets on any market day, or any day when there was an army presence in town, and ensuring that spirits were not sold on those days. The pairs would not overtly carry weapons while patrolling. While there were plenty of weapons in town, and the militia was aware of this, they were not permitted to overtly carry weapons. Usually, I should note, whenever a riot broke out, the militiamen would disappear, as they did not wish to get involved and appear as protectors of Jews. Therefore, in times of emergency, we had to rely only on ourselves. To fortify our defenses, we occasionally had a mounted unit appear, and once we managed to detain a gang of inciters and hand them over to the police.

Our *Samoobrona* gained a reputation in the region, and it was even called in once to a neighboring town, to keep the peace at market day. But our activity was only effective against civilian inciters and raiders; it would be helpless if we had to confront a marauding army.

And then, when the Germans invaded the Ukraine, they instilled Skoropadsky as *Hetman*, in charge of the entire region, as they viewed him as an effective shield against Bolshevism. Of course, this was followed by the establishment of the State Guard (*Derzhavna Varta*), and the formation of the Cossack Cavalier Divisions. In those days the *Haidamakas*instigated riots in a number of places.

But the really great calamity befell the entire region, including Zinkov, once Petliura rose up against Skoropadsky. The Jews became the scapegoat. Entire towns were destroyed during those savage times. In our area, the greatest massacres were perpetrated in Proskurov, Felshtin, and Staro–Konstantinov ("Old Constantine"). Our town, distant from the center, escaped destruction, but occasionally, individual soldiers would appear, demanding a "contribution". Jews have always been prepared, and we were no exception, to pay money to redeem lives, but we always added a show of strength when paying the money, prepared to defend ourselves should the soldiers get out of control.

Avraham Gusakov

There was also one incident where money was deceitfully extorted from our townsfolk. One fine day the sound of continuous gunfire sounded. Panic broke out. The Ukrainians hitched their wagons and began closing their shops. Rumors spread that the army was entering town. The first pair of *Samoobrona* operatives who ran out towards the source of the gunfire, without rifles but with concealed pistols, were met by three mounted men, two of whom carried rifles, and the third a machine gun. They asked to meet with the mayor, and said the regiment had sent them to inform us to prepare a large "contribution", and to surrender to them the weapons that had fired upon them. If this was all given to them, the regiment would not pass through the town.

[Page 67]

In addition to the weapons that the *Samoobrona* and certain individuals possessed, we also had ten government–issue rifles, issued to ten licensed men led by Yisrael Greenman, nicknamed "Einkaufer". We decided to hand over the ten government–issue rifles to the riders. and properly explain it, as we were powerless to object to the demands of the army. I and one more of our members brought the rifles. They accepted them, but they trained the machine gun on us and threatened to obliterate us if they were not given a large sum of money, ransom for the townsfolk. In order to avert danger, the money was collected quickly. Moti Feuerman, president of the community, arrived with the money and handed it to the riders. They invited him to their lodging for a drink, and even issued him a receipt for the money. They ate, they drank, and they disappeared. We later found the rifles, their breeches removed, and cast away into the mangers. The entire tale about the regiment had been a complete fabrication.

We had many difficult and dangerous adventures with the Cossacks under the command of Petliura, who would devise any way to cause us grief and extort exorbitant sums of money from the townsfolk. We also had many clashes with the local Ukrainians, especially on Fair Days, when large numbers of farmers from neighboring villages would all gather in one place. At times, these clashes were quite serious, but they never escalated to bloodshed. Most noteworthy were the people of the village Vrebky who were very open with their propaganda and incitement to massacre Jews. But because we were constantly on guard, we succeeded in thwarting their plans beforehand.

We stood bravely and showed great fortitude. We instilled fear in the inciters and raiders who thought they would find us weak. Besides the hot and cold weapons[3] that we employed in case of emergency, we used sticks and bottles, and the *Samoobrona* strike force also had iron knuckle dusters. If you have not seen Yankel Petyotis in a fight, you have never seen a hero in action. He could strike at ten men at once, none of them able to hit him at all. There was also a guy, a water carrier who worked for David Wasserfeuer, a redhead, who possessed tremendous physical strength. He was a bit sluggish but immensely resolute. It was said of him that he could knock down a bull. He was capable of pushing back a crowd of people.

The power of the *Samoobrona* became especially apparent during one of the brawls that broke out between the Ukrainians and the haberdashers in the market. The brawl had likely been pre–arranged. It was a market day, and the square was crowded with people, mostly farmers from the neighboring villages. An unexpected frenzy broke out. Several of the Ukrainian shoppers attempted to escape without paying the merchants for the merchandise they were buying, and one of the Jews broke out shouting, "Help!

I'm being robbed!". The merchants began to hastily close up their shops. To call for help, several rounds were fired as well.

When pandemonium broke out, most of the Jews high–tailed it out of there, but amongst the crowd were people,

[Page 68]

among them some who were not young, and who were not *Samoobrona* members who are not accustomed to running from a fight; most of them were carriage drivers. There was Yehiel Tana, a broad and stout man, there was Berel Paysis, a muscular man, The Yantsis brothers, Chilikel "the Litvak"–they were the first to rush to the aid of the haberdashers. They snatched a new hat from one gentile, and grabbed a new hat off the head of another. A massive brawl broke out. The Ukrainians began striking the Jews. The Jews responded, blow for blow. The Ukrainians filled the market square, the incitement was overt. Some of the shops, whose owners could not close them up in time, were abandoned by their owners. These were small grocery shops that could not be robbed in a hurry. Gentiles began grabbing bars of soap, some stuck their arms into barrels of pickled fish. But even this, they did not get the chance to complete because, just at the right time, our considerable reinforcements arrived. Although we did carry weapons, they were mainly meant for intimidation purposes. Even the knives that both we and the Ukrainians carried, did not, fortunately come into use.

We used only sticks and bottles. The strike force members also had knuckle-dusters.

If you haven't seen Yankel Petyotis and the way he charged the raiders, you have never seen a hero. Avraham "the militiaman" was also outstanding that day in his bravery. By then he was already a bona fide militiaman–he wore a government–issued uniform–but his salary was paid by our community.

Eventually, the gentiles were vanquished, split up into little groups and chased by the Jews who outnumbered them. And when they began to flee, other Jews joined the *Samoobrona* people. We did not sustain any serious injury during that big brawl–just the odd broken arm or leg, and scrapes and bruises.

This entire campaign took place in the vicinity of Zinkov's famous pottery market, which was entirely under control of the "gentiles" who, that day, had primarily suffered losses, because during the scuffle, and specifically during the retreat and escape, pots whose owners were not able to collect inside, were trampled. The following day, the potters proposed that they would contribute people to the *Samoobrona*, and in return we would position guard details near them on market day, to prevent damage to their merchandise. We rejected their proposal.

Generally, we were successful in those days in protecting our fellow Jews in Zinkov and their property. But we were helpless against the army, and if we did occasionally manage to survive clashes with the army, it was not thanks to force but, rather, thanks to the implementation of some artfulness and artifice. But one particular night, disaster suddenly struck, delivering a terrible blow to *Samoobrona* as a whole, and each of us individually. We were stunned and crestfallen. We sustained what one would call a direct hit.

That night, Petliura forces entered the town. The instructions, given by *Samoobrona*, were for everyone to lock themselves inside their homes, as usual, at night, and to not open up for anyone, not to respond to any order from the army or the police, and should anyone attempt to force their way in, they were to begin shouting, to alert our people, who would then endeavor to arrive there from wherever they were grouped, and address the situation. This maneuver was usually effective, and the assailants would flee before they could act.

That night, we did not hear any shouting. I arose the next morning to find out that Petliura's men had assassinated Avrahamke, who was the central pillar of *Samoobrona*. They had attempted to rape his sister, and when he forcefully prevented them from committing this vile deed, they killed him.

[Page 69]

The savage army had meanwhile left town, leaving us stunned, crestfallen, orphaned, deep in mourning over Avrahamke, who literally was the *Samoobrona*. Sure, Gusakov was the commander, and Hendzels his second–in–command, but we never saw either of them in any dangerous situation. But Avrahamke would always turn up, and his very presence instilled in everyone a sense of security. When he said, "let's go!", anyone would follow him anywhere, no matter the danger.

This time, he had been alone and was unable to single–handedly contend with armed despicable thugs from Petliura's army.

May his memory be blessed!

Translator's footnotes:

1. A cold weapon is a weapon that does not involve fire or explosions (such as the act of combustion) as a result from the use of gunpowder or other explosive materials. (Wikipedia). A hot weapon, by contrast, is one that does use explosive power.

2. Обшивка is a Russian word that means sheath, coating, cover, skin, and other similar words. It is unclear if he's saying he ran for cover, or towards the perimeter, or maybe he ran towards the town furrier's shop, or a clothing store.

3. As mentioned above, Yevsektsiya warm weapons" are those that use explosions to work, such as gunpowder in standard guns. Yevsektsiya Cold weapons" are those that do not use explosions to work, such as knives and bayonets.

[Page 70]

The Years 1920–1940 in Zinkov
by M. G.
Translated by Yael Chaver

The purpose of our memorial book is to write the history of our murdered town. We must recount and narrate, as best we can, everything we know about life in Zinkov before the great destruction, and provide a documentary image of the bloody tragedy itself, based on the witness statements we possess. Examining the few memoirs that we have, we see that no one has provided materials about the period after the civil war, when the Soviet regime was establishing itself in our area. [1] The reason for this absence is very simple. During the civil war, when various armed bands stormed through our region, our town slowly lost its residents. Many died during the epidemic. [2] There was a time when three or four deaths would occur in a single night. The young folks, seeing no future for themselves in the town, left for the wide world– other countries, or the large cities of Russia; some went to Kiev, others to Odessa. Even later, when the regime stabilized, the stream of Zinkov natives leaving the town continued. It was then still possible to receive passports to leave the country. Even people who had lost their status (storekeepers with no stores, merchants with no merchandise) went to the large cities. They wanted to adjust to the new economy, either as clerks in a government shop or as managers; the Soviet government needed the long experience of the former merchants. Others went to work in the factories. Those who stayed behind also underwent a long process of adjustment. Worker and artisan cooperatives were formed. People from other towns started arriving in Zinkov, as well as Jews who had previously lived in villages. A difficult process of economic development began.

Over the years, contacts between those who had left the town and those who stayed faded. Everyone was busy establishing their positions and fashioning their lives under the new conditions. During the 1930s, a heavy silence fell over people. Those who still had correspondents wrote only about their health and family. No one wrote about life in Zinkov in general or about specific events. However, we will quote from the little information that has reached us from that time, and compare it with information about previous and later periods. For example, we know about the difficulties that faced Jewish youth who wanted to get a higher education under the Czarist regime, the economic problems of storekeepers and small merchants, and the sad state of poor artisans. True, the number of Jewish illiterates was much lower than among the peasants of the region. But at the same time, the older people did not know the official language of the country. Only few had newspapers and books, even among Jews. Of course, there were enough people in our area who knew a verse of Torah or a chapter of the Bible; there was also a small number of scholars. Many handed their children over to private tutors. Young people strove to educate themselves; but it was hard to attain higher, or even secondary, education.

[Page 71]

What were things like during the 1920s, under Soviet rule? It is well known that general education in schools was obligatory. There were schools everywhere comprising grades 1–7 or 1–10, where studies were almost of *gymnazya* standard. [3] Previously, only a few children could study at Sumnievitsh's two–class school, where a priest would teach the children religion ("God's Law"). He would terrify the children with his long black coat. The Christian children had to kneel and cross themselves, while the Jewish children stood frightened and confused, not knowing what they should be doing. Now, however, each child (regardless of ethnic origin or religion) could go to any school, free of charge. The young people really devoted themselves to studying. Zinkov had a special school where Yiddish was taught; it existed until the Stalinist edicts. [4]

The children of Zinkov began going to the higher schools. Those who completed their studies could be accepted for a government position, or as officers in the Soviet army. They entered industry, and became physicians, engineers, and scientists in all areas of Soviet science. This was a great change from the days of external students and the quota system of Czarist times, when many Jews were forced to convert in order to advance themselves. [5] Places where Jews were once forbidden to set foot, such as Holy Moscow with its 160 churches, or Kiev, now welcomed everyone equally, including many Jews. [6] Many Zinkov survivors now live in Kiev.

[Page 72]

We also heard of electric lights that had been installed in Zinkov itself, as well as regular cinema showings. We were told that Pinchesl's house had become a theater, in which pictures were shown on a screen. A club was founded for lectures as well as a library. We heard that a *kolkhoz* had existed in Zinkov before the destruction; unfortunately, we have no further details. [7]

We know nothing about the conditions under which people lived in Zinkov for the twenty years preceding the destruction, because they were all murdered by the Hitlerite killers. Yet, let us not forget after all that Zinkov still exists as a geographical location in the U.S.S.R., and that several Jewish families still live there. It may be possible for a Jewish community to develop there. Who knows? Let's hope for that. Jews always live with hope. They believe with all their hearts that Messiah will come, and they dream about a distant, bright future. And while we're expressing hopes, let's hope that Jewish culture will once again live and flourish on the soil of Zinkov, and that our heritage of two languages will be nurtured along with our folkways. [8] Who knows, our memorial book might reach the Zinkov library, and Jewish children of modern Zinkov will be able to read this book and get an idea of how we lived during the difficult, tragic period, and what Zinkov used to be like.

Translator's footnotes:

1. A multi–party civil war in the former Russian empire lasted for several years after the abolition of the monarchy in 1917.
2. There were outbreaks of typhus and cholera during these years.
3. The *gymnazya* provided secondary education.
4. Official anti–Semitic laws were passed in the U.S.S.R. beginning in the mid–1930s.
5. External students would study outside the university, aiming towards university standards.
6. "Holy Moscow" was one way of referring to the city.
7. *Kolkhoz* was a Soviet collective farm
8. The two languages are Yiddish and Hebrew.

[Page 73]

The First Strike in Our Home Town of Zinkov

by Moyshe Garber

Translated by Yael Chaver

It was when the spring storm of revolution raged the length and breadth of great Russia, when the enslaved masses shook their chains so that the foundations of the rotten Czarist order were shaken.

Moyshe Garber

Eventually, breezes and sounds of the great revolutionary turmoil reached Zinkov. New young people, students and workers, appeared; they had been sent out from the larger towns in our area, such as Proskurov, Vinnitsa, and Kamenetz. Their mission, as they expressed it, was to awaken the workers of Zinkov from their lethargy, educate and organize them, inform them how exploited they are because they work for negligible wages and inhumanely long hours. The working class of our town consisted of apprentices of tailors, shoemakers, carpenters; and a few tinsmiths and blacksmiths, as well as a few clerks. There was also a prominent group of milliners and "glove–makers" who sewed cotton–padded undershirts for the peasant women. [1]

[Page 74]

A long series of secret meetings followed, "secret propaganda" as they were termed. In summer they were held in the fields, in the "deep valley"; in winter they took place in a house on a side street, so that the "police" would not find out. Excited people crowded in, listening with tears in their eyes when the "agitator" described the bitter conditions of working people. For the first time in their lives, they heard words such as revolution, battle, exploitation, freedom, and the like. [2]

Shlime the baker, Binem's wife, with her family

People quickly learned revolutionary songs, and a library of Yiddish books was actually set up in our house. This is why I remember the episode of the Zinkov worker's movement so vividly, and the birth of the Jewish Revolutionary Workers' Organization – the Bund. [3] The workers in Zinkov began to be called *bundovtses*. [4] The leaders of the Bund in Zinkov were Avrom Abramovitch (or, as he was called, Avrom–Alter, Sani–Yitzchok's son), Noyekh Shpilerman (or Noyekh, Khaykl's son),

[Page 75]

Yoysef Shtrakhman (or Yoysef–Peretz, Yehuda Leyb's son), Berenzon (Khayim–Itzik Shaye's brother), and several others. [5] When the leaders saw that conditions were right, they decided to mount an "open battle" and call out the Zinkov "working class" for a strike, or, as it was then termed, a *zabastovke*. [6] One fine morning, all the workers – upon a signal from the leader – set down scissors and irons, and went out to the streets like soldiers mobilized for war. The bosses were stunned, and had no idea what was happening. They had never in their lives heard the word "strike." The strike committee assembled the bosses and clarified the strikers' demands: shorter work hours and higher wages. The bosses wouldn't even listen and categorically rejected these demands. For their part, they declared war on the strikers and their committee.

Now a series of denunciations and blows began. In return for a glass of brandy, the bosses hired the Zinkov underworld to fight the workers. These scoundrels got drunk on Shabbes, attacked any workers they encountered in the synagogue or on the street, and beat them up. Soon after that, the Bund organized a "beating brigade," a kind of "strong–arm squad," consisting of young men who could give as good as they got. This "commando" was headed by a carpenter's apprentice named Moyshe–Khayim (Snowstorm's son) or Moyshe Natanzon. [7] This Moyshe was a decent, hard–working laborer, who was proud and grateful to have become educated and understand what was happening in the world and in the proletarian revolutionary movement. After a hard day's work he liked to have a good wash, put on his nicest clothes, pick up a book, and walk the streets of Zinkov. If people asked him, "Moyshe, where are you going?" he would proudly answer, "To the *filitek*." [8] When the workers saw that the bosses were unyielding, continuing to rampage and make denunciations, they decided to take stronger measures. First, the "brigade" itself spread fear among the professional brawlers. They sought out the informers on their Shabbes walks, or at their homes, while they were napping after the Shabbes meal, and beat them up. That put a stop to the denunciations.

But the bosses would still not yield an inch, and the strike committee decided to employ a new strategy. There was a carpenter's apprentice named Mekhl (Sore–Khantse's son). This Mekhl was a precise copy of the character of Jimmie Higgins created by the American writer Upton Sinclair. [9] In this novel, Sinclair described a type of worker and Party member who is totally devoted to his organization, and always ready to take great risks, even death, if the Party required it. He was unremarkable, asked no questions, gave no talks, but blindly carried out whatever the leaders requested. This was Sinclair's portrait of Jimmie, and this was Mekhl the carpenter. Once, during a strike on the eve of Passover, Mekhl came to visit us and saw my mother, may she rest in peace, preparing chickens for the holiday meal. He said, "Rokhl, do me a favor, don't throw away the inner organs, that is, the chicken offal." Surprised, Mother asked him, "What do you need it for?" He smiled and said, "What do you care? I need it." He went outdoors and soon returned with two earthenware pots, filled them with all the offal, and left.

[Page 76]

Early the next morning we heard an uproar in the streets; the whole town was agitated. My father, may he rest in peace, went out to the market as usual, but soon came back saying that last night, during the first Seder, someone had thrown pots full of offal through the windows of Leyzer, the misshapen leather–worker, Nachman the tailor, and someone else whose name escapes me. The pots landed right on the Seder table, ruined the entire meal, and scared everyone to death.

The upshot was that during Passover week the bosses met with the members of the strike committee, and reached an understanding. Work conditions were greatly improved; the workers were better paid and their hours were shortened. The main thing, though, was that from then on the workers felt that they were not at the mercy of the bosses and that they were an organized force. The bosses realized this, and started dealing with the workers respectfully, man to man, and not like lords to slaves.

Translator's footnotes:

1. The Polish *katinashke* (transliterated in Yiddish and presented between quote marks) apparently refers to leather workers. There is no explanation of the quote marks.

2. The quote marks are in the original. Some of the terms are transliterated from Russian.

3. The Bund was a secular Jewish socialist party initially formed in the Russian Empire and active between 1897 and 1920.

4. A mildly pejorative way of saying "Bundists."

5. People in such Jewish communities were very familiar with the details of family relationships, which often counted for more than official last names.

6. The Russian term for "strike."

7. The quote marks are in the original. The English term "strong–arm squad" is transliterated into Yiddish. The name Snowstorm is not explained–it may be a nickname.

8. This is a mispronunciation of the Yiddish *bibliotek* (library).

9. In 1919, Upton Sinclair published the novel *Jimmie Higgins*, about a member of the Socialist party who is a labor organizer. Sinclair's work was widely translated into European languages, and was popular in Socialist circles of Eastern Europe.

———

[Page 77]

How Nicholas II was Overthrown in Zinkov:
A Tragicomic Scene from the Distant Past
by Moyshe Garber
Translated by Yael Chaver

Mayday finally came. People in Zinkov knew by now that May 1 was a holiday for all the workers of the world. Preparations for the festive holiday lasted for weeks. When the day came, everyone dressed in their finest, attached red ribbons to their lapels, and assembled on the butchers' meadow behind Dr. Garbotovsky's fence. I was then a small boy, curious to know, see, and hear everything. So I didn't go to *cheder* that day and joined in all the festivities. The mood was merry and elevated. The high point of the event was when four tall guys were set up in facing pairs. Two more guys were placed on their shoulders; they joined hands and formed a kind of chair. That was meant to signify the "czar's throne" (the "royal seat"), on which the "czar" sat. That was either Meir, Leybe's son (Meir Horovitz). One of the workers gave a festive speech. A red flag was unfurled and a resounding shout was heard: "Down with the czar!" The "throne" collapsed and the "czar" fell down so hard that the ground trembled. But it did not end there. Fashionable young men then wore very tight pants. Poor Meir fell from the "throne" with such force that the back seam of his pants ripped, and he was too embarrassed to stand up... When the audience caught sight of this, the solemnity of the occasion was forgotten, and they broke into resounding laughter that echoed across the fields and forests for a long time.

But who at that time could figure that only a few years later the mockery of the naïve Zinkov young men and women would develop into a bloody reality... The czar and his rotten organization was indeed overthrown. But everything that followed flung the world into a bloody mess for a long time, and the greatest victim of this violence was once again our Jewish people.

[Page 78]

Azi Zecherman's House

by Yisro'el Sanis, Roytburd

Translated by Yael Chaver

The best location on the street was that of Moyshe Zecherman (Yosl's son). He had a large house, whose entryway had apartments on both sides. The top floor of the house consisted of a labyrinth of unusually large rooms. It would be interesting to find out when and why such an odd house had been built. It was not a hotel, or apartments for tenants. On the other hand, the "storey" – as we shall call the upper floor – did not seem to be a palace for a rich and powerful man, or a landowner. During the decade from which I have clear enough memories of life in the town and before I left the town and the street, the "storey" was never occupied by permanent residents. The neighborhood changed from time to time, and went through various phases. Before World War I, Polish landowners ran a club there for a long time. They had wild parties with the eminent residents of the town. Music would be played, and people would spend long evenings there playing cards and drinking.

At the beginning of the Russo–German war, when the uncle of Czar Nikolai, Nikolai Nikolayevitch, started to expel Jews from of the border towns "on suspicion of treason," Zinkov became a haven for many refugees; many of these lived in the "storey." [1] Some of the refugee families settled in Zinkov permanently. Most, however, only stayed in town for a while, and our Zinkov Jews displayed the admirable trait of hospitality. They opened their own poor, cramped homes to their homeless brothers, and helped them with whatever they could. Those refugees who settled in the town brought not only a natural increase in the Jewish population, but also an intensity and liveliness to local commerce and community activity. They quickly became a familiar part of the Jewish community and made friends among its members.

[Page 79]

During World War I, a small unit of prisoners of war was brought to the town from somewhere; they were quartered in the "storey," which happened to be vacant at the time. These prisoners consisted of a mixture of Austrians, Germans, and even Turks. In the evening, they would sit on the metal steps of the building and sing songs. The songs of the Turkish prisoners songs were sad, with oriental tunes. Everyone stopped to listen. Even the glum Germans, who kept themselves apart from the Turks, would grow silent and listen to their songs.

It is impossible to provide a precise chronological account of events that happened earlier or later. Naturally, some details have become vague in my memory after so many years, especially years of suffering and painful experiences. During those years of unrest, revolution and counter–revolution, Zinkov was under several occupations;

there were even intervals with no sovereign power. These intervals were the most tragic. There were days and nights of anxiety and fear, hunger and poverty, as well as major epidemics. Robbers and bloodthirsty bands rampaged freely, rushing into town and rushing away. But the excitement that the first years of the revolution brought into community life never waned, despite the conditions and the surrounding tensions.

The "storey" was constant witness to all the wanderings and upheavals. The Austrians came and took over the "storey" for their officers; the Poles returned and occupied it for their officers. By the way, when the Poles stayed in Zinkov, I saw for myself, and realized, what bullying Jews meant. One of these episodes happened at Passover. As I was walking on the street in the morning of the first day of the holiday, I saw a group of Polish soldiers surrounding several bearded Jews, thrusting brooms into their hands, and commanding them to sweep the street while dancing. All this time, they tormented them, pulling and plucking at their beards with mockery and derision. Watching this, I sensed the helplessness and impotence of the Jews' condition. I realized the significance of such paralyzed rage and forcibly restrained hate and disgust towards the animal in uniform holding a firearm, and towards the miserable creatures who were, unfortunately, so numerous. Thinking that this was no more than a minor game compared with

[Page 80]

what happened 25 years later, it is hard to understand how this savage hatred and disgust could be instantly erased, and how our people –the collective victim of the most horrendous outrages – should be required to free the recent mass–murderers of responsibility and leave their crimes unpunished.

But the darkness that spread over our town in those days was infiltrated by rays of bright light and happy statements. Zecherman's house with its "storey" found its rectification when it was taken over by Zionist youth and became the town's center of Zionist activity and culture. [2] The large rooms of the "storey" were now transformed into classrooms. Benches were set around long tables, for the enthusiastic students who learned to read and write Hebrew and Yiddish. There was no shortage of students, but a shortage of books, and a great lack of teachers. However, studies progressed briskly. Those who already knew something shared their knowledge with those who knew less. Teachers who came to Zinkov from other places, such as Shteynberg and Fridman, made their contributions to enlightenment and education in the town. Students, who appeared out of nowhere, also began sharing local cultural life and were especially active in political gatherings. The upper level of the firehouse resounded with fiery arguments between Zionist and Bund speakers in a hall packed to the rafters with excited listeners. [3] However, the atmosphere on the upper "storey" of the Zecherman house was quite different. It was a place of study. *Halutzim* did exercises and sang their songs. [4] Amateurs prepared theatrical performances and a choir rehearsed concerts. The concert–master was a student from the Odessa Conservatory of Music, who had left Odessa because of the widespread famine there. He had two good qualities: he made gaiters, and he was a fiddler. An audience gathered the moment he began playing; and his music was very affecting. He enthusiastically organized a choir, and was remarkably good at working with groups of boys and girls, and even 10–14–year–olds on beautiful melodies. His repertoire consisted of songs such as "Do you know the land where lemons bloom and goats eat carobs like grass," and *Hatikvah* [5] with variations and as a duet. He also taught them a prelude; the Hebrew Shabbes song "The sun has left the treetops"; a landscape themed "Autumn is over and spring has returned to our country," and other melodies. Natives of Zinkov who participated in the choir in those days carry the melodies of those songs in their memories and occasionally hum them nostalgically. When they meet, they sing these beloved songs and remember that period of cultural revival, which continued regardless of the widespread unrest.

Amateur drama club in Zinkov

[Page 81]

As we have already noted, the center and main location of all activities was Azi Zecherman's house. However, our cultural work was not limited to the "storey"; it spread throughout the town. Two groups of *halutzim* had prepared themselves to emigrate to Palestine, and signs of their goal were visible everywhere in the town. On the street, they always walked together in a group. The only employment they could find in town at that time was occasionally chopping up a cartload of wood – so that is what they did. There was a vacant plot of land overgrown with weeds and surrounded by a tall fence near Shloyme Helman's house, at the edge of town. The *halutzim* who were preparing for pioneering work in Palestine organized in a kind of *hachshara* group and got permission to create a garden on that plot. [6] They started work enthusiastically, clearing the area, plowing with dull pickaxes, and planting a garden with things they brought from home: a few potatoes, several

[Page 82]

onions and heads of garlic, some kernels of corn, and cucumber seeds they somehow obtained. None of the eager *halutzim* knew about gardening, and there was no one to teach them. However, they worked with love and gusto, and achieved some results. They dug a large earthen pit, where they could store equipment and other things as well as shelter from rain and even spend a night. They guarded the young plants from the goats that eyed the fruits of the enthusiasts' work. The garden existed for two summers. The good, dark Ukrainian soil yielded abundant crops; there were enough vegetables to distribute freely to those interested. We can definitely say that the garden played an important role in feeding the poor of the surrounding villages in addition to the poor of the town.

At the end of the second summer, there was almost a tragedy. One of the groups of hooligans rampaging in the area decided to shoot a bomb into town. [8] The bomb landed right in this garden. Luckily, it did not explode, and no one was injured. However, the garden was abandoned because of the unrest, bringing that happy and productive work to a stop; the young enthusiasts no longer enjoyed the wholesome feeling that comes with farming, which was their end–goal. Unfortunately, this was also the end of the *hachshara*, although no one expressed it at the time.

Another project worth mentioning is the tobacco "plantations" (as they were termed). A virtual epidemic of plantations broke out at that time. Every vacant plot was soon occupied by a tobacco plantation. Outside the city limits large areas planted with tobacco suddenly appeared. The *halutzim* quickly applied for work, and they "killed the tobacco babies." They didn't know how to use the swing plow; instead of plowing under the delicate plants they often cut them down. Whenever that happened, a cry of regret was heard: "they killed a tobacco baby!" This phrase became an expression that many Zinkov natives of our generation remember to this day.

The Zinkov Hazamir club
Middle: the conductor, Ziegerman [7]

[Page 83]

A group of Zinkov emigrants en route to America

Political activity in the town was also organized and coordinated inside the "storey." Preparations started for the constituent assembly and for the elections. The first elections for the local municipality also took place. The election campaign was lively and heated. Each group and party put forth its list of candidates. By that time Moyshe, the town elder's son, had a printing press. [9] I believe it was the first printing press in Zinkov. He quickly had enough work, printing flyers and calls to action. His printing press was a center of activity and liveliness. The manually operated wheel of the machine never stopped clacking.

However, the elected town municipality unfortunately had only several stormy meetings, and was unable to continue functioning. The unrest caused by the Petlyura bands and other marauders destroyed the course of normal life, and only intensified the fear and terror of tomorrow. [10] Young people started to think seriously about the future. Many decided to leave, encouraged by their parents; and primarily – for *eretz–yisro'el* (then Palestine). [11]

[Page 84]

It is interesting to note that the varied and lively activity of the different social groups and circles in town at the time had no designated leader (except, possibly, for the Bund). There were many active workers, but no one gave orders and there was no hierarchy. Clear ideological groupings started to form. The group of *halutzim* set up productive work and "proletarianization" as its ideal. [12] They categorically renounced commerce as a profession. Collective farming was their ideal, and Socialism was their goal.

The local bosses, who had their own ballots even during these elections, were primarily concerned to hold on to the town's management, and were not pleased to see the young folks' interest in abandoning them. The activity of the local Bund was focused on the elections, and gave the impression that its members were really involved in the revolution and were the spokespersons of the local proletariat that opposed the householders. However, there were no true proletarians in our town. There were only artisans, manual workers who worked independently; some of them even employed several trained workers. Ideologically, they strongly opposed the Zionists; but in our town, at least, they had no long–range plans.

We cannot conclude this chapter on social life in Zinkov shortly after the Revolution without mentioning one joyous day that we experienced in that period: the celebration of the Balfour Declaration and of San Remo. [13] The celebration was organized and prepared inside the "storey." The crowd marched ceremoniously by the "storey." On the balcony, the most important people of the movement, as well as teachers and activists, stood among fluttering blue–and–white flags. [14] All faces glowed, as though salvation had already really come, and all problems were over. The young folks who joined that mass march surely felt that very soon they would surely fly to that land "on the wings of eagles," the land that was the subject of such beautiful songs, and the focus of such wonderful dreams. [15]

The family of Zusia and Babe Segal in 1926

[Page 85]

The way in which the celebration was carried out is fixed in our memory. Ten young folks, with Nokhem Yoshpeh at their head, went into the forest early one morning several days before the march. The forest lay on the road between the villages of Riventchke and Bebekh, about half a kilometer from town. [16] The way there was through a narrow road that continued as a path between fields. They sang as they went. It was a lovely summer day, and the wheat stalks in the fields greeted the happy youths, who marched, rosy–cheeked, with unbuttoned shirts. They grew silent when they entered the forest, fearing the forest guards, who could have punished them badly for what they were about to do. They could even have been beaten. The guys weren't afraid of the non–Jewish kids. Even if it came to blows, they had Nokhem with them, after all; he was far from a weakling, and could land a serious blow. The others would also not have held back.

The guys started in on the saplings, quietly and carefully. They would bend a sapling tree to the ground. Once the bark cracked, they would cut through the rest of the trunk with smaller knives. It didn't take long for them to make off, marching out of the forest through the fields, holding the broken saplings, on their way back to town. They wove the saplings into a garland, which they took up to the women's section of the synagogue and hung through the window–like openings in the wall. They decorated the entire synagogue in this way. It had never been so beautifully decorated. Nokhem Yoshpeh was a natural artist and decorator. He would paint beautiful pictures

[Page 86]

and had an artistic sense. There were additional decorations on the *bimah* and the *menorah*. [17] He also assembled a group of guys in costumes and blue–white caps whom he would drill. When the day came, they gathered on the street near Azi Zecherman's house. The costumed "honor guard" stood there holding flags and placards. All the important leaders stood on the balcony of the "storey." A crowd gathered, and the procession set out for the synagogue. Once they got there, the marchers stood around the lectern with their flags, while the speakers took the platform. The synagogue was large enough to accommodate the crowd, and the entire town came. In this way, Zinkov welcomed the first news that a Jewish homeland would be created in Palestine, and hopefully – a Jewish state as well.

In 1918 or 1919 two groups of *halutzim* left Zinkov. They set out with no money, no passports, and no permits, relying on God's mercy to reach *eretz–yisro'el.* They stole across the border to Galicia, made their way to Vienna, and then travelled to *eretz–yisro'el* with the help of Zionist organization offices. [18]

[Page 87]

The first group of *halutzim* consisted of the following members:

Nokhem Yoshpeh, Yitzchok Frenkel, Basya Shterntal, Berl Saliternik, Mune Averbukh, Avrom Shenkelman, Yisro'el Shvartzman, Yoyne Zayontshik, Mendel Kurtzman, Moyshe Zaltzman, Fishl Zaltzman, Dovid Feldman, Yitzchok Feder, Khayke Fenkel, Yisro'el Vekselman.

The second group included:

Mendl Vaysman, Dovid Fuks, Shloyme Goldberg, Shamai Shur, Ruvn Rozental, Velvl Nesis, Habe Nesis, Arke Nesis, Yoyne Zayontshik, Bunye Feder, Pinye Averbakh, Eliezer Shvartzman, Rokhl Rapoport, Pesye Fayerman, Shmuel the Rabbi's son, Karin.

Entire families of the town followed the groups of *halutzim* and emigrated to *eretz–yisro'el*. These were:

The Blinder family, Friedman the teacher, the Zaltzman family, the family of Arke Shenkelman, Shimen Saliternik and his wife, the entire Saliternik family (Shimen's father), Arke Frenkel with his wife and family, the Vertzman brothers, Khayke the daughter of Yoysef–Lozer (the butcher), the Yoshpeh family, Nokhem Katz. The others, whose names I have forgotten so many years later, or never knew, will certainly forgive me. Most of the ones mentioned are now established citizens of Israel, with extended families. Only a small number later left *eretz–yisro'el*, because of various reasons and situations, and settled in America. A few became ill in *eretz–yisro'el* and died at a young age. Let us honor their memory!

A group of Zinkov natives in Haifa, 1922–23

Berl Saliternik, Mune Averbukh, Fishl Zaltzman, Mune Averbukh, Shiyeh Shteynbas, Shloyme Goldberg, Shamai Shur, Mendl Vaysman, Aba Nesis, Mintz, Eliezer Shvartsman and his wife, Yitzchak Fayderman, Dovid Fuks

[Page 88]

The children of our Israelis, as well as their fathers, took part in the defense of Israel when it became independent and was attacked by the Arabs. Along with all their Israeli brothers, they made sacrifices for the land and were wounded. Nokhem Yoshpeh lost his son, a bright young man of seventeen. Some of our fellow Zinkov natives, who visited Israel and came to visit Nokhem, saw a special corner of his house dedicated to the memory of the beloved, fallen son. The family placed his rifle, his helmet, and other objects that he left behind, in that corner. We honor his bravery and the holy sacrifice that he made while defending the honor of his people and the existence of the State of Israel.*

---

* See "In Memoriam: Yekhiel Dovid Yoshpeh." [19]

Translator's footnotes:

1. Grand Duke Nikolai Nikolayevitch was actually the first cousin once removed of Czar Nikolai II. "Russo–German war" refers to the fighting in the early years of World War I (1914–1916). He served as Commander in Chief of the Russian army.

2. The writer uses the term *tikkun*, a term from Lurianic Kabbala, meaning in that context "rectification" of spiritual collapse.

3. The layout of the "firehouse" is not clearly described.

4. This Hebrew term is used to denote prospective Zionist emigrants to Palestine.

5. The first song referred to is a Yiddish version of a well–known poem by Wolfgang Goethe from his novel *Wilhelm Meister*, which was set to music by a variety of composers. Its first line is "Kennst du das land wo die zitronen blühn" (Do you know the land where the lemons bloom). Though Goethe's character Mignon is apparently referring to Italy, the poem was translated into Yiddish as expressing the age–old Jewish longing for Palestine. Schubert's melody was probably the best-known of its musical settings. *Hatikvah*, written in Hebrew by Naftali Herz Imber in 1878, became a hallmark of the Zionist movement and is the national anthem of Israel. The melody is apparently based on a Romanian folk tune. The poem *Shabbat ha–Malka* ("Queen Shabbat"), with the first line "The sun has left the treetops" was written by Hayyim Nahman Bialik, the pre-eminent Hebrew poet of the late 19th century, and set to music by Pinchas Minkovsky.

6. The Hebrew term *hachshara* was used for training programs and agricultural centers in Europe and elsewhere. At these centers, Zionist youths learned technical skills necessary for their emigration to

Palestine/Israel and subsequent life as members of *kibbutzim* (communal settlements).

7. The Hebrew *zamir* means "nightingale," and was a popular name for choral groups.

8. The type of "bomb" is not specified; possibly a hand–grenade.

9. The Russian term *starost* is used for "village elder." It seems that this position was held by a Jew at the time. The "printing press" is likely to have been a mimeograph machine, and the "wheel" – the drum.

10. Simon Petlyura (1879–1926) became a leading figure in Ukraine's struggle for independence after the Bolshevik revolution and eventually became the head of the State. He headed most of the pogroms against Jews in 1918–1921

11. Here, and below, the writer uses the traditional Hebraic name for the biblical Land of Israel.

12. Proletarianization called for increasing the size and importance of the working class as a precursor to social equality.

13. The Balfour Declaration was a public statement issued by the British government in 1917 during the First World War announcing its support for the establishment of a "national home for the Jewish people" in Palestine. At the San Remo conference of 1920, the Allies placed Palestine under British Mandatory rule and confirmed the pledge concerning Palestine contained in the Balfour Declaration.

14. These colors became identified with the Zionist movement.

15. The biblical quote is from Exodus 19, 4.

16. I could not identify the names of these villages.

17. A seven–branched candelabrum is often part of the eastern–wall accessories in a synagogue; it commemorates the Menorah that stood in the ancient Jewish Temple of Jerusalem.

18. Galicia (Yiddish *Galitziye*) is the area of the 18th–century kingdom of Galicia-Volhynia, later a crown land of Austria-Hungary; it had a very large Jewish population.

19. The starred note is in the original.

———

[Page 89]

Zinkov During the Years of Revolution and the Civil War (1917–1921)

by Moyshe Grinman

Translated by Yael Chaver

The years following World War I were difficult and impossible to forget. These were years of revolution and counter–revolution, years of massacres against Jews, such as those at Proskurov, Felshtin, and other, smaller, towns throughout the Jewish Pale of Settlement. [1] They were years of hunger, epidemics (typhus and scarlet fever); years during which Jewish lives were free for the taking, Jewish women were raped and tortured, and Jewish property was robbed. These are all facts that we natives of Zinkov, who lived through it all, can only remember with agony, and pass on in every detail to the next generations. Let me try to present a few memories of that time.

It is hard to describe how the Jews of Zinkov were able to navigate between the various rulers who constantly changed, in order to save themselves from extreme dangers that lay in wait almost daily. Armed bands, equipped with ammunition coming in from outside as well as with armaments left behind by Czarist army soldiers during their defeat, attacked the town repeatedly. Apparently, all the new rulers were only out to strangle the revolution and drown it in blood, and to eradicate the "Jewish Bolsheviks." In their drunken state, having spent all their money on drink, they were busy only with robbing, terrorizing, and murdering the civilian population–but not concerned with establishing any kind of order or normal life and work.

Moyshe Grinman

[Page 90]

And if a regime was successfully established in our town for any length of time, it spelled the start of a great calamity for the Jews of Zinkov. The commander and his "guardians of the law" – those undisciplined, lawless robbers – held the fate, life, and death, of our brothers and sisters of Zinkov in their hands, as well as their meager properties. A series of demands and ultimatums began. With each successive ultimatum, the appetites of the commander or the *hetman* grew. When previous requirements had gradually been met, they came up with more demands of food for their soldiers and their horses, boots, cloth; and above all – special sums of money and other things for the commander himself.

[Page 91]

People needed to have courage and strong nerves, resignation and readiness for anything in order to negotiate with the bands. The townspeople also had to be patient, and ready to trust the emissaries they sent out on this perilous mission. The representatives had to be courageous enough to go into the den of lions, negotiate with the bandits and argue with them in order to avert the terrible decrees; it was quite impossible to yield to all the demands. The main person active in all these missions was Motti Fayerman – who, by the way, was killed along with his brother–in–law on the road from Derazhne to Zinkov. At the time, he almost had the chance to leave the country and go through Galicia to Vienna; his wife and child were already on the other side of the border, near Lemberg. [2] Other emissaries were Yisro'el Aynkoyfer; my father, may he rest in peace; Gusakov the dentist; Avstravnik the lawyer; Trachtenberg; and the Christian Markivski, who lived in the town and had good relations with his Jewish neighbors.

Family of Avromke Nesis, the son of Netta Belhus, with his wife and children

"Headquarters," from which the representatives were sent to the commander, and where the major deliberations took place, was the house of the Rabbi, Moyshele, may his memory be for a blessing, who took part in the meetings himself; he was a very liberal person, and a true leader of the community. He was beloved by all and his house welcomed everyone: householders, artisans, students, and all young people. Among the attendees were Khayim (Royze's son), Arke Shenkelman, Sani Alter Sanis, Itzik (Binem's son), Yekhiel Yoshpeh, Yehoshua Fayershteyn, Fukelman the bookkeeper, Berl Kubrik the town elder, and others whose names escape me after such a long time. Meetings were also held at the house of Gusakov, the dentist. What the delegations endured defies description. One thing is certain: at the time, Zinkov didn't do too badly, after all. Compared with other Jewish towns, the number of fatalities was relatively small, and the "delegations" saved our town from mass slaughter more than once. [3]

From time to time, an elected committee, or municipal council, also functioned in the town. The participants came from all strata of the population – storekeepers, artisans, merchants, and laborers. The representatives on behalf of the artisans were Shmuel–Lipe, Idel Koval, Abramovitch (who was also the leader of the Bund), Levi Stoler, and the dentist Gusakov who identified with the so–called "Leftist" elements of the town and was their spokesperson, speaker, and representative. [4] In general, there were no serious differences of opinion or major opposing interests among the townspeople. The merchants and storekeepers (with a few exceptions), artisans and journeymen – all were similarly poor, more or less, and there were no terrible class conflicts.

[Page 92]

As early as during World War I, great hardships developed in the town. Worst off of all were the children of mobilized soldiers, and the women whose husbands had gone away to America before the war, were later cut off from their families by circumstance, and could not send them money for living expenses. A relief committee was formed in town. Every week, pairs of people would go through town with a list of people who had committed to weekly contributions to help the women (who were nicknamed "the American wives"). Almost all the donors were locals, and the pairs would actually go from house to house and collect the money that was then distributed among those in need.

The situation became much worse during the periods of unrest following the war. The town was cut off from its environs. Peasants were not able to bring their products into town, and merchants and storekeepers couldn't take wares into the villages to be sold to the peasants in return for their products. It was impossible even to get salt. At one point there was such a shortage of salt that major epidemics broke out for lack of salt in food, and there were many deaths. [5] There were no sugar, kerosene, or bread either. In addition, there was an influx of immigrants (*bezhentses*). [6] These were the Jews whom the Czar's uncle Nikolai Nikolaevich, as commander of the army, expelled from the border areas of the former Austria and Russia, considering them all to be "spies." [7] All these new arrivals came with no possessions and were penniless, starved, and terrorized, and did not know where to turn. But Jews, after all, are Jews; the Jews of Zinkov took their brothers and sisters into their own homes, cramped and impoverished as they were, and shared food with them.

[Page 93]

The relief committee was swamped with work. The activists were the same as before. Gusakov, the dentist, was also a committee member and did remarkable work. For their part, the committee linked up with a central relief organization in

Kamianets–Podilskyi. Aid indeed came: money, and clothing. Not too much, but nonetheless aid. It might have come from a Jewish relief organization in America, or in Russia proper. We were never told the details of how the aid reached us through all the fighting and the insecure roads; the Red Cross may have been involved. At the initiative of the committee's leaders, Abramovich and Gusakov and their group, as well as the artisans and others, a cooperative store was established. This store somehow managed to obtain flour, salt, sugar, soap, and other necessities, and thus slightly alleviate the shortage of elementary products. This is how Zinkov survived the difficult times after World War I, days of revolution and counter–revolution.

Berl Kubrik, the town elder, and his family

But the later – and much worse – problems during the rule of Hitler, when death lay in wait at each and every house, almost obliterated the memory of earlier shortages and suffering. All the brave and devoted activists of Zinkov were wiped out: my father and the entire family were murdered by the Nazi killers. Khayim Royzes, Abramovich, and Motti Fayerman were murdered, as noted elsewhere in this memorial book. The Rabbi, Reb Moyshele, died in Zinkov when young. [8] Arik Shenkelman and his family made their way to Israel. Sani Alter Sanis and his wife made their way to America, to their son Yisro'el. Gusakov and his wife emigrated to America. Here, in

America, he had trouble adapting himself professionally to local requirements. In addition, there was a state of crisis. [9] He found no way to do community work, lacking the language, friends, and a familiar environment. He remained withdrawn, disappointed, and embittered and eventually died here at an advanced age. The natives of Zinkov in New York gave him a plot in their cemetery, though he did not join our local organization. The merits of his earlier activity and devoted community work served him well.

[Page 94]

Translator's footnotes:

1. The Proskurov pogrom, in which at least 1,500 Jews were murdered, occurred on February 15, 1919 in the town now known as Khmelnitskyi, which was taken over from Bolshevik control by the Haidamaks (Ukrainian paramilitary bands). The Felshtin pogrom of February 1919, in which at least 500 Jews were killed, was part of the same wave of pogroms. The Pale of Settlement was the western region of Imperial Russia, which existed with varying borders between 1791 and 1917, in which permanent residency by Jews was permitted.

2. Lemberg is the name given by the German occupiers to present–day Lviv, Ukraine. The reference to a border is unclear.

3. The quote marks are in the original.

4. Some of the names in this list may convey the trade of the bearers: Koval means "blacksmith", and Stoler means "carpenter."

5. The link between lack of salt and disease outbreaks is unclear.

6. The Russian word is inserted in Yiddish transliteration, between quote marks and parentheses.

7. See Translator's note 69.

8. Original note: His family stayed in Russia and was saved when they evacuated Zinkov for eastern Russia.

9. The reference to crisis is unclear.

[Page 97]

Zinkov before the destruction: personal memories from home

Memories from My Hometown Zinkov

by Shmuel Korin

Translated by Aryeh Sklar

It is very hard for me, after nearly a lifetime, to recount the memories of my childhood and youth in that town where I was born and raised. After all, forty–four years have passed since I left its confines and made *Aliyah*, the only one of my family to do so. The rest of my family remained there, living their lives under the Soviet regime.

I was able to maintain a written correspondence with them until the destruction of the town in the hands of the accursed Nazi enemy.

Most of my family, including my father and mother, were murdered. The only ones who survived were my brother, who served during the war in the Red Army, and my sister, who was living near Leningrad at that time, and was able to escape with her life before the enemy arrived there. It is thanks to my brother and sister that I even know the exact date when my family, as well as many others of the townsfolk, were put to death–it was August 4th, 1942.

My father, whose name was Meir Yosef Korin, had been called in by the *Rebbe* Reb Moshele and his acolytes who were from that town to assume the rabbinical pulpit and serve as teacher and halachic ruler for their parish.

I was the eldest, and I was about five years old when we followed my father to live in Zinkov, and from then until I reached adulthood, there in our town I grew up and there I was raised.

In his capacity as the rabbi, my father, of blessed memory, was not just the authority on matters of kosher law, but he was also an arbiter on interpersonal matters, and he was dedicated to his parishioners–tending to the sick and providing for widows and orphans. Our home was wide open to them, and throughout the day many different people would be coming and going. One came seeking counsel, another to ask for aid for someone who was sick, or assistance in tuition for orphans. There were also people who would come and appoint my father, of blessed memory, as arbitrator in their disputes. And there were even times when a dispute broke out between a Jew and a non–Jew and both parties, choosing to avoid appearing before a state court, would come to argue their case before my father, each of them confident in receiving a true and just ruling from my father.

One interesting and important detail comes to mind. There were four esteemed families from our town, who were leasing a large nearby flour mill, and a dispute broke out among them, and some of them wanted to take the case to the state court. My father, knowing that such an act would greatly entangle them, potentially bankrupting them, used his influence to prevent them from doing so, and for an entire month, night and day, worked with them to resolve the dispute and effect reconciliation among them. Long afterwards, the parties involved would cite this good deed and express their gratitude to him.

Although the people of our town were not wealthy, and most of them labored for a living, they were kind, and whenever there was a need, they always contributed generously to the best of their ability.

[Page 98]

I must bring up one detail in this context: at the outbreak of the First World War in 1914, an order was issued by Gen. Ivanov, commander of the southwestern front, that, since the Jews are suspected of spying for the enemy, any of them who live within 50 verst (1 verst = 3500 ft.) from the frontline, must, within 24 hours, leave their homes and go farther from the frontline. This was on a Thursday, and from the entire region surrounding our town, a flow of refugees arrived. Hundreds of families with their belongings arrived on farmers wagons, all in need of shelter. Our townsfolk, without exception, all responded to the present need and each home took in several families.

I remember that five or six families took refuge in our home. With the assistance of several of the town dignitaries, my father immediately organized a relief committee that set out to raise money for the families who had been rendered destitute. The next day, Friday morning, we youths set out, sacks on our backs, to collect *Challah* for the Sabbath from every home in town, to provide for the poor who had not yet had the opportunity to fend for themselves. Only after the Sabbath did a portion of the refugees set out to neighboring towns, and still, in almost every home, a family of refugees remained until the battlefront shifted away from us and the refugees could return home.

It is also noteworthy that in Zinkov lived the offspring of the *Apta Rebbe*. There were those who said that they had chosen our town as a residence because there were no Christian churches within it, unlike the nearby towns who all had standing at their center, at the market square, a Christian church. Not so in our town, where the Catholic and Orthodox churches were located in the valley by the Turkish fortress, out of the view of the Jews. And occasionally, when a Jew would come to town to visit the *Rebbe* or one of our townsfolk, or when on occasion a local Jew would head out to the synagogue to pray or to prostrate himself on the tombs of the rabbis, during the month of Elul, he would not encounter even a single symbol of the foreign religion on his way.

It is known that in Zinkov there were two Hassidic courts, that of Reb Moshe'le and that of Reb Pinchas'l. They were brothers, but did not get along, and the dispute between the two brothers extended to their acolytes, and to the townsfolk in general. The town was, therefore, divided into two: One faction included Reb Moshele and his acolytes and friends and family, and the second faction included Reb Pinchas'l and his acolytes and friends and family. My father and his family were among the acolytes of Reb Moshele. As a result, all I knew about the *Rebbe* and his court, was limited to Reb Moshele's faction. As it is known, around the holidays up to hundreds of Hassidim would arrive from out of town, many of them with their families in tow, to spend the festival within the court of the *Rebbe*. But from among the townsfolk at large, many would join one faction or the other, not only devout acolytes, but also people from among the "Jewish Enlightenment", and even from among the youth, would come to bask in the light of the *Rebbe*'s court. The *Rebbe* Reb Moshele was outstandingly noble, and many were his friends, and friends of his family, and the *Rebbe* and his family returned love and friendship to all.

Another memory comes to mind, when I was already eight years old and able to freely pray and even understand most of the liturgy. That year, I went with my father to the *Kol Nidre* service in the synagogue that was in Reb Moshele's courtyard. The spacious synagogue was packed with congregants of all ages, very old to very young. Many a *Neshama* (memorial) candle stood burning. By the prayer dais near the Holy Ark, sat the *Rebbe*, in his armchair, wearing a white *Kittel*, his prayer shawl over his back, on his head a white *yarmulke* interwoven with silver threads, and a crowd of acolytes and admirers surrounding him, handing him notes with requests. All of a sudden, it became quiet, and the *Rebbe* stood up, approached the dais, and began with the opening verses of the *Kol Nidre* service. And there was something special about his voice, about the impassioned words coming out of his mouth, and the utterance of his lips left an impression on the congregation. To this day, whenever I enter a synagogue on *Kol Nidre* night, that impassioned vision resurfaces before my eyes, and the noble image of the *Rebbe* reappears to me in all its glory, just like in those distant childhood days.

[Page 99]

In our town there were not many state–operated educational institutions. There was one public school, attended by the children of the nearby farmers, and even some Jewish children, mostly girls. Boys were not sent to that school, because they had classes on Saturday and there were no Judaic studies in the curriculum, and they learned nothing except the official language and some math.

Parents made great efforts to provide their children with a Jewish education at their own expense, and they could not always afford the costs this entailed, even though for all of them the study of Torah took precedence even over food. The community operated and funded the *Talmud Torah*, which staffed educated teachers. In our town there were also many a private *heder*, where teachers drilled Torah into students for ten hours every day. Even on Saturday afternoons, learning did not cease, and they would study *Ethics of the Fathers*. Even during the intermediate days of Passover and Sukkot, study continued in the *Cheiders*. There were various types of *Cheider*, and they were adjusted to the age of the children, from six years to fifteen. Only Judaic studies were taught there, and for official language and math they would go to private tutors. There were also teachers from among the "*Haskalah*" – the "Jewish Enlightenment", who possessed outstanding knowledge in Hebrew grammar and literature, and it was they who taught the youth a love and devotion to the Hebrew language and modern literature. And it was they who raised up a generation of students who made their parents proud, and when the first call came to make *Aliyah*, scores of Zinkovian youngsters arose and joined the camp of the pioneer rebuilders of the land of Israel.

The Hebrew School in Zinkov, faculty and students

[Page 100]

Memories of My Home in Zinkov 1900–1930
by Yisro'el (Sani's son) Roytburd[1]
Translated by Yael Chaver
Thanks to the editor, the writer Moyshe Grossman

"Oh, somewhere, somewhere far away, far
far away,
My childish heart dumbly desired
And longed so–

* * *

What did I want? I myself don't know.
I know only that it will never return"

Hayim Nahman Bialik[2]

In Zinkov, Podolia province, Ukraine, there once stood a house. It had stood there since ancient times. If one took the time and trouble to rummage among the oldest gravestones in the cemetery, one could find the names of the ancestors of the family that had lived in the house. And these ancestors, I was told, had built the house with their own hands. The house was strong and solid, built of hard stone, with thick walls. It seems to me that the house stands to this day; I cannot believe that it was destroyed. The entrance to the house led over a low hill to the beginning of a narrow alley that was called "the between–stores." It was a corner house, with a ground–floor apartment below and an upper floor with windows facing both sides of the street. Looking out of the eastern window, one could see not only the street but the fields as well, in the distance, across the valley on the slopes that led down to the valley and to the Ushytsia River.

In summer, it was a pleasure to see the changing colors over the hills; from the black cultivated fields to the green grass, from green grass to the golden waves of ripe grain. You could also see flocks of sheep in the early morning climbing up the winding white paths among the fields

[Page 101]

and see them again rolling down at twilight, like a marvelous, constantly shifting, wool carpet. In the fall, the fields were reaped and fine haystacks of stacked sheaves rose in straight lines, like drilling soldiers. When the sheaves vanished, leaving the fields bare, you'd know that winter was coming, and the starkness would soon be covered with a white quilt of crystal–clear snow. The house would start preparing for winter, buying all the necessities, fitting in the double windows, strewing sand between the panes, and cleaning out the chimneys of the central stove.[3]

Let me point out, for the children "who did not know" Zinkov, that the Zinkov Jews could enjoy the beauty of the surrounding fields and orchards only from a distance, but could not benefit from their bounty.[4] The wide fields did not belong to the Jews of Zinkov. The town bordered on its rural surroundings, but Jews could not settle anywhere outside the gate. They had to buy their food and earn money by negotiating their needs with the surrounding Christian population.

As everyone knows, windows are not used only for looking out. They also serve for looking in. Let's drop in for a short visit to the house. The first thing we notice is that the sunlight streams in, first encountering the polished cupboard that stretched half the length of the wall. This cupboard was built by Yoysef (Tesi's son), a local carpenter. These days, such a fine piece of work would be considered a treasure, a real work of art. Yoysef spent long days planing and smoothing out the wood, until the surface was as lustrous as silk; then he lacquered and polished it with chopped walnuts tied up in cloth.[5] He decorated the door with thin strips of veneer. Finally, he crowned the cupboard with an elegant, delicately worked head–tefillin.[6] The subdued sheen gleamed in the sunlight like polished glass. Oh, Yosl![7] You gave so much joy to the children you allowed into your workshop to watch you work. They marvelled at the shavings, spinning out from under the plane as though they were alive, and snatched them up by the handful; the movement and rhythm of the saw cutting the boards was a source of wonder to them.

In addition to the cupboard made by Yosl, the room also contained a large rectangular table with bulbous, carved legs. The table was surrounded by the inevitable "Vienna" chairs with woven cane seats.[8] The wall was decorated with two large photographs of Grandfather and Grandmother. The original photographs were originally made by Yehoshua Photographer.[9] Uncle Shloyme asked for them to be sent to America; they came back to us enlarged and colored.[10] The wall clock hung between the pictures. This was a large–faced modern clock, powered by a spring that had to be key–wound every 24 hours. This was an innovation, compared to the heavy pendulum in most contemporary wall clocks. Incidentally, I was never able to discover the age of the clock, or how long it had occupied its important place in our house. In any case, it had certainly happened before I first opened my eyes and took a first look at the world I had entered. The clock was surely showing the hours and minutes accurately, but who would be interested in noticing that? It was probably doing the same thing and showing the hour and minute when I left the house, never to see it again. And once again, no one paid attention... Only the clock itself knew, ticking away the flying time and ringing out the hour, day or night.

[Page 102]

So life flowed comfortably and happily–but only for a few years. The clock chimed the hours of Friday evenings.[11] In summer, soon after the festive meal, everyone would go out into the street. Women would sit on the earthen benches adjoining the house walls and discuss the quality of this week's *challahs*, the high price of the fish for Shabbes, and the like. Young men went for walks with their wives. Children, of course, would be outdoors. In winter, more people went out on Shabbes evening; most people stayed home on Friday nights. Later in the evening on clear moonlit nights, when the Shabbes candles had gone out and the kerosene lamp's wick had run out of fuel, the moon would appear from somewhere and send an exploring ray of light into the house.

The house is quiet. The household members, sitting in the lively darkness with neighbors and friends, have exhausted their conversation and remained seated around the warm central stove, each immersed in thoughts. Now the moon sends a stream of light into the room, driving the darkness out of the corners, throwing a veil of light over everything; minutes later, its round face is looking through the windows. It sees itself mirrored in the polished brass candlesticks on the table, and smiles teasingly at Queen Shabbes, who is visiting here until tomorrow evening and shakes people up a bit.[12] The conversation starts up again. Arye Shenkelman starts singing a psalm to a traditional tune, more and more devoutly, and the long hours of the winter night drag on. No one notices that the moon has disappeared, and is hiding behind the tip of the synagogue roof. A trumpet call slices the air, reverberating from somewhere far away, sharp and oddly sorrowful. It suddenly stops, starting again sporadically until it goes completely silent. The watchman at Divishek's factory down in the valley is letting people know that he is awake, and that the hour is late. The trumpet's call has broken the idyll of absolute peace. People wake up, each grab their fur coats and caps, and go out into the cold street. Each person went to his own corner. The cold plucked at people's faces, bringing them wide awake. The nighttime streets lie frozen under the untouched virgin snow. House roofs and tree branches are robed in white, standing asleep as though by a magic spell. Wrapped in dark shadows, the houses leaned against each other. A thin thread of smoke emerged from a chimney somewhere, and stretched straight up to heaven. A glowing ember had breathed out its last bit of fire; or a witch had cooked up her broth.

[Page 103]

In the houses, all the windows are dark, not a glimmer of light to be seen. Everything is asleep. Only the startled barking of a dog comes from somewhere. It barks desolately and is soon silent. A stride, a creak. Feet rise up on their own, boldly. I'd love to stride like this to the end of the world... The alleys are now so peaceful and quiet, "how blessed are your tents, Jacob."[13] Sleep, you familiar, kind people. I'd like to remember you as existing under the reign of Queen Shabbes, and no other regime...

———

Translator's Footnotes:

1. Sani seems to have been the name, or nickname, of Yisro'el Roytburd's father. People were often referred to by a patronymic; thus, Yisro'el Sani's was Yisro'el, Sani's son.

2. The quote is from a Yiddish poem by Hayim Nahman Bialik (1873–1934), the pre–eminent Hebrew poet of the late 19th and early 20th centuries; my translation This excerpt is from one of his few Yiddish poems, first printed in a Polish Yiddish magazine in 1899.

3. I was not able to clarify the reference to sand being strewn between the windowpanes.

4. The biblical phrase "a new Pharaoh who did not know Joseph" (Exodus 1, 8) is often used to refer to a younger generation that is not familiar with the old ways.

5. Walnut oil can be used to treat wooden furniture.

6. *Tefillin* is the ritual term for the phylacteries that Jewish men wear on their forehead and left arm for praying on certain occasions. They are small leather boxes that contain verses from the Torah. The head–*tefillin* is the more elaborate of the two.

7. Yosl is a diminutive of Yoysef.

8. These bentwood chairs with cane seats were very popular in 19th–century Europe.

9. "Photographer" is presented as Yehoshua's last name; professions often served as last names.

10. Presumably, Uncle Shloyme was living in America.

11. Friday night, the start of Shabbes, is a time for family and social gatherings.

12. "Queen Shabbes" is a term for the weekly day of rest.

13. The quote alludes to Numbers 24, 5.

———

[Page 104]

Memories of My Zinkov Home
by Yitzchak Frenkel[1]
Translated by Yael Chaver

Zinkov stood firmly on the top of a tall hill and was a major center for the Jews throughout the province of Podolia, Ukraine. There were very few non–Jews in town: the judge, the doctor, the medic, the post–office manager, and a small number of hospital workers. The chief of police, his constable, and the police officers they commanded lived out of town.

Yitzchak Frenkel

The hill where Zinkov stood is surrounded by a valley dotted with Ukrainian villages. The Ushytsia River flows gently through the villages; on its way to join the Dniester, its waters power grain mills, usually standing in pairs on either side of the river. The river section that flows through a village is often named for that village: the Kalinovka River, the Krivuli River, and the Men's River, so named for its deep water, suitable for "masculine" swimming. On hot summer days, all the Jews of Zinkov – old and young – would go down to the river to wash off their sweat in the Kalinovka River east of the mill, where the water was shallow. The young folks would go to swim in the deep water of Men's River. On their way to the river and back, the bathers would pluck juicy fruit off the branches overhanging orchard fences.

[Page 105]

No trained engineers had planned the streets and houses of Zinkov, yet the main streets of the town were straight, and the houses on either side were tall and wide, the whitewashed walls gleaming brightly in the sun. The two main streets crossed at a wide square, with a high pole bearing a bright "Lux" kerosene lantern. This was the town center. The Jews of Zinkov would gather on the square in their free time and talk about their livelihoods, town affairs, and the reports in the newspapers. They talked about ordinary matters: whose son or daughter was getting married, a *bris* or *bar-mitzvah* in the family; the quality of the cantor's chanting on recent holidays; who was granted which blessing before a Torah reading last Shabbes or holiday; the number of followers who came from towns near and far to the "courts" of *Rebbe* Moyshele or *Rebbe* Pinchesl (may their memory be for a blessing) and the gifts they brought.[2]

Other topics of conversation were about the best places to walk on summer evenings and on Shabbes (behind the Christian cemetery (the *tsvinter*) or behind the city hall; about who needed the services of the court because of a debt or a quarrel; etc.[3]

The Jews of Zinkov made their living in various ways: leasing forests or flour mills, as lumber merchants, trading in flour (both wholesale and retail), fabric, groceries, and notions. There were owners of taverns and hotels, bakers, dealers in medicines, pharmacy owners, teachers, and various artisans. These were the "householders," the most important men in town, and constituted most of Zinkov's residents. They lived in the homes they owned on the town's streets and squares. The lower street was the home of the poor: patchers of fur garments and shoes; millers; tailors making clothes for peasants, synagogue sextons, the indigents, and the town's gravedigger.

My father, Aharon Frenkel, came to Zinkov in 1898 from his home town of Michalpole, where he was born to his father Yoyne and his mother Toyve; in Zinkov, he married my mother Nekha, the daughter of Henekh and Khaye Gornshteyn (may their memories be for a blessing). Father was proud of being Jewish. He was learned, loved to read, and was sociable. He was generous, and always gave freely to the poor of the town and indeed, to anyone in need. He loved young people who were interested in knowledge and culture, advised the municipal library about book acquisitions and even contributed money for this purpose. The local theater troupe took his advice concerning choice of works and performance style. He was a regular at the small synagogue, and donated generously to its maintenance. He would take his seat at the prestigious east wall of the synagogue and participate in choosing the readers for the *aliyahs*; he would buy the most important *aliyah* for himself.[4] If there were disputes between grantors of aid and its receivers who did not repay the aid, or between storekeepers about attracting customers, or other financial disputes, the two sides would turn to Father and lay out their arguments. His opinion would be accepted as a judgment, with which both sides were satisfied.[5] Father devoted most of his energy to educating his children. He made sure the children did their homework; he would first help them, then quiz them. Mother was his assistant. He made a living by managing two grain mills on the banks of the Kalinovka, which he leased from the authorities. Each mill employed 10–12 workers.

Nekha Frenkel
(may her memory be for a blessing)

Aharon Frenkel
(may his memory be for a blessing)

[Page 106]

The Jews of Zinkov lived peacefully. It was not hard to earn a living, and their living conditions were good. The children were healthy and happy; their clothes and shoes were clean and intact. On Shabbes and holidays, their homes were happy and contented. On summer Saturdays, after the Shabbes meal and a nap, each family would go for a walk outside the town limits for fresh air, beyond the non-Jewish cemetery and the *vlost*, to the square surrounding the old fort (the *shloss*). The hikers would reach the nearby villages and strike up conversations with peasant acquaintances resting on their fences. These peasants often gave them gifts from their farms – flowers, apples, plums, sunflowers.[6] Relations with the villagers were normal. Things changed with the outbreak of the first World War, in the late summer of 1914. Not all Jewish men of draft age were in a hurry to enlist for the defense of their "step-homeland," with good reason.[7] Searches for conscripts in Zinkov became common and kept people on edge day and night. The members of the Jewish community council were constantly negotiating with the Chief of Police and the constable, asking them to stop the searches or at least give advance notice... During the first years of the war the food supply was still steady, and trade continued as usual. At the end of 1916 a lack of kerosene, salt, and fabric began to be marked. As a result, tensions with the peasants began to rise. They falsely accused the Zinkov Jews of hiding goods. Discontent and signs of coming revolution were noticeable in Zinkov as well.

[Page 107]

At the first news of the 1917 February Revolution, the Zinkov Chief of Police and the constable vanished, as well as all the policemen.[8] The town was left with no authorities. The city council decided to organize self-defense, without consulting with the public. Most of the townspeople, however, thought that it was too early to take such an independent step, because they were not sure that the revolution was stable; the deposed government might return, God forbid, and such a hasty step would bring disaster upon the town. However, one night we heard knocking at the door. The Chief of Police came in with his Chief Constable, proposing that Father keep their swords and the few firearms they had, until the unrest died down. This great deed would work in the Jews' favor, when the old regime eventually returned. Father sent me to call for the advocate Abstryanik, Gusakov the dentist, Motya Fayerman, and few young men. After a brief consultation, they decided to take the weapons, hand them out to the young folks, and set Father at their head. The Jews of Zinkov could not believe their eyes the next morning: Jews carrying police swords were out on the street for the first time in Jewish history, with all its calamities and humiliations.

The Zionist ideal and the longing for the historic homeland of our people, which Father had suppressed for many years for fear of the authorities (who opposed any movement of national liberation), now burst forth. Zionism became popular in our town, Zionist education was carried out in the synagogues, the schools, and the streets, and captivated the Zinkov natives.

Zinkov natives building a road in Rishon Le–Zion:
1. Yitzchak Frenkel 2. Reuven Rozental 3. Netanel Frenkel

[Page 108]

When the members of the Regional Zionist Committee came to Zinkov to collect contributions for Eretz–Yisra'el, the ground was ready: women and men of the town donated jewelry, wedding rings, and gold watches. Father and Mother, of course, were among the first to donate. The young people started to organize in a HeHalutz group.[9] In order to finance their activities, they chopped wood for school stoves. Father, may his memory be for a blessing, was at the forefront of the young people, fanning their enthusiasm and desire to immigrate to Eretz–Yisra'el.

The October revolution, which swept through all of Russia, led to an extreme nationalist counter–revolution throughout Ukraine.[10] Jewish life and property became free for the taking. Ukrainian armed bands stole, robbed, and killed indiscriminately. Two days after the Proskurov pogrom, Petlyura's forces murdered most of the Jews of

Felstin.[11]Representatives of the Jewish community came to Zinkov for help burying the dead and caring for the wounded. Their community distress deeply affected the town's Jews . Father, along with the other council members, organized a delegation of ten young men and two young women; one of the women was a newly certified physician, the other a pharmacist. I was one of the members of the group. We braved the dangers of travel through villages with their gangs seeking to murder Jews, en route to help our brothers and sisters in Felstin. It became imperative to organize self–defense in our town. The best and finest, as well as the young people headed by Nokhem Yoshpe, answered the call; Nokhem describes this project in detail elsewhere in this volume.

A group of Zinkov natives in Haifa:
1) Dovid Fuks 2) Zevulun Rund (not a Zinkov native) 3) Shloyme Goldenberg 4) Unknown 5) Nissan, from Husyatin 6) Zev Nesis (may his memory be for a blessing) 7–9) Unknown 10) Mandel 11) Menachem Vaysman 12) Shmuel Korn 13–14) Unknown 15) Shamai Shor

[Page 109]

The Jews of Zinkov lived under the protection of this "Defense" force for about two years, cut off from the center of the country,

with no reliable news of events. They were also cut off from supplies; there was a severe shortage of kerosene, salt, sugar, and other staples. The value of money dropped; whatever supplies were available disappeared and could be acquired only on the black market in return for grain, or silver and gold coins. Our skies were darkened; there was almost no way to survive. Once again, my father sounded the alarm: Brothers, don't wait for the empty fleshpot to refill itself. Let's leave while we are still alive, and go to Eretz–Yisra'el.

And indeed, a pioneering Zionist movement developed in our town; it overcame all the external obstacles and problems, as recounted by the first pioneer, Nokhem Yoshpe, in his detailed account. Groups of pioneers from Zinkov arrived in Eretz–Yisra'el. Their adjustment to the country was extremely difficult, as was their adaptation to the hard labor of road–building; and even more so – to the unemployment that followed. They could barely subsist until the next job came along. We shared all our experiences with Father, in letters to him. We concealed nothing. All the descriptions of our difficulties did not deter him. In 1923, he arrived in Eretz–Yisra'el with my brother Yekhi'el, and a year later Mother arrived with the remaining four children. They set out with youthful energy to build their new home in the age-old homeland. Father leased 10 dunams of land from the Jewish National Fund, bought a horse and a plow, and started to plant tobacco, assisted by his children.[112] Mother contributed by caring for the modest cabin on the outskirts of Rishon Le–Tziyon, in which the family lived. Over the years, the sons and daughters married, and all settled down in Eretz–Yisra'el. The children helped their parents buy the land on which their home was built. Father planted fruit trees, bought cows, and made a respectable living through his own efforts. All the sons and daughters would gather at the parents' cabin on holidays and celebrate. Father's yearning for the homeland and his lifelong goal was fulfilled. Father died at age 72; Mother lived for 14 more years. May their memory be blessed forever!

Below is the list of pioneers from Zinkov:

The first group included:

Nakhum Yoshpe, one of the organizers of this group, went to Eretz–Yisra'el as early as 1920. The following people came in 1921.

David Feldman (the carpenter, may his memory be for a blessing), and his wife.

Pearl Feldman

Mendl Kurtzman (may his memory be for a blessing), founder of *kibbutz* En Harod

Yeshaya Shteynbas, *moshav* Kfar Vitkin

Moshe (Muni) Averbukh, *moshav* Havatzelet

Khaye Frenkel–Vekslman, Tel Aviv

[Page 110]

Yisra'el Vekslman, Tel Aviv

Yitzchak Frenkel, Haifa

Batya Shterntal, *kibbutz* Ayelet HaShahar

Yisra'el Shvartsman, Haifa

Yona Zayntchik, left for America[13]

Yitzchak Fayderman, left for America

Avraham Shenkelman, left for America

The second group included:

Shlomo Shapira (may his memory be for a blessing), a pioneering road–builder

Zev Nesis (may his memory be for a blessing), died in America

Abba Nesis (may his memory be for a blessing), died in a traffic accident on the Rishon LeZion road.

Mendl Vaysman (may his memory be for a blessing), Haifa, died in 1956

Shlomo Goldberg, Haifa

Reuven Rozental, Haifa

David Fuks, left for America

Shamai Shor, left for Argentina

Dov Saliternik (may his memory be for a blessing), a founder of En–Harod

Shmuel Koren, *moshav* Neta'im[14]

Besides these two organized groups, isolated halutzim as well as families from Zinkov went to *Eretz Yisra'el* at various times. Among them were those who had previously been exiled to Siberia. Most of them became rooted in the country and participated in different ways in the establishment of the community.

———

Translator's Footnotes:

1. Pages 104–110, have been translated from the original Hebrew. I have transliterated names according to their Hebrew pronunciation.

2. Specific blessings are said before and after reading a Torah portion; certain blessings are considered more prestigious than others.

3. I could not translate *vlosts*, which apparently refers to an official or governmental building.

4. In this context, *aliyah* refers to the honor of being called up for a Torah reading, which usually involves a monetary contribution to the synagogue. The income from the sale of aliyot helps to maintain the synagogue and its

functions. The relative importance of different *aliyahs* is decided by custom and by the congregation.

5. No repayment of charity (tzedakah) is expected, whereas financial and other aid (*gemilut–hasadim*) is often granted by a mutual fund, and repayment is expected.

6. Sunflower seeds are a favorite snack in Ukraine.

7. This observation is not elaborated on.

8. This was the first of two revolutions in Russia in 1917. The February revolution culminated in the Czar's abdication.

9. HeHalutz was a Jewish youth movement that trained young people for agricultural settlement in Eretz–Yisra'el. It became an umbrella organization of the pioneering Zionist youth movements.

10. The October Revolution, (October 7–8, 1917), officially known in Soviet historiography as the Great October Socialist Revolution, was a revolution led by Lenin's Bolshevik party. It toppled the interim government that was instituted after the fall of the Czar in February 1917.

11. The Proskurov and Felstin pogroms occurred in February 1919. Symon Petlyura was the Chief of Military Forces in the Ukrainian republic.

12. One dunam is roughly the equivalent of ¼ acre. The Jewish National Fund was founded in 1901 to buy and develop land in Ottoman Palestine for Jewish settlement.

13. The writer uses the common Hebrew verb *yarad* (literally "descended") for the act of leaving the Land of Israel, an act of leaving that is traditionally construed as negative. The noun *yored* ("one who descends") is used somewhat pejoratively.

14. *Kibbutz* and *moshav* are two of the forms of Zionist settlement practiced in pre–Zionist times. A kibbutz is a collective community, traditionally based on agriculture. A *moshav* is a cooperative agricultural community of individual farms.

———

[Page 111]

Zinkov, Our Town

by Moyshe Garber

Translated by Yael Chaver

Oh, God! Inspire my imagination and strengthen my pen, so that I can use all my might to revive you, my very dear former home and all of you, my dearly beloved sacred martyrs. I, too, would like to add a few bricks to this memorial monument; bricks mixed and molded with blood from my heart and tears from my eyes.

I was not intimate with my town, Zinkov, from 1921 to its destruction. I don't know how people lived there under Soviet rule, whether better or worse, and will not dare to judge; I have no memories and no impressions of that period. But I remember very well Zinkov and its residents during my early childhood, up to the day I left my town, at the end of 1920. Oh, I remember it very well. It is deeply engraved in my memory, in my heart, and in every part of my body.

Often, when I am alone, my heart yearns nostalgically so that I become detached from the reality around me. I shut my eyes and fall into a kind of trance. I let my thoughts carry me back many years, to my distant, impoverished, beloved town, where I was born, where my cradle stood, where Mother and Father trembled as they watched over me, and where I lived through so much joy and suffering together with my family, my friends, and my neighbors. As though through a thick fog, it all comes nearer and nearer, until I see everything so clearly that I can almost touch it. I see the houses, the streets, the alleys, the paths and trails in the fields and hills, where I ran around as a child, and played with my friends. As though on a movie screen, I see the images, the people, and the events that are still so dear to me.

Here is my own home, on the Taravitza, near the field, where I was born and lived until the day I left, never to set eyes on it again.[1] No one was out in that cold, dark winter night before we went away, to see me standing outside leaning against the wall, parting from my home and weeping bitterly. I see all the neighbors who lived with us in the same house, such as my uncle Yehoshua Sender's son (Shaye Fotografshchik).[2] Others who lived in the house were Efroyim (Batchke's son) and his father–in–law, the snub–nosed synagogue caretaker, who would call everyone into the synagogue for prayers. Next were the houses of Hersh Foydnik, Shmuel Stolier, Mordkhe Boykes, Shmuel Mishandzenik, Yisro'el Shnayder, Tsalay (Leybl's son), Itzi–Meir Khmelenker, Ben–Tziyon (Shaye's son), Yankl Haritan, and many more.

[Page 112]

I see my *kheyder*, with my kind *melamed* Sani (may be rest in peace); right next to it is the *talmud–toyre*, on the butcher's meadow; the house of Mendel the *shoykhet*, the teachers Bronfman, Koyfman, Kretshmar, Osher Altman, and others.[3] It was in the *talmud–toyre* that I spent my happiest and best childhood years. That is where my solid foundation of knowledge and learning was laid, the basis for my later cultural education and development. I felt boundless love for my beautiful natural surroundings. When the grain in the field grew tall and ripe, waving like a golden sea, I loved to walk along the narrow path to the Libak valley. Cut off from the world, I would stretch out on the soft, fragrant grass, my face upturned to the clear blue sky, and ruminate, dreaming the golden dreams of youth, and marvel at the beauty of God's world. Oh, how good it was then to be young and free of worry!

Shmuel–Lipe (son of Sender) Garber and his wife Rokhl (may their memory be for a blessing), the parents of Moyshe Garber

[Page 113]

I remember the hot Shabbes days of summer. After morning prayers, we would eat a good midday meal, with *cholent* and a fatty *kugel*.[4] The older folks lay down for a nap, and we youngsters were off to the fields and woods, through hills and dales. Once we were tired and sweaty enough, we'd climb up the cramped, narrow path along the old Turkish fort, then let ourselves down to the spring. We'd quench our thirst with the ice–cold, crystal–clear water that flowed down a stone channel. Once we were refreshed, we sat in the shadow of the willows, among the lively rivulets of water. We stuffed our pockets full of *putr–krayt* (a type of bluish stone we used for carving toys).[5] Afterwards everyone felt like taking a swim. The river was not far away; we headed over there, or to the Grebleye, or the Men's River.[6] Oh, how I envied those who could swim across the river. In my child's eyes, they were more heroic than those who swim across the English Channel today.

And do you remember, dear Zinkov natives, the Shabbes twilight hours, when young and old, dressed in their best clothes, would stroll calmly across the green hills below the fort, below the non–Jewish cemetery, or simply along the fields, all the way to the black cross and back? We gulped in the refreshing air and feasted our eyes on the beautiful sunset and the beautiful panorama of the valley with the curving river bordered by colorful cottages, orchards, and gardens.

Once again, the amazing images pass before my eyes. They rush one after the other, in no special order: the massive building – our famous synagogue, which I always viewed with so much wonder; it was constantly a mysterious riddle. I really wanted to know how a small poor town such as ours came to have such a gigantic, imposing structure, such an architectural masterpiece; who the artists were, who carved the beautiful Torah ark that defies description, the likes of which I have never seen since. After all, who were the builders and creators of such an expensive project? I never received a satisfactory answer. I'm sure that no one knew.

The image of the market, with its stores, stalls, and sellers, emerges from the farthest reaches of my memory. The non–Jewish women are set up with their wares – fruit and vegetables. The Jewish women selling in the market sit further along with their baked goods. At the side is a long row of the earthenware pots for which Zinkov is renowned. The most prominent buildings in Zinkov are the brick house of Yosl (Shaye's son), and Khayim Kliger's oversized building, surrounded by stores. Close by, I can see the rounded well near Shloyme Shor and Sore Yosi Mekhtsis. The well, which had cost a fortune to dig, never produced water.

[Page 114]

I see it all before my eyes again. I see the patches of deep mud and the cold, dark, winter days and nights. Most of the population lived in dire poverty, need, and hopelessness, but I do not want to think about that too long. I want to remember that which was beautiful, good, and beloved; that which is so closely linked with my romantic, dreamy youth. I seem to hear the whistle of Divishek's brewery, which woke the workers at 6 a.m. The Divishek name and its beer added to the popularity of our Zinkov. Not far from the brewery were the tanneries, with their pungent smell of *kvass*,[7] in which the pelts were soaked; these pelts were later made into fur jackets for peasants, and used for leather. And here, at the foot of the hill, is the bathhouse. It played an important role in the life of the Zinkovites. That is where the poor washed every Friday, and refreshed their exhausted bodies in the steam bath. Scary voices would scream down from the top bench, *"Podovoy paru!"* ("More steam!").[8]

Itzik Hersh Volfbayn's wife
(may her memory be for a blessing)

Itzik Hirsh Volfbayn
(may his memory be for a blessing)

[Page 115]

Dear fellow Zinkovites, you certainly remember the fire brigade (*pozharne komande*), with their gray uniforms and shiny brass helmets. You remember how they would go out and train with all their gear, climb onto roofs and spray water from their "pumps." But they could never actually extinguish a fire, because there was a serious shortage of water; water had to be brought up a long way from the foot of the hill. The brigade's center was called "the fire brigade's depot." Its upper floor consisted of a hall where weddings would be held, visiting theater troupes would have performances, and even we young amateurs would play there, and bring some light and joy into the quiet, monotonous life of the Zinkovites.

* * *

Suddenly, the day came which spelled the end of the quiet, peaceful, impoverished life of Zinkov, and of the normal life of the whole world. That was the day when the First World War was declared. The bloodbath and widespread slaughter lasted for two years, before Russia reached the abyss of complete breakup. At that point the democratic Kerensky revolution broke out, putting an end to the Czar and his rotten, incompetent clique, and we breathed more freely and happily, participated in demonstrations, and held inspiring talks. But the Kerensky regime was weak and did not know how to establish and consolidate its power. It continued the futile, senseless war, until the Bolsheviks came and promised a speedy end to it. This had a powerful effect on the weary people, and even more so – on the hungry, bloodied armies, who were rotting in the trenches. In this way, the Bolsheviks, headed by Lenin and Trotsky, rose to power. The internal and external counter–revolutionary forces did not surrender easily, and made repeated attempts to regain power. Denikin, Kolchak, Petlyura, the Poles, and more and more armed bands succeeded each other.[9] Jewish blood and Jewish property became free for the taking. We lived in constant fear of death and terror, lying in cellars and attics like terrified shackled sheep, waiting for the slaughter. The armed bands rampaged, robbed, murdered, and raped Jewish women. Death was hard, but life was even harder. Hunger and typhus finished off the rest.

The devilish dance finally slacked off a bit. Anyone who had the chance ran off, as panicked animals flee from ravenous flames. We ran, and ran again, to all the corners of the world: to America, Canada, Argentina, *Eretz–yisro'el*, and wherever possible.

[Page 116]

* * *

But when the terrible plague of Hitler came, our unfortunate brothers and sisters could run no more, because the blood–drenched enemy was persistent, strong, and merciless. With real German precision, it completely and forever destroyed our Zinkov, its people, and its life.

Now we survivors of Zinkov, call ourselves *landslayt*; the word *landsman* overflows with love, intimacy, and brotherly feelings.[10] We are organized in societies and associations bearing the name of Zinkov, of Zinkovites, of Zinkov life. Even when our inevitable end comes, Zinkov natives find their eternal rest in the cemetery that is Zinkov soil; over its entrance is the inscription "Zinkov – Podolia" in large Yiddish letters. God rescued us from the hellish fire, and it is our destiny to continue the existence of Zinkov and of the Jewish people. This we do, and will continue to do, with love and devotion, to our last breaths.

Translator's Footnotes:

1. This may refer to Targowica, which is 66 miles away.
2. People were often known by their profession or trade.
3. The *kheyder* teacher was termed *melamed*; *shoykhet* is the term for a ritual slaughterer.
4. The *cholent* is a traditional stew that is usually simmered overnight for 12 hours or more, and eaten for lunch on Shabbes. *Kugel* is a casserole–style dish, made with either potatoes or noodles in sweet or savory varieties.
5. I could not identify the Yiddish term *putr* (or *futr*)–*krayt*.
6. I could not identify the Grebleye River.
7. *Kvass* is a traditional fermented Slavic and Baltic beverage commonly made from rye bread.
8. Here and in the following sentence, the Russian is presented in Yiddish transliteration, with a Yiddish translation.
9. Anton Denikin (1872–1947) led the anti–Bolshevik ("White") forces on the southern front during the Russian Civil War (1918–20). Admiral Alexander Kolchak (1874–1920) was an Arctic explorer and a naval officer, who was recognized in 1919–20 by the "Whites" as supreme ruler of Russia.
10. *Landsman* and *landslayt* can be translated as "compatriot" and "fellow countrymen."

[Page 117]

Memories of Bygone Times[1]

by Y. Ben–David

Translated by Yael Chaver

Two intersecting roads divided Zinkov into four parts. At the crossroads stood a tall pole with a kerosene lamp, which created a pool of light underneath. The children were drawn to the light like moths, continuing their play that had stopped when it grew dark.

Yosef Ben–David

It was the time of the First World War. The supervision of children by parents and teachers slacked off. From time to time, the schools would close, because the ruling gangs requisitioned them; the buildings seemed to have been planned to house soldiers. The children were affected by their surroundings, and tried to imitate the adults as they played. Their favorite game was "soldiers." Each street would have its own army unit, complete with officers, to fight the children of the next street. There were imaginary captives and casualties in these battles; sometimes, the wounds were far from imaginary.

Control of the town often changed hands. Every once in a while a gang that had formed in the vicinity appeared. Bullets began flying about. The residents would hide indoors until it grew quieter. That was life in those days: economic concerns on the one hand, and mortal danger on the other hand. Our fatalities were relatively low, compared with the other towns in the area. This was apparently due to the "self–

defense" group, which was well–organized and deterred the robbers and thugs. The core of the group was students who had returned home from Odessa, and brought weapons with them.[2] Many homes also had their own weapons. Our house, for example, contained a long–barreled Parabellum pistol, which I often took out of its drawer and examined.[3] I was very proud of myself when I held the large instrument in my small hands, and sometimes tried to use it. To this day, I can't understand how I escaped injury in those exercises.

* * *

[Page 118]

It was nighttime, frosty, snowy. Suddenly, shots rang out. As we were experienced, and prepared for disaster, we gathered in an inner room whose walls did not face the street, where we would be safe from intentional, or stray, bullets. Once the first moments of panic were over, we listened intently to gauge the amount and direction from which the shots came. We found that they were coming from the area of *rebbe* Moyshele's house. Once the shooting stopped and things grew a bit calmer, we found out that the tavern just behind the rabbi's house was occupied by a gang that was planning to take over the town. Once the self–defense group found this out, they decided to foil the plan. A face–to–face battle broke out between gang members and self–defense fighters. Our guys advanced, taking one room after another from the gang in the tavern, all the way up to the attic. In this way, they managed to overpower the gang and place them under arrest in the firehouse. A serious problem now arose: they had no way to shackle the gang members. The answer was supplied by the Yoshpe family, many of whom belonged to the self–defense group. That night, they opened up their store, brought out iron chains, and the gang members were secured.

* * *

It was Friday evening. All was quiet and peaceful in the town; but we had not finished our meal before shots were heard once again. Within a few seconds, shots and explosion echoed from every corner of town. Father (may his memory be for a blessing) took his weapon and went out. All Mother's efforts to get us to bed were in vain. We sneaked out of our beds, rushed down the stairs, and stood on the ground floor, in the living room. We were very curious about what was going on outside. Late that night, we found out that a gang had been organized in the "Kalinovka" neighborhood, with the goal of taking over the town; it was only thanks to the efforts of the "self–defense" group that the gang was fended off and the town was saved.

* * *

Eventually, we became used to the rumors that swept over town every now and then about robberies and murders perpetrated by gangs in various towns. These became a regular part of our childhood experiences, until we got word one Friday night about approaching danger. The sun was still high. Grandma (may she rest in peace) ordered us to come in, wash, and change our clothes for Shabbes. At first we refused, because it was still early and we could have played outdoors for a while. But I understood the situation after hearing Grandma's conversation with the adults. She told my parents, "If we have to die, at least we'll be buried with clean bodies and fresh clothes." The rumors were that the threatening gang had decided to carry out a massacre in Zinkov, like the one it had earlier perpetrated in Proskurov.[4]

* * *

It was night. We were already in bed, when the wall next to my bed suddenly lit up.

[Page 119]

Flames from a nearby house illuminated the entire neighborhood. Immediately, there was a commotion on the street. The firefighter's carts hurried toward the fire. Alarmed people ran around, trying as they ran to find out what had happened. It soon became clear that the house of Levi the carpenter was on fire. Rescue operations were soon under way and the firefighters started to extinguish the fire, but suddenly stopped because explosions were coming from the attic of the house. It turned out that the owner, a member of the self-defense organization, had stored different types of ammunition in the attic for safe-keeping. The firefighting efforts had to stop until all the ammunition was gone.

* * *

One day we heard that the school was closed. A gang that had taken over the town took up housing in the large school building and its spacious rooms. As this "vacation" went on, Father (may his memory be for a blessing) decided that I had to fill in the gap in my studies with the aid of a tutor. Our family friend Shmuel Fridman (may his memory be for a blessing) was to be the tutor. I went to his home, near the slaughterhouse, every day. One day, when I showed up for my regular lesson, the tutor was surprised: "Are you coming to study today? How could they let you leave the house in this situation?" I was surprised; Fridman began explaining that a gang had entered the town and it was dangerous to be on the street, especially as it was a long way from my home to his. As generous and warm-hearted as he was, he could not understand me: was I, a child, to blame for the war, and the presence of gangs in cities and towns? Was that a reason to deny myself the pleasure of learning?

* * *

The *Rebbe*, Moyshele (may his memory be for a blessing) lived next door, in a large, spacious house. One wing of the house was vacant, as it had been damaged by a fire. The rabbi and his extended family lived on the ground floor, and the upper floor was used as a synagogue, including a womens' section as well as a private room for the rabbi. The synagogue was large and well-lit, and the light coming from outside was amplified by the rabbi's inner light. *Rebbe* Moyshele was young. His behavior was unassuming and pleasant with everyone. He greeted everyone graciously, whether unlearned or scholarly, old or young, or someone who had simply come to ask his advice. People knew that the rabbi would find an answer to their questions and a remedy for problems that bothered them. The rabbi (may his memory be for a blessing) was especially fond of children, and would greet them with a friendly tug on the cheek.

* * *

The last night of *Sukkes, Simkhes–Toyre*, was celebrated with *hakofes*—circles of people dancing inside the synagogue.[5] Despite the late hour, a large crowd of the *Rebbe's* followers waited reverently for him to emerge from his room. The synagogue was very crowded. When the *Rebbe* appeared, his followers started clapping and singing. Each circuit around the hall added more enthusiasts to the dancing circles. The *Rebbe* himself would join the celebrants later. He held a small Torah scroll as he danced, and his followers would dance along with him deep into the night. The people of Zinkov certainly knew how to rejoice, even if it was only on *Simkhes–Toyre*.

———

Translator's Footnotes:

1. Pages 117 through119 have been translated from the Hebrew original.
2. Odessa was a major center of higher education.
3. Semi–automatic Parabellum pistols were in widespread use in Europe at the time.
4. The massacre in Proskurov was on February 15, 1919.
5. *Sukkes* (Sukkot, literally "booths"), the autumn harvest holiday, lasts for seven days and is the last of the High Holidays. It is named for the temporary dwellings of the Israelites during their wanderings in the desert. An additional day at its end, *Simkhes–Toyre* (Simhat Torah, "the joy of the Torah"), marks the end of the annual weekly cycle of Torah–readings. In the celebration, which starts on the eve of the holiday, the last reading of the previous year is immediately followed by the first reading of the new year. All the Torah scrolls are taken out of the ark and paraded around the synagogue seven times, accompanied by dancing, singing, and rejoicing. The celebration continues the next day. *Hakofes* is the plural of *hakofe–* circular procession.

[Page 120]

My Childhood in Zinkov
by Dovid Fuks
Translated by Yael Chaver

If God had miraculously commanded the four towns of Zinkov, Michalpole, Vinkivci, and Salapkovits to become one city and adjoin each other on the semicircular area of the clifftop near the former Turkish fortress, which we called "the castle," Zinkov would have been a large city, and I would have been happy to introduce myself whole–heartedly as "a Zinkovite."[1] However, the four towns were spread over a large area. Vinkivci was separated from Zinkov by a large, dense forest; Salapkovits – by a valley and a steep path; and Michalpole, especially, was separated from the other three towns by a small lake that had to be skirted along a clayey uphill road. On most days, the road was covered with thick, clayey mud that never dried between rains. It was even worse in winter. Severe frost would harden the wet clay into jagged lumps that were again hard to cross.

It was in this "clayey town," of all places, that my mother chose to bring me into the world, though her own family was in Zinkov. My father Fayvish (may he rest in peace) soon moved with his family to the village of Pakutenits, several *versts* away from Zinkov, and was known as "Fayvish of Pakutenits."[2] My great–grandfather had already been a *yishuvnik* in that village.[3] When I was all of three years old, my parents took me to Michalpole, where I had been born, and handed me over to my grandfather, Eliyohu the cantor, so that he would bring me up and send me to *kheyder* along with other Jewish children and I would not become a non–Jewish child, God forbid. I would be brought home for the High Holidays, and taken back to Michalpole afterwards. The foundations of my Jewish education were laid in that isolated Jewish town, Michalpole, which I will remember fondly all my life. Hitler, may his name be blotted out, turned all these Jewish towns into a giant rubble heap, but at that quiet, calm time, everyone all lived as good neighbors.

[Page 121]

The most deeply engraved on my heart is Zinkov, because the few years that I spent there were the best of my youth. As I mentioned, my parents settled in the village of Pakutenits, about 5 *versts* from Zinkov. A few Jewish families already lived there, and when the children grew a bit older they brought a teacher to the village. Those were the peaceful years, before the First World War. A small boy had a very good life in the village. Apples and pears grew profusely in the orchard behind the house, and juicy plums as well. It was a joy to run barefoot in the grass, even if it was not your home or your grass; who cared? The other Jewish families also had children, with whom I could play; it was such a joy to run from one end of the village to the other, up to the mill (the miller was Jewish), and bathe there with the other guys under the waterfalls created by the mill's paddles. We lived peacefully with our peasant neighbors. It seemed that we could go on living like this happily for years, but the war fell upon us, followed by the turmoil of the armed bands which turned their murderous instincts primarily towards Jews.

While I lived in the village with my parents, we would often go to Zinkov, either together or separately. We would go to buy necessities or to sell something we had bought from the peasants. Family members also lived there: my aunt Gitl (may she rest in peace) with her family; one of these was her daughter Sonia, now my wife. They had previously lived near the Austrian–Russian border, moved to Zinkov when the war began, and lived in a house on the same street that has been so eloquently described by our friend Yisro'el Roytburd. The first friend I made in Zinkov was actually Yisro'el Sani's (Sani Roytburd's son). First of all, his house was always open to young people. Yisro'el's father liked to spend time and have fun in company with young people. A relative of theirs also lived in the house, a pretty girl named

[Page 122]

Basya, who was an orphan; both her parents had died. She was a good friend of my cousin Sonia. We all formed a strong bond.

Sani's house was also the place where my intellectual education began. Sani would initiate conversations about various issues; by then, Yisro'el had already subscribed to the Russian illustrated journal *Nivo*, which would award prizes to the work of the best Russian writers.[4] Those books, which I read with enthusiasm, had a decisive effect on my intellectual development. From time to time I would also read the Yiddish daily newspapers *Moment* and *Haynt*, to which my father in the village subscribed, as well as the *Kievskaya Misl*, to which one of the Jews in the village subscribed.[5]

* * *

Our quiet lives did not last long. The difficult days of conflict between revolutionary and counter–revolutionary forces now began. Murderous bandits started to rampage in our area. There was a pogrom at my parents' house in the village. Everything was robbed, and my library, that I had worked so hard to collect, was turned into a pile of Hebrew words that scattered in every direction with the winds that blew through the broken windows.[6] The situation was such that the entire family moved to Zinkov, "under duress," as it were.

On my earlier visits to Zinkov, I had come to know all the young people who were involved in community activism. Now we grew closer, and I became a member of *HeHalutz*, despite the opposition of my parents, who did not want to let their only son vanish into the wide world. They succeeded only in stopping me from joining the first group of Zionist settlers from Zinkov. I left with the second group, in spite of my parents' protests. I assured them that I would bring them to *Eretz–Yisro'el* at the first opportunity. Unfortunately, this was not to be. My father died of natural causes in Zinkov, and my mother was slaughtered by the Nazi murderers. May their memory be honored forever, along with that of Zinkov, where I spent my youthful years.

———

Translator's Footnotes:

1. I could not identify the place name transliterated as Salapkovits, Solopkovits, Salafkovits, or Solofkovits. The corresponding Yiddish letters in the text lack vowel signs.

2. I could not identify the place name transliterated as Pakutenitz or Pokutenits. A *verst* is a Russian measure of length, about 0.66 mile.

3. A *yishuvnik* was a Jew who lived in a village with no Jewish community and was considered unlearned, and thus inferior to Jews more involved in Jewish culture.

4. I was not able to identify a periodical by that name. The Russian "Nivo" is roughly "level" (as in "level of achievement").

5. The *Kievskaya Misl* was a major Ukrainian newspaper. *Der Moment* (1910–1939) and *Haynt* were the two main Yiddish daily newspapers in Poland, published in Warsaw; they were in very wide circulation.

6. The writer uses the Hebraic term *sheymes* (which I have translated as "words"), to indicate the importance of these books for him. *Sheymes* is the Yiddish word for fragments of a holy book written in Hebrew letters that are not to be discarded, but buried in consecrated ground. It is not clear whether all these books were holy, in the conventional meaning of the term, or in Hebrew, but he clearly considered them sacred.

———

[Page 123]

My Childhood Years in Zinkov

by Moyshe Grinman

Translated by Yael Chaver

My father Yisro'el (may he rest in peace) was a community activist in our town, Zinkov, along with a group of friends who joined him in working for the good of the community. In those years, there were several *kheyders* in Zinkov, with teachers who taught the children Torah with Rashi, as well as Talmud.[1] There was also a *talmud-toyre*, which was more progressive than the *kheyders*, but used almost the same methods. The community activists, including my father, realized that the children also needed to be taught Russian and to receive a secular education. They therefore decided to establish a new *talmud–toyre* near the existing one and to bring in teachers from larger cities, who could point education in a new direction.

They also decided to build a new bathhouse in town, so that Jews should not have to walk far in the winter cold to the old bathhouse, outside town. With this in mind, two large buildings were erected on the old meadow, near the old *talmud–toyre*. However, when the walls were finished, the structures could not be completed; the town treasury had run out of money. The community activists then started collecting money throughout the city, to complete the buildings. At first, they turned to the few rich men in town and demanded a larger contribution for this purpose. However, as is well known, rich people are not too considerate. A few of them flatly refused to donate money. What's to be done in such a situation? A solution was found: "If they won't contribute in life, they'll contribute after death." Simply put, these people would not be buried until their heirs made good on the important social debt imposed on them by the town: to complete the two buildings that were so vital to the Jewish population. Surprisingly, the rich misers were in no hurry to die, and the buildings remained unfinished for a very long time. However, we youngsters wished the rich misers long lives; we used the two unfinished structures as forts when we played war: one group barricaded itself in one of the buildings and the other – in the second. We would climb up the walls and discover the positions of the "enemy." Over time, the walls crumbled completely.

[Page 124]

My father (may he rest in peace) realized that there was no point in waiting for the completion of the modern *talmud–toyre*, and turned to the only Russian school in Zinkov. However, they had a quota for Jewish children. My father overcame this decree by using the time–honored method that had served during the Czarist regime… and Simnevitch, the principal of the Russian school, allowed me through the doors of the school.[2] At this point, I would like to recount an episode that happened in the school. One of the few Jewish students in the school was our friend Nokhem Yoshpe. He was the son of Yekhiel–Itzi (Manish's son) and has been living in Israel for years. His only son was killed in Israel's War of Independence (honor to his memory!). Nokhem Yoshpe was than a boy of about twelve. One day at noon, when the children were let out of school for their midday meal, Nokhem made a "fig" gesture at the image of Czar Nikolai the Second, that was hanging on the wall.[3] One of the Christian students noticed this and told Principal Simnevitch, who then took Nokhem into a separate room and gave him a beating. Nokhem emerged from the room black and blue. We Jewish children sat trembling with fear that there would be new regulations affecting Jewish children. But Simnevitch made better use of the incident,

and extorted money from Nokhem's father for the "crime," as it were, of his 12–year–old son.

This incident was typical of Jewish life in Zinkov during the Czarist period; and not only in Zinkov.

———

Translator's Footnotes:

1. Rashi is the acronym for Rabbi Shlomo Yitzchaki (1040–1105), a medieval French rabbi and author of a comprehensive commentary on the Bible and the Talmud. His commentaries are still in very wide use.

2. There is no description of this "method," but it was most likely bribery. The ellipsis is in the original.

3. The "fig" sign is a mildly obscene gesture that apparently originated in the Mediterranean region and was adopted Slavic cultures. The gesture uses a thumb wedged in between two fingers.

———

[Page 124]

The Life and Death of a Jewish Family
Translated by Yael Chaver

I will begin with my own distant past, with my own family.

My father (may he rest in peace) was Yisro'el Aynkoyfer; everyone in Zinkov knew Yisro'el Aynkoyfer?[1] He was so called because he would travel to the larger cities of our region, such as Proskurov, Kamenetz, and even as far as

[Page 125]

Odessa, to buy merchandise for the Zinkov shopkeepers as well as other things needed in the town that were difficult to obtain. When a storekeeper needed goods to fill the shelves in his business, he couldn't allow himself to travel and make the purchases. He would write out a list and give it to my father. When enough lists had accumulated, my father would hire a pair of peasant carts and go to the larger cities, to buy everything and bring it to Zinkov. Of course, my father received some compensation for his work; nowadays we would term it a commission. My father also took care of the *talmud–toyre*, the Russian school, and students who had private tutors, and supplied them with the necessary schoolbooks. I can still see the mountains of books throughout our home, books of different colors and languages; I would happily go through them to satisfy my curiosity. My father even supplied the Jews of Zinkov with wine for Peysekh (Passover). He would bring anything people ordered. That is why he was called Yisro'el Aynkoyfer rather than by his actual last name (Grinman); in general, Zinkov did not approve of last names. My mother's name was Miriam, and she was called by her father's name: Miriam, Shloyme's daughter.

Yisro'el Aynkoyfer's family. Except for one survivor, the entire family of 30 was murdered

[Page 126]

I begin my memories with my earliest childhood, when we were still only two children in the home, before more children appeared in succession, and our family tree grew and branched out more and more.

My father was not a rich man, but he made a good living. He sent all his children to school, first to *kheyders* and then to the two–class Russian school.[2] He gave girls and boys equal chances to study. He also had an iron–goods store in Khayim Kluger's house. When I grew older I helped to run this store, and later managed it almost completely on my own. This freed my father to continue his purchasing travels.

The First World War came along, and disrupted life in the whole world, including my family. The time came when I was called up. I was good looking, healthy and strong. We knew that "Fonye" would snatch me up with both arms and make a soldier of me.[3] My parents could not let their son go into Czarist military service, especially during wartime. Jews were second–class citizens, possibly even lower than that. In addition, they were treated badly once they were in the army; they were hated and persecuted. People accused the Jews of cowardice, plain and simple. All these accusations were proven absolutely false. The heroic actions of our young people were soon famous in every place where they had a specific goal, such as later, in the Red Army, or in America, or, especially, in Israel's army during the War of Independence. My father therefore made every effort to make sure I would not have to join the Czarist war.

In the meantime, the stormy days of revolution and counter–revolution came. For a while, chaos and anarchy reigned in the region. Young people stopped going into the army, and we were called "non–Kosher hares" and "wicker–covered jars."[4] The police carried out frequent raids in the town to catch deserters; but there was always advance word of these raids, as the policeman received a suitable "gift"... Much later, when the Soviet regime was established, we – a group of young men from Zinkov – started working for the provisioning office of the Soviet army and the civilian population. This released us from active military duty. It was soon announced that Petlyura's bands were nearing Proskurov. The office in which we worked was quickly evacuated and we were supposed to travel with them. However, we Zinkov natives decided to make our way back to our home town.

[Page 127]

Rabbi Meir Yoysef (the "Black Rabbi") with some family members.
The parents and some of their children were murdered.
Shachna and Sore Vasserman, their son Yoysef and his family.
All were murdered.[5]

Here I must tell a story of an event that was very typical of that chaotic time. The cart–drivers of Zinkov, who drove passengers to Proskurov and back, no longer dared to make the trip, fearing they would fall into the hands of the Petlyura bandits. We didn't think too long, and decided to walk. One bright summer's day we, four guys from Zinkov (myself, Moyshe Garber, Izi Baytlman, and Lyova Finkl – who later became my brother–in–law) set out for Michalpole. We were so naÃ¯ve that we did not inquire about the direction from which the murderous bands were coming. Scared and sweaty, we arrived at a nearby village; our hearts sank when we saw that the village was full of soldiers. It was too late to turn back–they had already noticed us. We continued on our way nervously, pretending we did not know what had happened. Our dread was even greater, because we had dared to place the Bolshevik papers inside the lining of our hats. However, we were happily surprised: it was a Red Army unit. We could continue our trip from the village in peace, with no questioning.

Translator's Footnotes:

1. "Aynkoyfer" translates as "buyer."

2. I'm not sure what the "two–class" qualifier refers to.

3. "Fonye" is a derogatory *Yiddish* personification of Russia and/or the Czar. It may be derived from "Vanya," a diminutive of the common Russian name Ivan.

4. Hares are considered non–Kosher, and are synonymous with "cowards" in Russian; the nickname "wicker–covered jar" may refer to the supposed physical fragility of Jews.

5. The translation follows the original text.

———

[Page 128]

Zinkov–My Home Town![1]

by Shlomo Ben–David (Blinder), Netanya

Translated by Yael Chaver

I vaguely remember you, my town, fifty years after my departure. When my dear father, David Blinder (may his memory be for a blessing) married our beloved mother, Ahuva (daughter of Ya'akov and Rivka Hasid, may their memory be for a blessing), they moved to the border town of Husiatyn. As he was a pharmacist, he opened a pharmacy there. I returned to you, my town, after the First World War broke out, when we were expelled from the border town; I left you forever when I was Bar–

Mitzvah, on our way to *Eretz–Yisra'el*.[2] After many long years, I portray you, my town, and present memories which, though fragmented, are very typical.

I remember well that our town was divided into four quarters by the main streets, which intersected. The crossing was occupied by the tall lamp, which functioned as the center for news and town talk, especially in the evenings. One quarter was focused on the home of the rabbi, *Rebbe* Moyshele (may the memory of the righteous be for a blessing), where his many followers would gather.[3] My grandfather, Ya'akov, also lived nearby. Another quarter consisted of the large market square with its lodgings and the well from which the townspeople, bearing yokes with buckets, drew water for home use and filled barrels for using all week.[4]

[Page 129]

The third quarter was centered around the home of *Rebbe* Pinkhesl (may the memory of the righteous be for a blessing), who had followers of his own. The fourth quarter was the oldest, with the synagogue at its center. The synagogue was said to date to the times of Khmelnitsky.[5] It was called "Movshivka," apparently because of the name's connection to sewing; tailors and shoemakers lived nearby.[6] Most of the townspeople made their living as small shopkeepers and peddlers. There were some larger stores in town as well. As in other small towns, most commercial life occurred on market days (every Tuesday), when peasants from nearby villages would bring their farm produce to sell and would buy merchandise that they needed.

After we returned to Zinkov, and my father took care of our basic livelihood, as it were, he devoted much energy to his childrens' education. Being an ardent Zionist and a delegate to the 11th Zionist Congress in Vienna, he did not want us to be educated in the old–style *kheyder* or *talmud–toyre*, or in the Russian school, and started agitating for the establishment of a Hebrew school in town.[7] And in fact, after much struggle and thanks to the work of a few other devotees, such a school was created. Among its teachers were S. Fridman (may his memory be for a blessing), S. Steinberg (brother of the writer Yehuda Steinberg), Goldshteyn, and Himelfarb.[8] My father's organizational work in education was helped mainly by the Vartzman, Aberbukh, Kaplan, and Frenkel families, as well as by my uncle Yekhiel Yoshpe (may his memory be for a blessing) and my uncle Yitzchak Sadikov, who were Zionist activists in our town.

At that time, a drama club for older youth was founded, and staged plays in Hebrew and Yiddish. We younger children created the "Flowers of Zion" association, and used our savings as well as some contributions, established the first Hebrew library in the hall of the firehouse (which had become a cultural and entertainment center for youth and adults). We received our earliest Zionist education in this library, and the library books in this library supplied the raw material for our dreams of immigrating to *Eretz Yisra'el*.

The famous Turkish fort and the winding path that led down from it to the spring, 100 meters away, were an unexpected source of special fun and activities for the young people of Zinkov. It was also the way to the nearby river in summer. The way to the fort passed through the village, where we were often ambushed by the non–Jewish boys and encountered sticks and stones. We often came back with ripped clothes; but sometimes we fought back properly, especially when our cousin Nokhem Yoshpe was the leader. The non–Jewish boys called him "Red–Haired Tribe."[9] He frightened not only the boys from the nearby villages; even hardened criminals were afraid to meet him due to his reputation. Nokhem headed the self–defense group during the time of pogroms, and we younger kids were his squires.

As we were *Rebbe* Moyshele's neighbors, we spent time in his home and played with his children. I remember that one year, on the eve of Sukkes, he tweaked my ear and told me, speaking Ashkenazi Hebrew (he usually talked Yiddish), "Go to Zerach and get me the *sukkah–sher*." At first, I thought he was asking for shears to cut the greenery, but after I had gone back and forth and come back empty–handed, I understood that he had been joking.[10]

I was embarrassed when I returned to his home, but the *rebbe* patted me and promised that he would come and grace us with his presence on the holiday.

[Page 130]

One more episode. The *rebbe*, who was a wonderful person, modest and highly educated, liked to debate Father on philosophical issues. If I remember correctly, they spoke of Hegel, Kant, and mainly Spinoza. I especially remember the vivid images I conjured up of the burning candles and the resounding *shofars* when Baruch Spinoza was excommunicated.[11]The *rebbe* would end the conversation with a keen comment: "We'll see how you behave there in the Holy Land."

After the pogroms in Proskurov and elsewhere in our vicinity, Father (may his memory be for a blessing) started to pressure Grandfather and Grandmother to close their businesses and make *aliyah* to *Eretz–Yisra'el*. The Balfour Declaration made an indelible impression.[12] We considered it a harbinger of national salvation. The Zionists of Zinkov donated their jewelry to the salvation fund, as an expression of support and participation in the great historical events.[13] The first *He–Halutz* group was organized, headed by our cousin Nokhem Yoshpe, and we stole across the Polish border at Husyatin in the winter of 1919, on our way to *Eretz–Yisra'el*. Our dear father did not live to reach the goal of his aspirations and dreams. He died when we were on our way, and was buried in a foreign land. It is our great good fortune to have been able to reach *Eretz–Yisra'el* and take part in the defense of the community while *Haganah* was still underground, and later to join the Israel Defense Army and do our part to liberate our homeland.[14]

It is our sacred duty to pass on to our children and grandchildren, down to the last generation, information about their parents' birthplace. Let them know and remember that we came to the land to preserve our people's life flame, and our future as a free and independent nation. We hold very dear the pledge entrusted to us by former generations.

Translator's Footnotes:

1. Original pp. 128–130 have been translated from Hebrew.
2. Boys have their Bar–Mitzvah ceremony at age 13.
3. The phrase "may the memory of the righteous be for a blessing" usually follows the name of a deceased rabbi.
4. The lodgings served travellers who would come to the market.
5. Bohdan Khmelnitsky was a 17th–century Cossack leader who led a revolt against the Polish–Lithuanian regime; he is revered in Ukraine as a freedom fighter but infamous in Jewish history. Between 1648 and 1656, tens of thousands of Jews–due to the lack of reliable data, it is impossible to establish more accurate figures–were killed in pogroms by the rebels. The massacres spread to other parts of Europe. The Khmelnitsky uprising and its accompanying pogroms is still considered by Jews to be one of the

most devastating events in their history. The trauma contributed to a contemporaneous revival of the ideas of Isaac Luria, who revered the Kabbalah, and the identification of Sabbatai Zevi as the Messiah.

6. I could not find any connection between "Movshiv" with the Russian for "sewing."

7. Hebrew for centuries had been used by Jews solely for religious purposes. It was brought into use as a modern secular language in the late 19th century, and became a linchpin of Zionist ideology.

8. Yehuda Steinberg (1863–1908) was a well–known Hebrew and Yiddish writer.

9. There is a long–standing tradition identifying red–haired people as Jews which deserve persecution. The anti–Semitic association persisted into modern times in Soviet Russia.

10. This practical joke is particularly suitable for Sukkes, when the *sukkah* roof is covered with foliage. The Yiddish *sher* means "scissors," and the child Shlomo understood it literally as a tool for cutting the greenery. However, the phrase *Sukkah–sher* means "wild–goose chase." Evidently, Shlomo was not familiar with the phrase. His reward–having the Rabbi join his family for the holiday–was an honor.

11. Baruch Spinoza (1632–1677) was a Dutch philosopher of Portuguese Sephardi origin. One of the early thinkers of the Enlightenment and modern biblical criticism, including modern conceptions of the self and the universe, he is considered one of the great rationalists of 17th–century philosophy. He was excommunicated as a heretic in 1656. Excommunication (*cherem*) is an extremely solemn ceremony, which involves candle–lighting and *shofar*–blowing.

12. The Balfour Declaration (named for Arthur James Balfour, then the British Foreign Secretary) was a public statement issued by the British government in 1917, during the First World War, announcing its support for the establishment of a "national home for the Jewish people" in then–Ottoman Palestine.

13. I could not identify the "salvation fund."

14. *Haganah* is the Hebrew word for "defense" and was the name of the main paramilitary organization of the Zionist Jewish community in Mandatory Palestine between 1920 and 1948.

[Page 131]

Our Town

by Rivka Katz

Translated by Yael Chaver

The town of Zinkov was sprawled over a high hill, and had a population of five thousand Jews. Looking across the deep valley, one could see many similar hills, covered in a soft lush carpet of grass, stretching all the way to the horizon. This valley surrounded the town on three sides and contained hundreds of small peasant homes. Winding around the banks of the calm little Ushitsa River were many orchards and gardens that yielded various fruits and vegetables. A wide road stretched along the fourth side of the town, between large areas of flourishing fields, surrounded in turn by dense forests. Thus, the vicinity of Zinkov presented a truly beautiful panorama that captivated all onlookers.

All these forests and fields, fruit orchards and gardens, supplied the town with rich produce. Many Jews earned a comfortable living by dealing with this produce. The poorer segments of the population also dealt with the peasants who would bring their wares into market daily. These wares consisted of fruit, vegetables, and eggs. Thus, the market and stores that were located in the center of town were constantly humming, and Ukrainian villagers were always in contact with the town's Jews. Zinkov was also famous for its manufacture of clay pots. Peasants (so–called *antchars*) in the region made clay pots, which were a cheap and important product at the time.[1] Jews would buy up wagon–loads of pots, which were then sent off to be sold elsewhere places for good prices. At some distance from the town lay "phosphorus pits," and those who dealt in that substance became rich. All these forests and fields, fruit orchards and gardens, supplied the town with rich produce. Many Jews earned a comfortable living by dealing with this produce. The poorer segments of the population also dealt with the peasants who would bring their wares into market daily. These wares consisted of fruit, vegetables, and eggs. Thus, the market and stores that were located in the center of town were constantly humming, and Ukrainian villagers were always in contact with the town's Jews. Zinkov was also famous for its manufacture of clay pots. Peasants (so–called *antchars*) in the region made clay pots, which were a cheap and important product at the time.[2]

Any conversation about the spiritual life of Zinkov should start

[Page 132]

by mentioning the two rabbis, *Rebbe* Moyshele and *Rebbe* Pinchesl, who played a prominent role in the life of the town. Although there weren't many observant Jews in Zinkov, the rabbis added much variety to town life and attracted numerous followers from the surrounding towns and cities. Zinkov had many fine, capable, and idealistic young people, who had, since the late 19th century, become famous for their initiative and rejection of all the superstitions of the time. They quickly adopted the new winds that were blowing in from western Europe: winds of freedom, education, and progress. These young people constantly nudged the town toward a new way of life. As early as the beginning of 20th century, Zinkov could confidently call itself a modern, civilized town. Everyone was reading, studying, and working to achieve a better, finer life. The town already had a private library where all could come to read, spend leisure time, and discuss various issues. It also had a modern *talmud–toyre* with capable teachers, which had higher standards than the outdated old *kheyders*. Various clubs and political organizations were created in the town: Zionists, Bundists, and others. Each of these addressed current issues very seriously.

How interesting that time was, how beautiful, how lovely life was in our Zinkov. How hard it is to forget it all!

Translator's Footnotes:

1. I could not translate *antchar*.
2. These "pits" were apparently a source of phosphate deposits.

[Page 133]

From the Distant Past: People and Life
by Moyshe Grinman
Translated by Yael Chaver

I have taken up much space with the sad and sentimental story of my own family in Zinkov, and incidentally included events of general life in the town. However, I cannot ignore some episodes in the lives of people who remain so prominent in my memory, and which have not been mentioned in other chapters of our documentary book.

Our two rabbis, the brothers *Rebbe* Moyshele and *Rebbe* Pinkhesl (may the memory of the righteous be for a blessing), have been mentioned several times. But nothing has been said about the old *Rebbe* Yisro'elke, who was a close relative of the above–mentioned rabbis. His house was old and unusually, with a broken roof full of holes. It stood off in a corner close to the greenhouse, behind Moyshe's courtyard, not far from the house where we lived, and not far from the place where the large stone building used to stand; it used to be called "the history" and later belonged to Markivsky, the tavern–keeper. Old Rabbi Yisro'elke was still making every effort to continue his rabbinical leadership. He even had a manager, Motl. The manager and his wife were quiet, sincere people. They were childless, and would invite the congregation to *kiddush* on holidays.[1]

I remember my father taking me along as a child, which made me very happy.

Someone has already written about the community leadership of Zinkov, whose mission it was to manage all the town affairs at that time (when the authorities were not yet obstructing them). I would like to present some episodes and names of people whom the previous writer did not know or remember. Among others elected were Sani Alter (Sani's son), Yisro'el Grinman, Avstrayanik the lawyer, Trachtenberg, as well as Leybl–Itzi (Mayke's son) or Leybl Shraybman. The leadership did much to help the poor

[Page 134]

of the town. Most noteworthy, however, is the organized help extended to women and children of local Jews who had gone to America and were cut off from their families in 1914 because of the war. At the initiative of Sani Roytburd, Arke Shenkelman (the secretary), *Rebbe* Moyshele, and several others, a plan for basic help was set out. Representatives went through the town, going from house to house and asking for voluntary weekly contributions for the needy. A group of young people was also designated to go through the town every Friday with bags over their shoulders, collecting *challahs* for the hungry. People were generous with their own food.

Above all, I would like to mention our close neighbor Sani Alter (Sani's son) and his gentle wife, Itta (may she rest in peace). Sani was an eminent and fine householder in Zinkov. He was handsome, with a short, trimmed beard and dressed in modern style.[2] However, he did not give himself airs, and was very unpretentious. He was observant, but not a *frumak*–a hypocritical religious fanatic. He was a product of the Enlightenment movement, a good Hebraist, familiar with the old literature, and an enthusiastic Zionist. His closest friend was Arke Avrom (Idl's son). Sani would often visit *Rebbe* Moyshele, and was good friends with the *Rebbe's* entire family. *Rebbe* Moyshele liked to spend long hours in Sani's company; they had extended conversations concerning everyday matters as well as world problems. A special topic was Jewish religious and cultural issues.

Sani was unremarkable. He wasn't influential, he never shouted, but worked for the community quietly and calmly. In addition to this work, he also played a major role in the organization and maintenance of the *Linas–Tzedek* and *Bikur–Khoilim* societies.[3] At that time, there were no hospitals or nurses in Zinkov to serve the sick. When someone was sick, and no one in the family could tend to them, people would turn to *Linas–Tzedek*. The society would send little Hershele to the member whose turn it was, and that person would go and fulfil his duty. This humanitarian act was really a great *mitzvah*.[4]

During the harrowing time when everyone fled from Zinkov, Sani sold his home and abandoned his grain business, which was hardly a business at all by then.

[Page 135]

He and his loyal wife crossed the border, and their son Yisro'el then brought them to America. As far as I know, Sani could not adjust to his new location here in America. He missed the atmosphere he had been used to his entire life. He missed his friends and those with whom he could continue to live a meaningful intellectual life. Unfortunately, he lived here for only a few years, and died. He found eternal rest in the Zinkov cemetery.

Sani's wife, Itta, could be termed a compassionate and pious woman. She was kind, quiet, and gentle. She greeted everyone in a friendly manner, and found negative traits in no one. She was a truly caring mother, who lived for many more years with her children, and found solace in her only grandchild, Moyshele, to whom she was deeply devoted. Now she rests alongside her husband, the formerly respected business owner and community activist in their home town, Zinkov.

Ezra Kagan (Aaron's son) and his family, 1914

Translator's Footnotes:

1. *Kiddush* is the blessing said over wine. The term also refers to a small meal held on Shabbes or festival mornings in the synagogue after the prayer services.

2. At the time, a trimmed beard and non–traditional dress were hallmarks of Jews who were less observant.

3. *Linas–Tzedek* and *Bikur–Khoilim* were community societies that lodged travelers and aided the sick.

4. *Mitzvah* in the biblical sense means "one of God's commandments." It also refers to a deed performed in order to fulfill such a commandment. As such, the term *mitzvah* has come to express an individual act of human kindness in keeping with the law.

[Page 136]

Short Sketches

by Avrom Shenkelman (Arke's son), Philadelphia

Translated by Yael Chaver

I remember my cozy home town, Zinkov. It was not a listless town. After the First World War, it was only napping, out of exhaustion and the heavy burden its residents had to bear. Hundreds of its young people were mobilized, and had laid down their lives for the unfortunate exploits of Czar Nikolai. But not everyone was willing to do this; people spent months hiding in various refuges, never seeing the light of day. Surprisingly, they were not discovered. Degenerate as the Czarist empire was, they could easily have been located. Apparently, the regime was not too interested in finding our boys and giving them rifles.

When the revolution took place, a volcano seemed to have exploded among the Jewish population of Zinkov (there were no non–Jews in our town). People suddenly woke into political awareness, and political movements developed. The Zionist movement occupied a very prominent position, especially the halutz pioneers. We young folks were organized under the leadership of Nokhem Yoshpe and began preparing to move to *Eretz–Yisro'el* (then Palestine). It's important to mention and honor the members of the first group of *halutzim*, who left for *Eretz–Yisro'el* at that time; this has been done elsewhere in our Yizkor Book.

[Page 137]

Zinkov Folklore[1]

[Page 138]

[no text]

[Page 139]

a. Memories from My Hometown Zinkov

by Moyshe Garber

Translated by Yael Chaver

I must admit that we young folks did not take the solemnity of the High Holidays too much to heart. So, when we heard the final *shofar* blast at the end of Yom Kippur, and the congregation quickly murmured the evening prayer and went outdoors to sanctify the new moon, we felt relieved and were overcome by a special joyous feeling.[2] We children knew that the joyous holiday of *Sukkes* was now coming, with *Simchas–Toyre*, and most importantly, with the *hakofes*.

At home, I, as the only son, was entrusted with the pleasure of preparing and arranging the *sukkah*. I crawled onto the roof and opened the "road."[3] I laid all the poles, spades, and sticks on top and spread the *sekhakh* over them. I used two barrels and some noodle boards to create benches for sitting. My sister decorated the walls with flowers, and it became (as Sholem Aleikhem would say), "Quite a *sukkah*!" How proud and happy I was later, when the neighbors who joined us were full of praise for our beautiful *sukkah*.

My father, Shmuel–Lipe, my grandfather Sender, and (I believe) even my great–grandfather Itze Tcherkises (may they rest in peace) had all prayed in Gad's *minyan* at various times; it was called Gad's *minyan* because the person who had donated his house to serve as a synagogue was named Gad). The synagogue was next to the house of Khayim (Royze's son) Itzikson. Across the street was Mordechai Vertzman's house and Tzufenai's old synagogue. When the *hakofes* evening began, the householders went to the tavern of Elye's wife, and spent a few comfortable hours over a glass of sour wine accompanied by nuts.[4] Once "the king's heart was merry with wine," and people felt *simkhas–toyre*–like, they joyfully went to join in the *hakofes*.[5]

[Page 140]

One of the members of Gad's *minyan* was the well–off Peysi Sitchkarnik, who claimed the right to chant the *Ato horeyso loda'as*.[6] As he was really exhilarated both by the wine and by the joy of the holiday, he would sing the verse out at the top of his hoarse voice: "*Ato horeyso loda'as*" etc. The *hakofes* around the lectern started immediately afterwards. The children were standing on the chairs holding candles, and flags bearing apples.[7] Their faces shining, they would kiss the Torah scrolls as they were carried by, and would call out in their chirping voices "May you live to celebrate next year! May you live to celebrate next year!"

For me, it was just a prelude to the real holiday that would come later, during the *hakofes* ceremony with the two *rebbes*, Moyshele and Pinchesl (may the memory of the righteous be for a blessing). Life in a town as small as Zinkov was boring and monotonous. Young people instinctively yearned for life and sought stimulation and entertainment. *Simkhes–toyre*, the *hakofes*, and accompanying the *rebbe* out of the *sukkah* were therefore a truly marvelous experience for us. We were not devout *hasids*; to tell the truth, it wasn't the religious content of the celebration we were after, but the fun.[8] I'm a bit embarrassed now to add that we treated the *hakofes* as a kind of carnival (if you'll excuse the comparison).

Once *Rebbe* Pinchesl had slept for a while, the brightest lamps were turned on, and the synagogue soon became packed with a joyous holiday crowd. Most of the *hasids*, those from our town and from other towns, lined the walls to make way for the *rebbe*. A bit later, the *Rebbitzin* appeared with her children, all of them dressed in finery – like a queen with her princes and princesses.[9] Everyone gazed at them with respect and admiration. With every minute that passed, I felt happier and livelier. After each *hakofe* the *hasids* sang and danced in a circle, with real *hasidic* elation, their heads thrown back and eyes turned up to God in religious ecstasy.[10] The *rebbe* danced at the center, holding a small Torah scroll high above his head in one hand, with his other hand in his sash.[11] In this manner, he kept moving to the rhythmic clapping of the *hasids* and the entire assembly. People climbed up on tables and chairs to watch. With pounding hearts, flushed faces, and shining eyes, boys and girls surveyed and flirted with each other.

[Page 141]

There were also pranksters in the crowd, who liked to trick the *hasids*. They would strew the floor with a powder that caused sneezing and itching, or stick a pin into the sensitive flesh of a dancing *hasid's* backside. Sometimes they would let a bird loose in the synagogue; the bird became very agitated by the tumult and bright lights and would fly around flapping its wings from one corner of the ceiling to another, while the amused audience shook with laughter. When the noise reached a peak, the *rebbe* uttered a sigh: "*Oy!*"[12] The *hasids* immediately took it up and repeated, ever more loudly, like an echo in the Swiss alps: "*Oy, oy, oy, oy, oy...!*" And when the *rebbe* demanded quiet, "*Sha!*" the *hasids* would echo him: "*Sha, sha, sha, sha...*"

We called the Jewish guys who had to report for conscription "Twenty–oners" or "conscripts."[13] At *Simkhes–toyre*, they would come and stand in a row, and each one placed a bottle of wine on the table as he passed the *rebbe*. The *rebbe* wished each and every one of them a release from military service.

This is how the night of *Simkhes–toyre* passed. The first faint bluish light of the coming day was visible on the horizon. By now, all were tired, sleepy, with pale faces, and it was no longer as noisy as earlier. We went home for some sleep and rest, and to go to the synagogue again the next day, for the second round of *hakofes* and to accompany the *rebbe* out of the Sukkah once again.

The crush, noise, and joy of the holiday were strongest and most noticeable in *Rebbe* Pinchesl's synagogue. We would often sneak out to take a look at the events at *Rebbe*Moyshele's. Things there were very different. The crowd was much smaller, quiet, and behaved more respectfully.

In this manner, we young people would have fun during *Sukkes*, and would anticipate next year's *Sukkes*, *Simkhes–toyre*, and *hakofes*. We believed that this would continue all our lives long. Little did we know that war was in store for us, with its terrible consequences, and that this location of Jewish life would be erased forever.

Translator's Footnotes:

1. This title is repeated twice, once in Hebrew and once in Yiddish.

2. The single *shofar* blast at the end of Yom Kippur is the final one during the High Holidays. As the Jewish calendar follows the cycles of the moon, the appearance of the new moon at the beginning of the month is marked by a special ceremony and prayer of sanctification. However, during the period of the High Holidays (1–10 Tishrei), when the first ten days are devoted to repentance for wrongdoings done in the past year, the ceremony is postponed to the night after Yom Kippur.

3. The Slavic word *shliakh*, used here, means "dirt road." Its use here is unusual. Apparently, there was a special opening in the roof, normally covered over, which could be uncovered to make accessible a space that would be turned into a *sukkah*. The *sukkah* must be mostly open to the sky, though its top is covered with branches (*sekhakh*) or other means to simulate a partly open roof. It is decorated with greenery and colored fabrics. Sholem–Aleikhem is the pseudonym of perhaps the best–know Yiddish writer, Sholem Rabinovich. Having meals in the *sukkah*, sleeping there, and inviting guests in are important features of the seven–day holiday.

4. In keeping with the Jewish calendar, the *Simkhes–toyre* holiday begins at dusk of the preceding day. There are two rounds of *hakofes*: that evening, and on the next day. I could not determine the reference to "sour wine."

5. The quote is from the biblical book of Esther, 1, 10.

6. *Ata horeyso loda'as* is the beginning of a verse that has been incorporated into prayer: "Unto thee it was shown, that thou mightest know that the Lord, He is God; there is none else beside Him." (Deut. 4, 35). The verse,

which is linked with the reception of the Torah by the Israelites, is often sung at *Simkhes–Toyre*.

7. It was the custom children to carry a candle stuck into an apple on top of a flag. The flags were decorated with a variety of Jewish symbols.

8. The writer uses the Yiddish phrase "Not the *Haggada* but the dumplings," meaning "not the actual occasion, only the pleasure."

9. *Rebbitzin* is an honorific for the wife of a Rabbi.

10. For *hasids*, dance is a tool to express joy and worship; it promotes spiritual elation, and unifies the community.

11. Many Jewish men (primarily *hasids*) wear a special belt during prayer and on religious occasions.

12. The Yiddish *oy*! is an abbreviation of oy vey, expressing exasperation or dismay.

13. In the late 19|th century, military service was made compulsory for all males at the age of 21.

—

b. "Doctor" substitutes in Zinkov — *royfes*[1]
by Moyshe Garber
Translated by Yael Chaver

It is well known that studying to be a medical doctor takes years and years, and a tremendous amount of work and effort. One needs a formal education starting with elementary school all the way to university, then completing medical school, followed by several years interning in a hospital. Only then, after a rigorous examination, does one receive a license to practice medicine and to be officially acknowledged as a physician. However, among us in Zinkov things were much easier and simpler. The profession of doctor was hereditary.[2] The grandfather was a *royfe*, the father was a *royfe*, and, naturally, the son was also automatically a *royfe*. And, miracle of miracles! Not only had none of them studied at universities and medical schools; they had not even crossed the threshold of an elementary school. And yet, they became *royfes*, healed the townspeople of illnesses, wrote prescriptions (in Latin, of all things), and poor people believed in them and sought their help; he rich went to the official doctor. Of course, you will say, "What do you mean? How is this possible?" The answer: "As you see."

[Page 142]

I remember one *royfe*, Moyshele, whose image is now faint, like a distant dream. He was short and stout, with curly *peyes*[3] and a bald spot, and always had a black visored cap and thick eyeglasses. He wore snow boots, to jump over the mud puddles, and a woman's shawl wrapped around his shoulders, against the cold. This Moyshele the *royfe* had several sons. Of course, they all became *royfes*. However, I would like to linger on one of them in particular. He was called Shmuel, the son of Moyshe Royfe. He was our family *royfe*, who would administer smallpox vaccinations and heal croup and whooping–cough; or, at least, do his best to heal us, He pulled our teeth when the pain became too much to bear.

My tonsils were very bad; we called them "plums" ("tonsils" is the word in America). They would get inflamed and swell every winter. Shmuel (Moyshe Royfe's son) would come every day, use a small contraption that produced steam, coat my throat with iodine and glycerine, and tell me to wrap my neck in a sock covered in tallow. I really loved him, and we became good friends when I grew up.

But Shmuel was not only a *royfe*. He was, as they say in America, "three in one": he was at one and the same time a *royfe*, a barber, and a pharmacist. He had a small pharmacy, and his wife Miriam–Freyde (Ranye's daughter) was his deputy pharmacist. When one opened the door of his house, a bell would ring. The Czar's portrait hung opposite the door. When a peasant came in, heard the bell, and saw the Czar's image, he would take off his cap reverently, and meekly state what he needed.

[Page 143]

Let's pay a visit to Shmuel's barbershop on a Friday. A long rod extended outside from under the eaves, bearing a round red disc. A sign at the entrance depicted a man sitting in a chair, wrapped in a white sheet, with the barber standing behind him holding scissors. The man on the chair and the barber resembled rigid twins, both with thick stiff hair and large curled mustaches. Above them were inscriptions in Russian: "Parisian Hair Salon," "Salon for Haircuts and Shaving," in so many words.[4] Now, let's go in and see what's happening inside the "Salon." A few people are sitting and waiting, but Shmuel isn't in yet. Influenza is spreading in the town, and Shmuel can't leave his patients. Meanwhile, a helper is there, doing his best. I think it was either Mordkhe Buke's son or Shmuel Stoler's son. Shmuel soon rushes in, breathless. He quickly empties out his pockets, producing a heap of ten–kopek and forty–groschen coins, and hands them over to his wife Miriam.[5] In addition to us, a peasant man and woman are waiting for him. He takes them into the kitchen, quickly diagnoses their problem, and before I know it the woman's back is covered with a forest of cupping glasses, and the man has sets of leeches on his neck, happily sucking his blood. Once he has finished his medical work, he starts shaving and cutting hair, talking incessantly and telling various tales. Whenever too much soap has accumulated on the razor, he wipes it off with a finger and tosses it at the nearby wall. The soap collected on the wall dries out and looks like a three–dimensional geographical map of the Asian Himalayas.

Meanwhile, Shmuel remembers that he needs to make up a prescription for a sick patient. As he is very busy with hair–cutting and shaving, he calls in to the kitchen, where his helper is standing at the oven, all sweaty, and tells her the following: "Miriam, my dear, please make up this mixture," and starts instructing her as to what and how much, so that everyone can hear him and be impressed. Everything is in Latin, such as "*acidum salicylicum, acidum censaicum*," or something else that sounds very mysterious and medically professional.[6]When a medical prescription is made up and a certain amount of water is called for, distilled water is used. This is water produced by water vapor that has been cooled and condensed back into liquid. The Latin term is *aqua distillate*. But Shmuel doesn't believe in such foolishness as distilled water. He tells Miriam, "Have you weighed everything? Now mix it and add six ounces of 'aqua dishkalis'." In simple Yiddish, this means "water from the basin."[7]

[Page 144]

I remember Shmuel best of all from the time when a terrible epidemic of typhus raged in Zinkov, in 1919. Hundreds of lives were lost. My father (may he rest in peace) died then, and I myself hovered between life and death for five weeks; miraculously, I survived. Shmuel watched over me the whole time, like a devoted brother. The town's young folks organized a *Linas–tzedek* association of their own, and each of us stayed overnight with a sick person at least twice a week. There were homes in which the entire family was sick in bed, and there was no one to even offer them a glass of water. Shmuel worked tirelessly, day and night, running from one house to another, and doing everything he could. During this period, he did not eat regularly or sleep. Pale and exhausted, he could barely stand. To this day, I really cannot understand how he himself avoided this terrible disease, unless it was God himself who watched over him.

This is how Shmuel (son of Moyshele Royfe), in his own way, served the poor population of our home town – a town that is no more.

We honor your memory, Shmuel Royfe!

———

Translator's Footnotes:

1. The Hebraic term *royfe* is roughly equal to a barber–surgeon: someone who could perform surgical procedures including bloodletting, cupping therapy, teeth–pulling, and bone–setting.

2. "Hereditary" is emphasized in the original.

3. Many observant Jews do not shave the sides of their head but grow sidelocks, following the Biblical injunction (Lev. 9, 27).

4. Both inscriptions are presented in Yiddish transliteration, followed by a translation.

5. A kopek was a coin, of the smallest denomination, of a number of countries in Eastern Europe, closely associated with Russia. A groschen is a small German silver coin, of very small denomination. Both were in wide circulation in the region at this time.

6. "Acidum salicylicum" is salicylic acid. *Censaicum* may be an invented word meant to sound Latin–like.

7. The Yiddish word for "water basin" is *dayzhe*; the speaker is apparently trying to make it sound more like Latin.

---

c. Judges in Zinkov
by Moyshe Garber
Translated by Yael Chaver

How a Christian Justice of the Peace made efforts to beautify and illuminate our town, and the end result of these efforts.

Our Zinkov had a peace court, and, of course, a justice of the peace as well. This judge was the president of the town ("head of the city"), though no one had asked us whether we wanted him.[1] The judge was a quiet, calm person, who evoked respect and politeness. Well, this judge/"city–head" thought up a way to make our town more respectable. We don't know whether he did this for our sake or for his own. Of course, he lost nothing by this deal. He approached a higher authority, and received a certain sum of money for the purpose of improving the appearance of our Zinkov. He wanted to pave the entire length of our main street, which ran from "city hall" to the bustling area near Rabbi Pinchesl's courtyard. He therefore brought over a whole group of laborers who were experts at this type of work from somewhere in the depths of Russia,. Stones were brought from the mountains in the vicinity, and sand was quarried from the area next to the Jewish cemetery. Unfortunately, a disaster occurred in the course of this work: Yisro'el Sichkarnik, a native of Zinkov, was buried alive under a hill of sand that broke down and covered him.

[Page 145]

For us children, the best entertainment was to watch the construction and paving work. When our town president had finished dealing with the paved road, he gave instructions to plant trees on either side. He had the trees surrounded with wooden guard structure, to prevent damage from the town's goats and children. Next, he decided to make a "park" for us. Menashe Skulnik would have said of such a park, "Huh, you call this a park?"[2] It was actually more like a large garden planted on a vacant lot that stretched along the houses of Avrom Paripker, Itzik Khazn, Itzi Tayman, and Dudi Melamed, not far from Avstaryanik's house and the pharmacy. The park was not like a city park, where one could take walks and sit under shade trees.

Our park was surrounded by a fence and had a gate that was always locked. In short, it was a park good only to look at, a decoration for the town.

When he was done with the park, he decided to do something about the dark nights when you could barely make out your own hand, especially during the muddy periods in the fall and before Peysekh.[3] He ordered large kerosene lamps, and had very tall poles installed in the four main points of the town. The lamps were set on the top of these poles; due to their great height, the lamps illuminated the sky rather than the town. I will always remember the wonder and pleasure of all the townspeople, myself included, the first time we saw the dazzling light cast by the lamps before they were hoisted to the tops of the poles. I doubt if any world's fair today could include objects as wondrous–looking as those lamps.

Unfortunately, the efforts of this industrious judge did not yield the hoped–for results. Within less than a year, the paved

[Page 146]

road developed deep pits that filled with mud and water, and interfered with human and wheeled traffic more than the unpaved road would have. The large volumes of water that flowed during snowmelt in spring simply undermined and swept away the sand, and the pavement that had inspired so much hope –and had cost so much money – failed completely. We did not get much pleasure out of the trees that had been planted, either. The poor removed away the wooden guard structures around the trees and used them to warm their cold, bare homes and their frozen limbs. The goats and the children finished off the job. During the war, no one cared for the park and everything withered away and shriveled away. The only relics of the judge's innovations were the lamps; but they, too, often hung there unlit, due to a shortage of kerosene. Besides, there was no one to take care of them.

So ended the efforts of our Christian judge to adorn the Jewish town. His dream, too, fell victim to war, revolution, and anarchy.

——

Translator's Footnotes:

1. The term "head of the city" appears in transliteration from Russian.
2. Menashe Skulnik (1890–1970) was a popular American Jewish actor, primarily known for his roles in Yiddish theater in New York City.
3. Peysekh occurs in the spring.

——

d. Our Zinkov *melameds*

by Moyshe Garber

Translated by Yael Chaver

As I never studied with a Talmud *melamed*, I will linger only on three *melameds* of young children.[1] These three were Sani the *melamed*, Dovid the *melamed*, and Gedalya–Hirsh.

At that time, Sani was already a progressive. He was not at all the type of *melamed* that our great artist Sholem–Aleichem describes so richly in his stories about children. It is rare that children love their *rebbe*; yet we did love our *rebbe* Sani.[2] He wasn't too strict with us, didn't terrorize us, and rarely used the rod. We respected him, carried out his instructions, and could learn more than children in other *kheyders*. For us, *kheyder* was not a hardship, as it was considered to be in those years. Our *rebbitzin* Rivka was kind–hearted and a good housewife. She kept her home and the *kheyder* clean and neat.[3] And we never heard any arguments between the *rebbe* and the *rebbitzin*.

[Page 147]

Rebbe Sani never told us any preposterous tales, nothing about demons and ghosts, and never frightened us with descriptions of hell and beatings with flaming whips for sins, lies, and other such transgressions – as other *melameds* did as a matter of course. I believe Sani was the only *melamed* who went to people's homes and taught young girls who were already ashamed to go to *kheyder*.[4] He even taught modern Hebrew to those who insisted. But Sani never really loved this job. First of all, he made very little money. Second, it was physically difficult for him, as he suffered from asthma; we called it *adushleyeve*.[5] Every now and then he would have a coughing fit and could not catch his breath. Finally, he decided to close his *kheyder* and go off to America. This meant that he would first go himself, and later bring his family over: his wife, his oldest son Itzi and second son Nachmen, and the youngest child and only daughter, Frumele. I had the rare privilege of being allowed by the *rebbitzin* to rock the baby's cradle.

The news that *Rebbe* Sani was leaving and going away to America led to much concern and displeasure among the pupils, especially as we knew, of course, that we would be handed over to the *melamed* Dovid. He was the complete opposite of Sani, with all the features found in Sholem–Aleichem's collection of *melamdim*. He was unusually large and stout, with a huge, wildly overgrown beard; and was confrontational. The lash never left his hand, and he would strike out right and left, whether justified or not. He often clashed with his wife, and the children had to hear all the mutual scolding and cursing, in murderous anger. You can imagine how our spirits sank when we realized what was in store for us. But no one dared to complain, because we had to obey the unwritten law that there was no tattling about *kheyder*. So we silently bore the heavy burden, suffering, and longing for our good *rebbe*Sani and his *kheyder*. Once, when the *rebbe* wasn't in the room, two pupils had a fight. In the midst of this uproar, the *rebbe* unexpectedly returned. He flew into a murderous rage and started lashing out blindly at all the pupils. I was small and quiet; my chin barely reached the table. I clamped my tongue between my teeth in fright.

[Page 148]

When the *rebbe* struck my head from behind, my teeth sank deep into my tongue, and the blood started pouring. In sheer terror and pain, I let out a scream, broke out in tears, and fled home. After this incident, I could no longer be silent; I poured out my bitter heart to my parents and told them what a hellish place the *kheyder* was, probably exaggerating quite a bit. From then on, there was no more *kheyder* and no more Dovid the *melamed*. A while later the good news came that our *rebbe* Sani was returning. Because of his poor health, he hadn't been allowed into America. I now understand very well how disappointed, embittered, and disheartened Sani must have been then, and how hard it must have been for him to return to being a *melamed*, an occupation he had hoped to leave. But we children never fully grasped such things. We felt fortunate and happy. Each of us was overjoyed to return to our beloved *melamed* and his *kheyder*.

Let us now turn to our third *melamed*, Gedalya–Hersh. Because he lived not far from us, I had the opportunity to get to know him well; besides, for a while his son, Moyshe, and I were friends. Gedalya–Hersh was completely different from the other two *melameds*, Sani and Dovid. He was easy–going, calm, and not too worried about poverty, health, or similar topics, which so affected Sani. Neither did he have the sullen and malicious disposition that led to Dovid's bad reputation. He was not highly regarded as a *melamed*. His pupils did not have to work hard. Besides, he was not overly observant, and not a fanatic. Who would have believed that a *melamed* of that period would have a "hobby!"[6] Gedalya–Hersh's "hobby" was pigeons; yes, pigeons.[7] He loved pigeons with a passion, and constructed an entire pigeon–house in the attic of his house. The pigeons would fly in and out freely through small windows that he installed; and, knock on wood, they increased and multiplied. No one was happier than Gedalya–Hersh when he stood on a summer's day without a *kapote*, dressed only in an undershirt and the *tallis–kotn*, his head covered by a *kippah*.[8] Holding a stick, he would guide his pigeons as they flew calmly around him, wings fluttering, rising and sinking, finally covering their master's roof. Apparently, the birds were also greatly enjoying this game.

[Page 149]

Apparently, people said that he spent more time with his birds than with his pupils – may it be no disrespect to him and may he forgive me...

Translator's Footnotes:

1. Talmud was studied by older boys, who started between the ages of 8–10.

2. *Rebbe* is an honorific for a *melamed*.

3. The *kheyder* was usually housed in the home of the *rebbe* and his wife, who was addressed and referred to as *rebbitzin*.

4. Girls did not usually attend *kheyder*; the reference to "already" is not clear.

5. This is probably a variant of a Russian term for asthma.

6. The English word "hobby" is presented, here and elsewhere, in Yiddish transliteration.

7. Some Eastern European Jews associated pigeon–raising with non–Jewish boys, pejoratively.

8. A *kapote* is a long coat formerly worn by male Jews of eastern Europe and now worn chiefly by very Orthodox or Hasidic Jews. The *tallis–kotn* is a fringed garment traditionally worn by Jewish males either over or under one's clothing.

—

e. The Zinkov "photographer"
by Moyshe Garber
Translated by Yael Chaver

He was called "Shiye fotografshtchik," or Shiye (Sender's son); he was my father's younger brother, which made him my uncle. I loved this uncle very deeply, really idolizing him. After I describe him in more detail, you will better understand how I developed such love for my uncle Shiye, and my admiration for his personality. You will be able to visualize the enormous, unbelievable talents that were lost in our small, impoverished towns.

He started out as a wood–turner, making wooden legs for furniture–makers to use in tables, chairs, sets of shelves, etc. He also made curtain rods for windows and door, for hanging drapes and curtains. Soon, he became a wood–carver, using different types of chisels and other tools to carve beautiful figures, covered in gold; these were placed on top of the *orn–koydesh* in almost all the *bes–medresh* institutions as well as in the synagogues around Zinkov.[1] He also carved decorations for furniture. Everything he made was a real work of art. However, despite all this, Shiye did not lose his desire to do new things; he wasn't interested in making money as much as satisfying his need for artistic realization. We don't know how and where Shiye became interested in photography, and how he started to learn this new profession. The Zinkov pharmacist of the time knew a bit about photography and began practicing it to fill his spare time; and he certainly had enough time. As Uncle Shiye was a frequent visitor at the pharmacist's, he soon took up the idea of photography. Thanks to his gift of artistic intuition and talent, he gradually refined and developed his own photography, until he was so good at it that it became his new main occupation – though he occasionally still did wood–turning and carving. He used the one hundred rubles that he had received as a dowry to buy the basic equipment for his photographic work. As his little home was crowded, he built a shelf in the smaller room for all the precious photographic instruments. Under the shelf, he created a small, dark room that every photographer needs, a "camera obscura."[2] I often stood at his side in this small, dark, stuffy "holy of holies" in the magical ruddy light that came from a red–paned lantern; trembling, I would follow the wonder of his work to which he dedicated so much enthusiasm and talent, as he did to all his artistic projects. Once, when Shiye stood on top of a chair to retrieve something from the shelf, the chair broke. He caught the side of the shelf, and boom! He fell, pulling down all his precious equipment with him. Most of it became useless. This was a terrible catastrophe for Uncle Shiye. However, he did not give up. Slowly, bit by bit, he reassembled the materials and instruments he needed, and continued to be called "Shiye the Photographer" to the day I left Zinkov, the last time I saw him.

Yehoshua (Sender's son),
may his memory be for a blessing
("the photographer")

[Page 150]

But this was not the last of his boundless, incredible gifts. Uncle Shiye could make models of beautiful fruit, and statuettes out of a kind of grayish clay, now called "ceramic." He would also make beautiful objects out of gypsum, as well as portraits of people using a regular soft pencil; these likenesses were life–like. There was a fence behind his small, crowded house. Uncle Shiye himself built a kind of large glassed–in room, which he called "the gallery." He also painted a large cloth with trees, architectural columns, terraces, and flowers, and used it as a backdrop when photographing people.

[Page 151]

When the war devolved into conditions of murder, rape, hunger, and total anarchy, and no one was interested in being photographed –and besides, the necessary materials were not available–Uncle Shiye persevered. He used his gift for inventiveness and made soap, cut tobacco, and developed a method for softening the raw leather that the tanners of Zinkov were making at the time. He also found a medical book somewhere and thought of becoming an unofficial medical practitioner; but he never did do that. He also built a secret hideawaying place in his small house, which saved our lives more than once.

I don't remember under which regime it was. But it so happened that the nightmare had eased a bit, and Jews could breathe a bit more deeply. Uncle Shiye pulled strings so that he wouldn't have to serve in the army and would become a militiaman instead. I will never forget the sight: they slung a sword over his creased, everyday clothes, and he would patrol the market. Jews would gaze at the sight happily and smile, as if to say, "Look at who's keeping law and order and who's guarding our lives and property." I have never seen a more comical and pathetic sight since.

Though his Jewish and general education was extremely limited, he read a great deal of Jewish history, and understood politics well. He was a wonderful storyteller, recounting things he had heard or read about in books; I gulped down every word. When news came that Jews were settling in the Kherson province in order to be farmers, Uncle Shiye was the first to leave his home with all his occupations and "hobbies" with his family to become a farmer.[3] Regrettably, nothing came of this farming effort; and his wife also died there, unfortunately. Disappointed, depressed, and sick at heart, he returned home and had to start over again. Even his death at the hands of the Nazi murderers was more dramatic and tragic than that of other people. When the brown Hitlerite murderers drove together all the Jews of Zinkov, and everyone knew well that they were going to the slaughter, Shiye and his son still had enough courage to try and escape.[4] Sadly, they did not succeed, and were shot on the spot. This is what the grandson of Dadi (the butcher's son) or Dadi of Moldava recounted; he has miraculously survived and is now living in Tel–Aviv.

[Page 152]

This is the history of Shiye "the Photographer," the remarkable man whose roots in Zinkov went back dozens of generations, who never set eyes on the inside of a school (except for *kheyder*). Though he had the qualities of a true genius, he barely managed to make a living at several occupations, and no one acknowledged his unusual gifts. On the contrary: he was considered an odd person, a kind of eccentric. It is difficult to imagine what Uncle Shiye would have become, had he been able to study and utilize his phenomenal abilities; what a great and gifted artist he would have been... Beloved Uncle Shiye, your memory is so dear and holy to me! I will not forget you until my last breath. My heart will bleed each time I think of you and remember your bitter destiny and your horrible, tragic end.

———

Translator's Footnotes:

1. The decorations referred to would most likely be depictions of animals such as lions, doves, etc., due to the religious injunctions against portraying human figures. The gold is probably gold–colored paint. The *orn–koydesh* is the cabinet in a synagogue for the Torah scrolls ("holy ark").

2. A camera obscura device consists of a box, tent, or room with a small hole in one side. Light from an external scene passes through the hole and strikes a surface inside, where the scene is reproduced, inverted, (thus upside–down) and reversed (left to right), but with color and perspective preserved. However, the writer seems to be referring to a darkroom for the development of photographic negatives.

3. In the 19th century, the Cherson Province was settled by Jews who left the northwestern provinces of the Pale of Settlement for the southern provinces which were developing in this period. The English "hobbies" is transliterated in Yiddish.

4. "Brown Hitlerite murderers" would seem to indicate the participation of Nazi Stormtroopers (S.A.), who wore brown uniforms and were often called "Brownshirts," but I was unable to find any reference to their participation in the murder of the Jews of Zinkov.

———

f. The Two Daughters of the *Melameds* Who Lost Their Way

by Moyshe Garber

Translated by Yael Chaver

The structure of human memory and the thought apparatus – the brain–is so remarkable, mysterious, and complicated! I need only to take out that deeply buried box in my mind, which holds the treasure of memories of my distant childhood and youth, over 60 years ago, and I find an inexhaustible wellspring. Each event, each place, each person, reappear as fresh, as alive, and as clear as though it was only yesterday.

I have already mentioned how the first young revolutionary shoots appeared; how organizers and activists came to our town from the larger cities around us, how they roused the workers from their lethargy, and how they opened up the minds, hearts, and eyes of the enslaved laborers. The following event happened during one of the secret meetings: The Secret Gatherings, as we called them, took place mostly in the fields, about a *verst* away from town, in the "deep valley." I don't really know the reason for this name, as

[Page 153]

it was not deep at all. Yet it was a valley. A small narrow area was created at the junction of two sloping fields; we called that "the deep valley." The peasants did not cultivate that bit of land, because it was often flooded by rainwater and snowmelt. However, in summer, when the water dried out, the earth would be covered with tall, aromatic grass, and colorful wildflowers. Guarded on both sides by the high–lying fields and the tall vegetation, it was concealed from the police's "good eye" and suitable for secret gatherings.[1]

One Saturday evening after the traditional stroll, the crowd of young folks gathered there to hear a newly arrived activist. The summer day had been hot. The valley air was cool and a light breeze caressed us. The young people were in a good mood; they sang under their breath, and did not feel like going home. However, two women in the group were milliners, daughters of Leybl *melamed* and Yechiel *melamed*. They were afraid of their parents' reactions if they came home late, and decided to go back to town on their own. A narrow path led from the valley through the grass to the main road, at the black cross.[2] The road was split at that point; the left–hand road led to our town, and the right–hand road led toward Derazhnia and the train station, to the town of Michalpole and the peasant village of Petrashie.[3]

The gathering finally ended, and everyone went back to their home in town. Very early Sunday morning, we heard a buzzing, like bees. I looked out of the window that faced the field, and saw the entire area full of people. I quickly got dressed and went to see what was going on. Very soon, I heard the terrible news: the two women had not come home the previous night, and no one knew what had become of them. It was as if the sea had swallowed them up. The mothers were wailing, tearing their hair, wringing their hands, and already mourning the untimely death of their unfortunate children, who had either been dismembered by wolves or murdered by highway robbers. Simultaneously, they were cursing the Bundists, who had led their children astray. The afflicted fathers were silent, but they were miserable and their faces were pale and dejected.

[Page 154]

Almost the entire population of the town had gathered in the field and began looking and rummaging through every nook and cranny. Suddenly, they noticed, in the distance on the Petrashie road, a tiny dot that was moving ever closer. It soon became clear that this was a horse and cart, with what seemed to be people sitting on it. All those assembled, old and young, with the weeping parents at their head, set out to greet the cart. And who was sitting there if not both our lost girls? They were pale and embarrassed, their eyes downcast.

It took some time for the townspeople to calm down. Then, the girls who had been lost and undergone so much suffering and anguish before they were found, started to tell the following tale: By the time they arrived at the black cross, it was pitch dark. Instead of turning left to the town, they started walking right, to the village. By the time they noticed that the way was taking too long, it was too late to turn back. So they kept walking, eventually came to the village, and stopped at the first peasant hut they saw. Frightened, their hearts trembling, they knocked on the window. After a while, the peasant who lived there appeared at the window; in tears, they told him what had happened. He took them to a Jewish house in the village.[4] He knocked at the door and identified himself. A light came on. The girls were taken inside the house. They repeated the series of events, and asked to be taken home; they were calmed down and given some food, but the householder was reluctant to drive at night. The girls spent the night sitting up (they were unable to sleep in this situation); early in the morning, the Jew harnessed his horse and brought the two *melameds'* daughters to town. This is how the two girls made a small mistake and caused a commotion in our quiet town as well as frightening their parents out of their wits.

You may be sure that the girls were no longer allowed to attend the "secret gatherings." Their parents watched them carefully, and it was a topic of conversation in Zinkov for a long time. The wonderful tale was told and retold, with a slight smirk, as if to say, "After all, what can you expect of the daughters of *melameds*!"

Translator's Footnotes:

1. The writer uses the Yiddish euphemism "good eye" for "evil eye," as a way of avoiding the attention of any evil power.

2. Tall crosses were often set up at road intersections.

3. I could not identify this village.

4. Rural Jews were farmers, forest workers, tavern owners or mill leasers, and often served as managers of leased estates. Because of their distance from an organized Jewish community, town Jews often considered them uncultivated and coarse.

[Page 155]

Important Figures of Zinkov[1]

[Page 156]

[Blank page]

[Page 157]

Aharon Shenkelman, My Teacher and Mentor[2]

by Y. R.

Translated by Yael Chaver

Was there anyone who didn't know Aharon, Arkeh Shenkelman? In a town as small as Zinkov, everyone knew each other, even those who lived ten streets apart. And anyway, how many streets did Zinkov have? And yet, there were different grades of popularity.

Unlike most in our little town, Arkeh Shenkelman did not have a nickname. Arkeh Shenkelman, the Hebrew teacher and pharmaceuticals supplier, was simply called Arkeh, or Arkeh, Moyshe Idel's son, after his father. Both Arkeh and his father were teachers and educators in their time and place. My father, may he rest in peace, would often mention his teacher Moyshe (Idel's son), and describe him as a literalist, who liked the simple explanation rather than subtle, often casuistic explication. People who held their ground were called "blockheads" ("stupid brain"): "In any case, you don't know the difference between the right and wrong versions, so how can you be discussing the wrong version?"[3]

His son Arkeh was shrewd. He did not accept conventional ideas, always imagined the future, and dreamed of poetry. He had a vast knowledge of Hebrew, knew all the details of the verb conjugations, and was a stickler for style and grammar. Woe betide the student who didn't know the conjugations and who couldn't distinguish between a *dagesh hazak* and a *dagesh kal*.[4] I don't know whether he was an expert in Talmud, Halacha, and medieval Hebrew literature, but he would explain a chapter of *midrash* or the Ibn–Ezra commentary so simply and easily that even the slowest student could understand him.[5] He especially loved teaching Bible. The Bible was his pet–he could inspire the whole class to enthusiasm and exhilaration when he taught the Prophets. In these classes he would stand at the edge of the dais, recite the words of the specific prophet and punctuate them with excited commentary. The pupils would sit motionless, intently listening to his words; he seemed to be inspired by the prophet himself.

Arkeh's voice was pleasant, and when so moved, he would lead community services. Sometimes he would enter our house on the eve of Shabbat, after the ritual candles and the lamp had flickered out.[6] He would come in silently, without anyone noticing, and amaze everyone in the next room by singing religious or secular songs in his sweet voice. After he had finished singing, and the next room was silent, he would walk in and say *Gut Shabbes!*[7] Then he would leave. He had a permanent role in the *minyan* in which he and Father and their friends prayed: on *Tisha b'ov* he would be the one to recite the biblical Book of Lamentations. His emotion as he recited "I am the man" penetrated all hearts and moved everyone, and those few who are still alive will never forget his reading of this book.[8] Few knew that Arkeh Shenkelman also wrote poetry. My father would rarely show me one of these poems, saying, "Arkeh wrote this." I would recognize the handwriting even without Father's note. His penmanship was beautiful, harmonious and rhythmic, "like a flock of sheep [...] they match perfectly, not one is missing."[9] Nothing has survived of all the poems he wrote while living in Zinkov. His son, Avraham, has saved only those poems that he wrote in Israel, after he arrived and settled in Raanana.

[Page 158]

Aharon (Arkeh) Shenkelman, a Hebrew teacher and pharmacist in Zinkov, and his wife Yenta (may their memories be for a blessing)

We are publishing some of these poems in our Zinkov Memorial Book; let them be a modest memorial to the man who shared his inspiration and knowledge with his students. His poems were very lyrical, and we have selected some in which he expresses his mood and emotions. These include his poems about Yiddish and Hebrew, his great love for the Hebrew language, his affection for Raanana (where he lived), and a eulogy for the national poet, Hayim Nahman Bialik.[10] Arkeh would have long conversations with the young people who visited the back room of his business about social and political issues; he was the one who inspired them with a longing for pioneering and social progress.

May his memory be doubly blessed!

Translator's Footnotes:

1. The Hebrew heading is repeated in Yiddish.

2. This section is translated from Hebrew.

3. The writer presents the term *farshtopter kop*)literally, blocked head) in Yiddish and translates it into Hebrew as "stupid brain."

4. The *dagesh* is a diacritic used in the Hebrew alphabet, which takes the form of a dot placed inside a letter and modifies the sound. There are two types of *dagesh*; the difference between them is often subtle.

5. The Spanish–born Avraham Ibn–Ezra (1089–1164) was one of the most distinguished Jewish biblical commentators and philosophers of the Middle Ages. His commentaries are used to this day.

6. Observant Jews do not light any fire between the beginning of Shabbat, on Friday evening, and its end, after dark on Saturday.

7. *Gut Shabbes* (Good Sabbath) is the traditional greeting on Saturdays.

8. The biblical Book of Lamentations, which traditionally memorializes the destruction of Jerusalem by the Babylonians in 586 BCE, is chanted at the beginning of *Tisha be–av* (Ninth of Av). The quote is from Lamentations 3, 1: "I am the man who has seen affliction by the rod of His wrath."

9. The quote is from the Song of Songs, 4, 2. I have added the ellipsis.

10. Hayim Nahman Bialik (1873–1934) was one of the pioneers of modern Hebrew poetry, one of the Jewish thinkers who gave voice to new currents in Jewish life. Thanks mostly to his long nationalistic poems, he became hailed as the national Jewish poet and was greatly beloved. His childrens' poems were extremely popular. His death at a relatively young age caused widespread community mourning.

[Page 159]

Poems[1]

by Aharon Shenkelman
Translated by Yael Chaver

[Page 160]

Eulogy for a victim of the riots, 1936

Your blood cries out to me from the soil,
Angry at human savagery
That has sacrificed you.
The voice strengthens and is heard in Ramah.
It deafens city sounds
Penetrates the heart,
Infuriating the very sun.
Your terrible death fed my longing,
Laid waste my home
And made my life bitter.
Yet God continues to torture us,
You have caused us much bitterness,
God Almighty!

January 8, 1936

Your blood cries out to me from the soil
Against human savagery
That has sacrificed you.
The voice grows louder,
It thunders from the sky
And the furious whirlwind
Drowns out the hum of the world.
Your terrible death has awakened my longing,
Destroyed beauty and made life bitter.
And God is not finished causing us trouble,
Misfortune goes on, year after year,
Oh, God!

Anthem to the Hebrew Language!

How pleasant and beautiful, you old–young.
You alone were present at Creation.

You showed the way to the nations of the world
And provided blessings to your nation.

When you were in exilic lands
You never stopped creating in your own style,
And used the best of other literatures
To create gifts for us.

When our sun shone in the Spanish exile
And we were free of oppression,
You attained the heights
And gave us the poems of Yehuda HaLevi

And in the desert of Czarist Russia

You gave us everlasting hope and a future.

You supplied manna in the desolate desert,

In the poetry of Hayim Nahman (Bialik).

Raanana

a)
Among the settlements
In the land of our fathers
Lies a small town
Named Raanana.

She shows off her charms
As though she's full-grown,
Trying her best
To adopt
Features of
City life.

b)
Arise, arise, Raanana!
Arise, break out in song!
From a small town
You've become a city!

No longer a naughty girl
Running here and there.
Now you rise in the presence of the elderly
And honor the old.

1936

Eulogy for Hayim Nahman Bialik

How, how, and why, our Bialik,
Could you, who loved us so,
Have left us?!
And we thought: you'll bear fruit in your old age,
You'll regale us with your beautiful poetry,
And tweak the cheeks of boys and girls.

You ascended to heaven, where your lyre will play
To awaken the hosts of heavenly song.
When the morning stars trill together, we'll awaken the dawn
And say your name with reverence.

Language and Morality [2]

The laws of ethics and the Hebrew language
Have made a sacred covenant.
They will be joined forever,
Never to be parted.
A faithful wife caressing her husband
After returning from exile,
As her beauty and grace are restored,
She thanks her rescuer and redeemer
Returning to her original husband
Who will adorn and treasure her as the apple of his eye.

——

Translator's Footnotes:

1. I have translated these poems rather literally and have not tried to reproduce rhythms or rhyme schemes. They are rich in quotes and allusions to the Bible as well as to Bialik's poems. Most of the poems are in Hebrew, except for the second, which is in Yiddish.

2. The metaphor of marriage in this poem stems from the fact that the biblical Hebrew for laws and language ("torah" and "lashon") are feminine– and masculine–gendered, respectively.

——

[Page 161]

Avrom Shenkelman

by Y. R.

Translated by Yael Chaver

At the early age of 16, this only son of a refined father, a devoted mother, and a brother to three younger sisters, was courageous enough to stand guard over the garden at the edge of town, created and nurtured by the Zinkov *halutz* members, even spending the night there in a little hut. At 16 he also left home and went to *Eretz–Yisra'el* with the first group of *halutzim* from Zinkov. As he explained, he was going "to show the way to others." It was not an easy road. They did not "fly on the wings of eagles," had no legal passports, or covered travel expenses. Once they came to the country, they were not welcomed by open arms, but by malaria and hard labor. Avrom, or Avromtchik, as he was called, joined *Gedud Ha–avoda*, where he worked with the other members doing pioneering labor.[1] His older sister Dvoyre left for America, together with her aunt Basya and her two children. At that time, travelling was extremely hard, because of the Petlyura and Denikin bands who were rampaging through the region.

Both children, Avrom and Dvoyre, did not go to blaze new paths for themselves alone. Avrom went to help build a land for the nation, and Dvoyre became the caregiver for the family. Her boundless devotion to the family led her to work hard, sewing blouses for American girls in a shop, and sending money back home. She was able to bring the entire family to *Eretz–Yisra'el*.[2] She called on Avrom to come to America as well, and help her carry the burden of help for the entire family. Avrom had no choice, and came. He worked for many years, and witnessed the fate of workers in the "golden land." Those were the worst times of the great strikes

[Page 162]

in the coal mines of Pennsylvania, and the first attempts to organize the steelworkers. Avrom started to work in a steel factory, and joined the movement to organize the steelworkers. He was brutally beaten more than once, by the "Cossacks," the private storm–trooper army of the magnates, and barely escaped becoming an invalid.[3] He returned to Philadelphia, depressed and discouraged. In time, he met his future wife, and married. He established a fine family and had a good life, in both the private and the community sense. He was the chairman of the "Friends of Israel" organization, where he worked for the cause of Israel enthusiastically. But whenever he met his Zinkovites he would speak nostalgically about the years in Zinkov when they all worked in the *halutz* garden and dreamed about the future. He, and a nephew in Israel, were the only remnants of the noble Shenkelman family.

Translator's Footnotes:

1. *Gedud Ha-avoda* (Labor Battalion) (1920–1929) was a socialist Zionist work group in Mandate Palestine.

2. The mention of *Eretz Yisra'el* here seems to be in error.

3. Immigrants from Slavic-speaking countries called police mounted on horseback "Cossacks."

―――

[Page 163]

Ya'akov (Yankl) Hasid[1]

by Yosef ben–David

Translated by Yael Chaver

He was noble–spirited, imposing – in all senses of the word, with a silver beard that added to his impressive appearance. He had been accredited as a rabbi, but refused to turn his learning into a livelihood.[2] He spent all his time studying, following the command "You shall meditate on it day and night."[3] But with all his dedication to study, he did not lose touch with the surrounding world. He knew Russian, and was no stranger to secular study. When he needed to write letters to his children, who had emigrated to the U.S.A. (his daughter, may her memory be for a blessing, and his son Moyshe Fayngersh, may he live long), he decided not to ask anyone to write an address in a foreign language, but learned the Latin alphabet so as not to need anyone's help, even for writing out an address. He was very interested in his grandchildren's' education and tried to teach them, as pleasantly as possible, that a person should use every possible chance to increase his knowledge. He was busy with charitable and public affairs, with all possible modesty, so as not to appear a community leader. He had many clever, fine, and elegant sayings, such as, "Life in this world is nothing but a dream, but it is better to wake up from a good dream than from a nightmare."

[Page 164]

His wife, Rivka (neé Sadikov) was a true helpmate. She managed the business and the household, supervising everything. She was the one who assured the family's livelihood. All who knew her appreciated her intelligence, practicality, and kindness.

They did not fulfill their dream of immigrating to the Land of Israel. Along with their son–in–law David Blinder, they closed their business in order to go to the land they yearned for. But their plans ran into problems. They did leave Russian, but the events of 1920 prevented their plans to continue to the Land of Israel.[4] They had to split up the group. Ya'akov and Rivka Hasid unwillingly emigrated to the United

States, and never stopped dreaming and thinking of leaving for the Land of Israel. They were unable to do so, and died in a foreign country. It is a pity for those who are gone and no longer among us![5] May their souls be bound up in the bond of life.

His wife Rivke, neé Sadikov
(may her memory be for a blessing)

Ya'akov Hasid
(may his memory be for a blessing)

Translator's Footnotes:

1. Translated from Hebrew.

2. The Mishnaic tractate *Sayings of the Fathers* refers to learning as something that should be done for its own sake (Chapter 4).

3. Joshua 1,8.

4. Riots between Jews and Arabs broke out in April, 1920, in which five Jews and four Arabs were killed, and hundreds injured.

5. Often used in a eulogy, this is a phrase in the Talmud, Tractate Sanhedrin, 111a.

—

[Page 165]

David (Dudi) Blinder

by Yosef Ben–David

Translated by Yael Chaver

David Blinder z"l

He was a prodigy, a devoted student in the best sense of the word. He was engrossed in religious studies until the Enlightenment swept him into secular affairs. However, even after he began to be interested in secular studies and started studying to be a pharmacist, he was able to combine old and new, and derived the best and most useful from both domains. The pharmacy he managed in Zinkov became a center for Zionist youth, a type of club where people met and exchanged views on current affairs in both the general and the Jewish spheres. His compelling personality attracted young people, and he became a teacher, guide, and educator of the young generation in the town. He practiced what he preached. After he returned from the Zionist Congress in Vienna, he decided that the Russian spoken in his home would be replaced by Hebrew; his was the first home in Zinkov where Hebrew was the everyday language.[1] He organized evening classes for young people, which were held at the home of the Sadikov family. He and his friend Shmuel Fridman taught Hebrew to anyone who was interested. When contributions to "Keren Ha–Yesod" were requested, he asked his wife Liba (Ahuva, neé Hasid)–may she live long – to donate her most precious ring, as he believed that people should contribute something that was not only of material value, but, more importantly, had symbolic personal significance.[2] Dudi was not a great talker; deeds were more important to him. He donated and called on others to donate, and activated others as well as himself. He was able to energize every Zionist activity, whether it was for local purposes or for *Eretz Yisra'el*, and was always ready to act within the *HeHalutz* organization or gatherings in homes, on weekdays, Saturdays, or holidays. He was also willing to speak about Zionism in the synagogue on holidays and Saturdays, and advocate for Zionist ideology and emigration to Palestine.

[Page 166]

When it first became possible to emigrate to *Eretz-Yisra'el*, he sold his businesses, regardless of the prices, to achieve his goal as quickly as possible and emigrate to the land he yearned for. However, he did not reach his goal. After selling his businesses he and his family joined a wagon train bound for the Russian border. He left home, but never reached his goal. The riots of 1920 overtook him; entering Palestine became impossible. His life was lost at a young age, and he could not reach his goal.[3]

May his soul be bound up in the bond of life!

———

Translator's Footnotes:

1. The reference is to the 14th Zionist Congress, held in August 1925.
2. Keren Hayesod ("The Foundation Fund") was established at the World Zionist Congress of 1920, to provide the Zionist movement with resources needed for the Jews to establish a Jewish state in Palestine.
3. There is no further explanation of the end of David Blinder's life.

———

Moyshe Sadikov[1]

by Moshe Ben–Shmuel

Translated by Yael Chaver

He was the son of Itzik Sadikov, a well–off – though not wealthy–householder. He owned a fine two–storey house, and was a wine dealer, with a wine cellar and a large selection of the most expensive wines. The Jews of Zinkov, of course, could not afford such wines. These luxury products were bought only by the rich landowners in the Zinkov area.

Itzik Sadikov's only son was Moyshe, who was studying in a *gymnaziya* in Proskurow or Kamianetz.[2] This Moyshe was a happy, cheerful, vivacious kid, loved by all the young folks. He was a real artist at imitating people, making fun of them and their expressions – a born actor; or, as people in this area would say, "a real clown." Whenever Moyshe Sadikov came home for summer vacation, decked out in his school uniform, we would all feel happy. First, he would describe life in the *gymnaziya* with a real flair – the exams, the practical jokes on the teachers. He would especially mock the German and French teachers, when his acting talent would really shine. We guys would enjoy him and rock with laughter, full of envy for his uniform with the shiny buttons; and we envied even more the fact that he was studying in the *gymnaziya*, which we all longed for but could not attain. To this day, memories of Moyshe Sadikov evoke a warm feeling and a happy smile. Moyshe Sadikov is still alive somewhere, but no one knows exactly where. Some say that he's in Brazil, while others say that he's in Argentina.

Translator's Footnotes:

1. This, and all the following sections, have been translated from Yiddish.
2. The *gymnaziya* was a secondary school. Kamianets–Podilskyi and Proskurow were larger towns of the region.

[Page 167]

Yitzchok Itzikzon (Isaacson)

(may his memory be for a blessing)

by Moyshe Ben–Shmuel

Translated by Yael Chaver

Born in Zinkov, he emigrated to Argentina when young, where he lived a productive life and revealed all his talents as an activist of Yiddish culture and a journalist. His friend and colleague, Dr. Moyshe Merkin, who was greatly saddened at the news of Yitzchok Itzikzon's untimely death, wrote: "The deceased was not only a great scholar of Talmud and *halakha*,[1] but also a highly educated person in many secular domains. His industriousness, sense of responsibility, remarkable diligence, along with his modesty, earned him many friends and admirers. He was a very warm and dear friend, whom I really loved, and respected for his encyclopedic knowledge. It is a pity for those who are gone and no longer to be found! We honor his memory!"

One year after his death, his friend and colleague wrote a memorial article in the *Yidishe Tsaytung*, in which he said, "... during the forty years of his life in Argentina, he found his place working at the *Yidishe Tsaytung*.[2] His knowledge was vast and covered many areas, primarily in Jewish scholarship. He acquired this, first in his hometown of Zinkov (Podolia) and later expanding it in Jewish Odessa of the time, where he joined the circles of great Jewish scholars, headed by Yoysef Kloyzner.[3] He was an autodidact, constantly studying, never thinking of interrupting his ceaseless learning... He loved languages and knew many well, including Hebrew, Yiddish, Russian, and English. After Hebrew and Yiddish, he loved English most; he had studied it on his own. For the *Yidishe Tsaytung*, he would often translate political articles and commentary by important politicians and writers from English, as well as occasional brilliant, witty stories or articles by a great English writer.... Very few Yiddish writers in his circumstances have travelled as much as him. He was the only Yiddish writer in Argentina who travelled to Israel three times at his own expense... It took us a long time to grasp that Yitzchok Itzikzon had gone on a trip from which one does not return. We will remember him forever. Honor to his memory!"

[Page 168]

The famous American Yiddish–Hebrew writer and intellectual, Arn Tseytlin, wrote a belated eulogy about his friend, the playwright Yitzchok Isaacson, in the *Tog–Morgn–Zhurnal*(June 15, 1964): "Yitzchok Isaacson was 'a scholar who was not properly eulogized'.[4] Born in Zinkov, Ukraine, he emigrated to Argentina many years ago, where he was a journalist, lecturer and language–instructor. He was a highly educated autodidact, a natural student who was constantly learning. Whenever he was free of his journalism work, he read and studied. He may have been the most highly educated Yiddish author in Argentina. He also had a rare sense of poetry. His taste, refined by world poetry, helped him position himself in Yiddish and Hebrew poetry. I met him when he visited New York. His dream was to settle in the Jewish state, but that remained a dream. His great passion was Hebrew philology. He considered Hebrew the mother of all languages, and hoped he would write the major work about Hebrew philology; that, too, was not destined to happen."

———

Translator's Footnotes:

1. *Halakha* is the term for the corpus of Jewish religious laws based on the Talmud.

2. *Di Yidishe Tsaytung* was published in Buenos Aires.

3. Yoysef Kloyzner (better known as Joseph Klausner) (1974–1958) was a Jewish historian and professor of Hebrew literature, and a major Jewish cultural figure.

4. Arn Tsaytlin (better known as Aaron Zeitlin, 1898–1973), was a prolific Yiddish and Hebrew writer, and an influential intellectual. The quote is from the Mishna, Sukkah 29.

Pessie Shraybman

by Moyshe ben–Shmuel

Translated by Yael Chaver

Pessie was the oldest daughter of LeybleItzi–Maykes. Her father had a grocery, from which his family made a good living. She was very likable, medium–sized, with beautiful hair, symmetrical features, and slightly dreamy, affectionate eyes with the occasional flickering spark. Her voice was quiet, clear, and pleasant. Though she tried to conceal it, those who knew her well were aware that the quiet and modest demeanor masked a free temperament and a strong lust for life. Pessie Shraybman had a fine theatrical talent. She was known in the amateur theatrical group of Zinkov as the "prima donna." She really distinguished herself in such roles as "Khashe the Orphan," "Mirele Efros," "God, Man, and Devil," and other roles.[1] In general, she was a fine young girl, who was good company and a good conversationalist.

[Page 169]

Our friend Yisro'el Roytburd recounts that when he had already crossed the Russian border and was in the town of Czortkow, Pessie Shraybman also arrived with the goal of emigrating to America.[2] But she soon changed her mind. "I don't want to part from my parents, sisters and brothers, and go to such a distant country, and never see them again." She soon returned to Zinkov, issuing her own death sentence. She and her entire large family, for whose sake her sensitive conscience impelled her to return home, were murdered in 1943, during the grisly brown Nazi plague.

Translator's Footnotes:

1. "Khashe the Orphan," "Mirele Efros," and "God, Man, and Devil" are three famous plays by Jacob Gordin (1853–1909), who became known for introducing realism and naturalism into Yiddish theater.

2. Czortkow was part of Poland at the time.

Sima (Leybe's daughter)
by Moyshe Ben–Shmuel
Translated by Yael Chaver

Sima's parents were poor. Her father did not earn enough to sustain his family and give his children a proper education. They really struggled until the boys grew old enough to learn a trade; with their help, the family's life became a bit easier. Her older brother Meir was the guy who is mentioned in our memorial book, in the chapter headed "How Czar Nikolai II was removed from the throne in Zinkov," which described the first May 1 demonstration in Zinkov. Sima received no systematic education, but had the innate ambition and will to achieve a higher esthetic and cultural level. She did so, thanks to her own talents and resolute efforts to attain the goal she had set herself. She worked hard, and eventually became a wise, interesting person who could fit into any organization. She also acquired a good profession: as an outstanding milliner, she earned enough not only for her own needs but enough to help her family as well.

She grew up to be tall and slim, and was remarkable for her pleasant looks. She also had a talent for making friends, and was always the center of younger girls who were dreaming of the springtime of their lives and the ambition to achieve something they themselves could not express. These young, partly grown children approached Sima with love and wonder, and sought her inspiration and spiritual leadership. I remember a few of her devoted disciples – Leyke–Peysie, Sichkarnik's daughter; Liza, Zaynvl's daughter; Tsirl, the daughter of Froym Bontshik; the sister of Isaac Feldman; and others. Leyke is living in Buenos Aires and corresponds with Sima. Sima was especially close to Etl Kagan, or Etl, the daughter of Ezri Arn. Etl was small and not pretty, but was remarkably smart and was very knowledgeable. Sima learned much from her. Etl should have earned a status of her own, but was unable to achieve it due to local circumstances. Sima is still living, in the Soviet Union. Her personal history is very sad. The war with Nazism ruined her life: she lost her husband in the war, both her sons returned as invalids, and she herself is three–quarters blind by now.

[Page 170]

The few sketches we have presented here are characteristic of the fate of our young generation during that period. Some are scattered to the ends of the earth; others have been wiped out, obliterated, oppressed, or tortured. This is the road our persecuted, suffering nation of martyrs must walk. I would like to hope that the current younger generations of our people, and of other nations, will eventually find the way to a finer, better world.

[Page 170]

Izya Baytlman

by Moyshe Ben–Shmuel

Translated by Yael Chaver

Izya's father was Hershl Baytlman, one of the intellectuals who arrived in Zinkov in the second half of the 19th century. Those young people were not familiar with non–Jewish schools, colleges, or *gymnazyas*. Yet they attained a fine level of education for their time. They knew Russian and Hebrew well, and were familiar with the literature of both languages – all through self–learning. Hershl Baytlman was a teacher. He died in middle age, around 1904–1905, and left behind a wife and an 8–year old son, Izya.

[Page 171]

Some time later, his widow, Nechama, opened a tiny store devoted to medicines and cosmetics. She had a hard time making a living, and sent Izya to Sumnevich's school.[1] Izya loved music, and his mother managed to obtain a violin for him, which he learned to play by himself. When Izya finished school, he gradually started to help his mother in the store; Nechama, for her part, learned how to make false teeth. Life became easier for them.

 Izya was short, with a fine head of curly hair, a short, upturned nose, and beautiful brown eyes. He had a particular charm and a bearing that made him very popular with the Zinkov girls. His best friend was Moyshe Garber; the two were inseparable. They were therefore known as "the twins." They grew up together, experienced the happy prewar years together, and took private lessons to study for the position of pharmacist's helper. They traveled to Kamenetz for the examination, and suffered together. After the revolutionary upheavals of 1917, the two friends joined the army together in the struggle to safeguard their newly found freedom – as did many young Jewish men at the time. When conditions finally stabilized, the friends parted. Moyshe Garber went to America, and Izya joined the Communist party, where he gradually rose in the ranks and attained a high position in the government department of trade unions. Izya married one of the finest girls in Zinkov – Rokhl, Shloyme Gelman's daughter, who was a teacher in a government school.

Both were murdered by the German cannibals, in Vinnytsia.

Translator's Footnotes:

1. I was unable to identify the reference to Sumnevich. The writer uses the non–Yiddish term *shkole* for "school," signifying a non–Jewish school.

Izya Baytlman and his wife Rokhl (Shloyme Gelman's daughter), both murdered

[Page 172]

Rokhl (Rachel) Kuzminer

by Khayele Klassik

Translated by Yael Chaver

Rokhl Kuzminer was the owner of a notions shop in Zinkov. She was famous in the town and its vicinity as a very generous person, who was always ready to support anyone in need. She was best known for this admirable trait of charity. There were small shopkeepers in Zinkov who lived, as the saying goes, from hand to mouth. They never had enough savings to buy merchandise for a holiday or a fair, when they might have a chance to earn more. Wholesalers would not give them credit. If not for Rokhl Kuzminer, who gave them loans, their situation would have been dire. Often, she didn't have enough ready cash to satisfy the requests of all the shopkeepers. In such cases, she would borrow money from a moneylender at high interest rates, and give it to the shopkeeper as a free loan. She required no promissory notes from her debtors, but only wrote the loans down in a special book. Often, the shopkeeper was unable to repay his debts at one time, and had to incur additional debts before paying off the earlier ones. The list of debtors and the amounts of debt would thus increase. But this charitable woman was not discouraged, and continued her good deeds. It's worth adding that Rokhl's fine practice was a tradition she had inherited from her mother-in-law Basia and her husband Zosya Kuzminer.

[Page 173]

The Destruction of Zinkov[1]

[Page 174]

[Blank page]

[Page 175]

The Destruction of Zinkov,
as related by Yehudit Weissblatt–Loyfer
by Y. R.
Translated by Yael Chaver

We now come to the most painful chapter of our book.

We, who have undertaken the responsibility of collecting material for this important chapter, did not have original sources for authentic information about the destruction of our town. We were not lucky enough to find Jews of Zinkov who had survived and could give us details of the great disaster that overtook our town. This was truly our main goal in assembling this memorial book, because filling it with memories of the time before the destruction, 40–50 years ago, would have completely sidetracked us. We knew that there were several survivors living in Kiev and in other towns in the U.S.S.R. Unfortunately, we could not send them too many questions or contact them properly because of the restricted relations between the United States and the U.S.S.R. Although we were recently able to somehow contact them, they supplied only general information that we already knew: the destruction of our town was total. It had been wiped off the face of the earth. None of its former residents were alive. It is also important to realize that between the time we left Zinkov (early 1920) and the outbreak of the terrible Second World War, we had no clear idea of the life that had developed there, and no social connections with the home we had left.

We made many inquiries in Israel, and a woman named Yehudis Vaynblat–Loyfer recently responded. She had endured the entire horrible tragedy of the Hitler occupation in Zinkov, and had survived. In letters, she recounted everything she had undergone. We now present her testimony word for word, as she wrote it down for us in her letters: "I am one of the few survivors who were able to save themselves and to go to Israel. My name is Ida Vaynblat of Zinkov, the granddaughter of Dodi the butcher. My current name is Yehudis Loyfer, and I live in Herzliya, Israel. Mrs. Raydman, of Zinkov, informed me that you were seeking material about the destruction of Zinkov. I congratulate you on your mission, and extend my hand to you from Herzliya, to Brooklyn.

[Page 176]

Yehudis Vaynblat-Loyfer, her husband and daughter

I am ready, difficult as it may be, to tell you everything that I know and have gone through, so that it shall remain as a memorial.

When the war began, I was seventeen and a half, and was a history student at the Kiev University. I could not evacuate, as I was immediately mobilized to help defend the city. When we were ordered to evacuate, it was too late. That is how I was seized by the German occupying forces.

[Page 177]

So I decided to go back to Zinkov. When I came home, almost all the Jews were still alive. As you recall, there was a great number of synagogues in the town, with roofs of straw or shingles, and dirt floors. People lived according to Jewish tradition, righteously and honestly. Over time, the straw roofs were replaced by shingles, the dirt floors by wooden boards, and life went on happily. The children grew up and studied, and their parents took pride in them. There were other changes as well. Rabbi Moyshele's large house was turned into a school; Rabbi Pinchesl's synagogue became a cinema. The synagogue of the cart–drivers, known as the "Kinsky," became a granary for the rye grown in the Jewish kolkhoz. Prayers were held in the old synagogue of Mirele–Tsupe, and in a small anteroom. The older Jews sighed and moaned, and young people avoided the synagogue. So life went on.

Suddenly, a black cloud came over us – the plague of Hitler. They tortured us for a whole year, but let us live. It was life, yet not life. There was nothing to eat, and even a shortage of water. The water–carriers were not allowed to bring water from the two wells in the valley; besides, they would not have been able to do it, as their horses had immediately been seized. The minds of the Ukrainians, who had already been infected with racism, were easily poisoned by the Germans. Jews were now forbidden not only to work as individuals, but were even prohibited from selling anything, even water. Anything that could be bought from the peasants was in exchange for a coat, a dress, a shirt, or underwear–whatever could be bartered. People became swollen with hunger. Jews were no longer allowed even to draw or carry water from the well themselves, as before. Mothers had to stand by and watch their children suffer from thirst. It was hard, bitterly hard. Everything needed to be stolen; those who were caught either beaten or clubbed to death. Only when God sent rain could we collect a bit of water for drinking and cooking, if there was anything to cook...

My appearance was hardly Jewish, and I was taken for a Ukrainian woman. I would leave the city and buy, or barter, some flour, beans, or potatoes, to take to a different street every day. Only a few of us could do it. We were afraid that the Ukrainians would recognize us and hand us over to the Gestapo. This went on for an entire year. I, as well as the others, were concerned for the old and the sick, and nothing deterred us from helping them. Often, we were caught by the guards, who wanted to know why we visited the *zhids* so often.[2] But we were experts at evading them, sometimes escaping with only a few blows. Those who were in great need of help included the black rabbi, Yankev Ber, Moyshe Shoykhet, Mirl Tsupnis, Royze (the daughter of Tzale, Hershe's son), the old Kupitzes, Shiye Zayontchik, Shmuel Royfe, and others.

[Page 178]

One Sunday morning, we heard horses in the street – Germans riding, singing and playing music. Well, we knew that the great calamity had arrived. No one went out on the street. People ran to hide in the hideouts they had prepared. People rushed around as though they were insane, fleeing to anything available – cellars, attics–as though that would save them from disaster.

Then, it began. The most observant Jews were shot first, as well as others:

Khayim Shoykhet (Khayim, Royze's son), his wife and two daughters.
The black rabbi.
Moyshe Shoykhet.
Yitzchok Fayn with his wife and children.
His son, Moti, with his wife Feyge and two children.
Zaynvl Laytman (Leyzi's son) with his wife and daughter Frida.
Royze Vodovoz with her sister Rokhl
Basya Furman with her grandchild.

The Shnaydermans.

Kupets with his family.

Motl (the son of Peyse Sitchkarnik) with his mother and wife.

Moyshe Kopit and Meir Kopit (Meir Kopit fought back, and was beaten to death on his doorstep).

Hershl Vaynblat with his wife Dvoyre and three children.

Khane, of the Post, with her husband Moyshe.[3]

Mirl Tsufenis's son.

Feyge Shapiro with her daughter Itta and two sons.

The synagogue manager, and many others.

Afterwards, it grew silent – the silence of death. Those who are alive crawl out of the holes. The Germans order us to cover the graves of the dead. The wailing is immense. They find the daughter of Pinye the butcher (Petyuta), a beautiful sixteen-year–old girl who was beaten to death. Apparently, she fought off a guard, and prevented him from raping her. She was battered to death, untouched and pure, and was buried as a saint, in the holy ground of the Jewish cemetery.

[Page 179]

It was quiet for a short time. Apparently, they wanted for the Jews to come out of their holes…"

* * *

In a private letter to Moyshe Garber, who had asked Yehudis for news of his family, she wrote the following:

"I knew your uncle, Yehoshua, or, as he was known, Shiye Fotografshtchik. His daughter Feyge married my brother. Your uncle lived in Proskurow, where he was a photographer. During the first massacre that the Nazis carried out in that city, Shiye and his daughter with her baby were hiding in a concealed hideout, along with others. The baby, who was 11 months old, was crying loudly and could not be quieted. They placed a cushion over the baby. When the Germans nearby left, and the cushion was removed, they found that the baby was dead. Your uncle and his daughter returned to Zinkov. Shiye was killed during the first massacre, along with my brother. His daughter remained alive for the moment…"

Her accounts are sporadic. The terrible experiences burst out of her memory at random. Mrs. Yehudis Vaynblat–Loyfer recounts episodes–one event, then a different one. It is impossible to determine what happened first and what later. We understand, however, that this is actually unimportant. Suffice it to say that a normal person could not conceive of such things: how can human beings do these acts, and how could anyone see them and remain sane, even go on living? The fact is that Yehudis,

Dodi the butcher's grandchild, in her corner of our Zinkov, witnessed the catastrophe that overtook our people and its dreadful extermination. Let the world know, and be stunned; let us, the survivors remember it well. And let no frivolous persons come and start chattering that holding a grudge is not a Jewish quality. God of vengeance! Forgive them, these faint-hearted of our people. They are not concerned with good qualities, or kind-hearted. They simply do not want to think about horrors. They don't want their rest and happiness to be disturbed; all they want is to continue their foolish existence, occupied with everyday matters.

Rokhl Baskales and her daughter Esther, murdered

[Page 180]

All of us, and you who read this memorial book – remember – *Yizkor!*[4] May Heaven itself shout it out until the end of time, until the last of those who dipped their hands in the blood of our people will disappear from the world, until the appearance of the generation referred to by the prophet: "*Nation shall not lift up sword against nation*" and justice shall reign among people.[5]

Let us switch to the following letters and "Lamentations" chapters of Yehudis Vaynblat–Loyfer:[6] "This is what happened when the German murderers carried out their first *Aktion*.[7] At exactly 3 minutes past two o'clock, they shot anyone they could catch. They ripped the clothes off men and women, and chased them. Children were stabbed with bayonets, or thrown down alive. Children were grabbed from their mothers, to wild laughter, and tortured or killed in the home before their mothers' eyes. At the same time, an orchestra of possibly one hundred musicians was playing jazz, to drown out the voices of pain and fear. Some mothers resisted, such as Menashe Raydman's daughter Dvoyre (about whom I will write separately). The mass shootings took place among the hills of Stanislavchik, near the Vikovits roar.[8] Later, they sent people out to cover the bodies. However, there was a downpour shortly afterwards, and the bodies swam up to the surface; people were sent out again to cover the bodies. A few days later, a non–Jew came and told us that he had seen a *zhid* being hung from a tree. The Jews of the community went over there and found Khayim Izakson (Royze's son) hanging by both arms from a tree. He was one of those who had been shot; how he came to be on the tree will forever be a riddle. They went to the Gestapo and asked for permission to bury him. The Gestapo office demanded a great sum of money and fancy clothes. The Jews went to the town's householders requesting help. Lyova Finkel handed over gold objects, and his wife's earrings (Lyova Finkel was Moyshe Grinman's brother–in–law; his wife Rivke was Moyshe's sister). The wife of Yisro'el Aynkoyfer (Moyshe's mother) contributed two rings. The Fukelmans donated a good field coat, Basya Vinokur gave the entire trousseau of her daughter Slava.[9] So it was that they ransomed the corpse of Khayim (Royze's son) and buried him in the Jewish cemetery. The Germans ordered all the other victims to be buried in mass graves. There was not enough property to ransom everyone. Zinkov was small and poor. It was decided that anyone with possessions should use them to barter for food, to aid the survival of those who had nothing left to exchange.

[Page 181]

32 people were crowded into a hideout in a hole somewhere. One of them was a 19–month–old child. It was the same story once again:

[Page 182]

The child cried. It was quieted by various means, the end result of which was that the child was suffocated. The mother was almost insane. She would not surrender the child, not believing that it was dead. The mother lived for six more months. Their hideout was discovered in a later *aktion*; by that time she had completely lost her wits. She would not go out and surrender to the Germans, and was buried alive. The hideout became her grave. All the others were murdered."

* * *

Yehudis ends her letter thus:

"It is hard to live and remember everything. I write this letter with my heart's blood. But I must write nonetheless. Let people know what the Jews suffered.

Shakhna and Sore Vaserman, with their son Yoysef and his family
All were murdered

Some information about Shmuel Royfe. As he was a widower, he remarried with a girl who was much younger, and had a child with her. They were all murdered during the first *aktion.*

Efroyim (Froyem, Batchke's son) and his wife Tzivia were murdered, along with their children. Only their oldest daughter, who was married to a Christian, remained alive..."

* * *

Yehudis goes on:

"After the year in which we were allowed to stay alive, regular *aktions* began. The first one was followed, two weeks later, by the second; later came the third, the fourth, and the fifth. The murders continued for eight days. It grew quiet again. We returned from the Rivnich forest, crawled around to check on all the houses, and called out to the survivors. They were very confused. The dead lay everywhere: men, women, and children – murdered, suffocated in their hideouts for lack of air, with no food or drink, dead of fright. We dug pits and placed the dead in mass graves."

* * *

Yehudis writes to Moyshe Grinman (Yisro'el Aynkoyfer's son):

"...A few days pass. We are now in a ghetto. The ghetto is established not far from your street, on the meadow near the butcher shop, not far from the Jewish school, all the way to the house where Ayzik Fukelman used to live. They promise that the Jews will remain alive, because they are needed for labor... Now, no one has anything to barter in exchange for a bit of bread. We go begging in the villages, and succeed in bringing some food from acquaintances...

[Page 183]

Your sister Khane was still alive then, but completely broken and full of agony...

And another episode: Once, as I was leaving the ghetto, a Jewish policeman catches me, Avrom Vasilke. He hands me over to the Gestapo.

I am tortured and beaten terribly; my sin was that I left the ghetto without wearing the yellow patch, the stain of shame, that the Germans ordered Jews to wear. I lie in the Gestapo for five days, begging for death. But I have nothing on me with which to commit suicide. On the sixth day, I am sent with a transport of Jews "to work." By now, I know what "to work" means, and I jump off the truck when it is going at full speed. They shoot at me, but I run away. I come to the village of Petrashi and stay there with a Christian for two weeks. In the meantime, I learn that there are no more Jews in the town...

[Page 184]

I return to town. It's true: they have expelled all the Jews. Not a living soul remains. So I go back to the village, but my Christian tells me that he is afraid to hide me any longer. I have nowhere to go, and start walking towards Mogilev. It was held by Romanians, who did not carry out pogroms. I manage to get to Mogilev, and stay there for five months. I live there with almost no food. I eat one potato and half a beet each day, if they're available. Now I live as Jewish. They catch me and send me to a labor camp in Tulchyn, and from there – to Tiraspol. I was liberated in Tiraspol. This is how I survived, and, as you see, I stayed alive."

* * *

In another letter to Moyshe Garber, Yehudis recounts:

"...You certainly knew Itzik Shapirovitch. He was a teacher in the Jewish school. He, his wife, and three of his five children were murdered; the other two survived.

... Now I'll tell you about Sheva Abramovitch (the daughter of Alter–Mani–Yitzchok's son). I'm sure you knew her. Her married name was Foygleman. She was very intelligent. She had four sons; she, her husband, and their sons hid in a phosphate mine. They suffered there for four years. A peasant would bring them some food, to sustain them. But Sheva couldn't hold out, and died three months before the end of the war; in fact, she was buried in that very mine. Her husband and four sons survived. The oldest son was of military age; he was mobilized, and fell in battle three months later.

Shapse Zalas's father, his sister Itta and her husband, Leyzer Palatnik, with their two daughters, who later graduated. All were murdered.

Her brother, Avrom Abramovitch, his wife Itta–Lea, and their son were murdered. Another son fell in battle; the other children were in Moscow, and survived...

In your letter, you mentioned the local paramedic, Gerega. He treated Jews very badly during the German occupation. His daughter came to Zinkov from somewhere, with a five–year–old child. She moved in with an SS officer, and really abused the defenseless Jews of Zinkov. The moment she found out where a Jew was hiding, she immediately turned him over to the Gestapo; her son smashed the panes of all the Jewish windows. But I lived long enough to witness her terrible end. After Liberation, she poisoned herself and her son. Gerega himself became blind, and lived with a different daughter. During the occupation, he absolutely refused to help sick Jews, and gave permission to shoot Jews hauled out of their hideouts behind his fence. Several dozens of Jews were buried in this way.

[Page 185]

Shloyme–Yisro'el Aynkoyfer and his wife, murdered in the war. The entire family was murdered.

Quite the opposite of Gerega was another Christian paramedic, named Vatzik (or Vadik). He, on the contrary, helped many Jews. Sadly, he soon died. His wife and daughter couldn't stand the sufferings of the Jews, and entered a convent, so as not to witness the complete destruction of Zinkov.

Rubinshteyn, the teacher, evacuated in time, with his wife and children.

Mitelman was killed along with his entire family.

The only survivor of Yekhiel Royfe's family was his son, Hershl the cripple.

Levi Stoler, his wife and youngest son, were murdered. His son Motl fell in battle. The other children are living in Moscow.

Two children survived from Pini (the cripple) Goldshmid's family.

The entire Berkovich family was murdered.

[Page 186]

The fish–seller, his wife, and two daughters were all murdered together.

Fixler, the tailor, his wife, and two sons survived. His daughter was murdered shortly before Liberation."

* * *

In her letter of March 2, 1965, to Moyshe Grinman, Yehudis writes some details about German soldiers who were "quartered" in homes in Zinkov during the occupation:[10]

As I recall, Gestapo men stayed in your house. *Schutzpolizei* were quartered across from your house.[11] An SS man and his family stayed in Avrom Blecher's house. A Gestapo officer and his servants stayed in the house of Perl the *sveytshke* (I think she was the daughter of Hershl's son Yekhiel–Mordkhe,– Y. R.).[12] The *Gebietskommissar* was quartered in the house of Moyshe Foyglman.[13] An assembly point where Jews were taken before they were slaughtered was set up where Mirl Tsufenis's house used to stand. The Jewish community office was in the Vertsmans' house. In 1947, when I was in Zinkov, very few houses remained standing. They belonged to Rabbi Pinchesl, Khane of the post–office, Menashe Raydman, Funkelman, Milshteyn, Rabbi Moyshele, Moyshe Tsukernik (Shpialter), Avrom Abramovitch (Alter's son), Sender Garber, Avstryak, Hersh (Yekhiel Royfe's son), Shmuel Royfe, the Vinokurs, Khayim (Royze's son), the Garniks, the "Sage of Nehardea," the "Yantanikhe," and a few other buildings.[14] Most of the houses were burned; those which were not were torn down and used as firewood by the Ukrainians. Only a hill of clay remained for each house. Occasionally, a ripped feather–filled torn pillow was be found, or a child's shoe. It is terrible to imagine how the non–Jews helped to destroy the town. Ukrainian inscriptions were scrawled on the remnants of the destroyed walls: "End Jewish rule! Long live a free Ukraine! No entry to Jews and dogs! Beat the Jews, save Ukraine!" and other such "kind–hearted" messages. Only when they realized that Hitler didn't respect them, either, did they become a bit better. But by then it was too late."

In one of her letters to Moyshe Garber, Yehudis recounts her later horrible experiences in the Zinkov vale of tears, and includes additional tragic details:

"On one of those days we found the mother of Velvl Tuchman, tossed into a pit. We wanted to take her out, but were unsuccessful. Velvl Rozenberg then asked to call her daughter, to beg her to come out. We called the daughter. The daughter talked to the watchmen and requested permission to take her mother out of the pit and bury her. And, wonder of wonders: the daughter took her mother's hand and easily picked her up out of the pit (Y.R. adds: it is unclear whether she was still alive, and the watchman initially prevented the rescue, or whether it really was difficult to remove her. In any case, that place gave rise to one of the legends that often develop during times of disaster and community suffering.). The next day, a new pogrom occurred, and all Mrs. Tuchman's children were killed, as was Velvl Rozenberg.

[Page 187]

Yisro'el Aynkoyfer with his son and nephews. All murdered.

Now, I would like to tell you another episode (Y.R. adds: this is the term that Yehudis uses for this sad event) that is so tragic, yet true. You certainly remember the large synagogue that the Jews of Zinkov were so proud of; there is much to be said about it. As you surely remember, two lions adorned the top of the Torah Ark. The Germans demolished the synagogue and broke everything, but a large section of the Ark, with the gilded lions, survived. Apparently, the Germans thought that they were covered with real gold, and wanted to strip the gold. They threw grenades that hit the Ark and broke it. But the lions remained standing in spite of everything. Then they sent two Jewish children to remove the "gold," while the adults were still standing there. They then shot the two children, who fell; and the wall remained upright. I believe that it is still standing. (Y. R. adds: Clearly, when Yehudis says: 'the Jews remained standing there,' she means the children; or else she is saying that Jews were sent to remove the lions while the children were held as hostages. As soon as the Jews didn't want, or refused, to remove the lions or the "gold" from the lions, the Germans shot the children.)

[Page 188]

Now I would like to note the bravery of one Jewish girl. I must tell you that it wasn't only Yitzchok Leybush Peretz who brought us his three gifts, as an expression of the heroism of the Jewish people.[15] A few of our martyrs today have also exhibited heroism... I want to tell you about a girl of our town, Zinkov. There were two or three Gemeynerman brothers. One was Pini, the butcher, who had an only daughter of 16. She was beautiful, smart, well brought up, and intelligent. We studied in the same middle school. At the time, I had already finished school, and she had another year to go. During the second *Aktion*, she was caught by a police officer, a former student at the same school, who had graduated a few years earlier. He wanted to rape her, and she fought with the powerful giant, fought to the death, until her pure soul ascended to heaven. We found her in the pit where he had dragged her – beaten, bloody, bruised, but pure and virtuous. She paid for her Jewish name with her life, and died, not like a sheep, but like a heroine. (Y. R. adds: Many isolated instances of Jewish bravery disappeared into the abyss of blood and have remained unknown. Due to the absence of press correspondents and photographic apparatus, some people dare to accuse our martyrs and hallowed victims of going like sheep to the slaughter.[16])

Another instance: Menashe Raydman, his wife Charne, and daughter Dvorye, with her young child, were taken to be shot. They wanted to take the child, and send Dvoyre to work, saying, "You are still young' you can work well before they shoot you." Dvoyre spat in the policeman's face, yelling "Bloody murderer!" They then shot the child before her eyes, and shot her too immediately afterwards.

I am tired after writing all this and can write no more now, but will write again. I have vowed never to forget the nightmare of blood."

[Page 189]

* * *

In her next tragic report, Yehudis writes, "Moyshe (Fani's son) and his daughter Mani survived; his wife and son were killed. Woe to this father! He was hiding with his son, who went outside for a bit. The SS men caught and shot him, and Moyshe was left waiting for his father to come back; he is waiting to this day. His daughter was studying in Moscow, and survived.

The Shraybman famiily, Itzi (Mayke's son) and his children. The younger ones were murdered.

The Brezmans were cap–makers. They lived in the meadow near the Vinkovitz *brum*. All were murdered, except for one daughter.

Leyzer Vouler was a smart boy, and was studying to be a history teacher. He was murdered during the second *Aktion*, along with his father, mother, and grandmother.

The Shundermans were all murdered. Unfortunately, their son Avrom, who was a university student, had come home for a vacation, and was murdered together with his family.

[Page 190]

Yosl Vodovoz, his wife, and children. His daughter was married to the son of Perl the *sveytshke*. His son Yankl was caught by SS men and was sent to work on the road. While there, he somehow annoyed the SS man. The latter picked him up and threw him, feet first, into a barrel of boiling tar. He later took him out and laid him down. People brought him back to the ghetto. He was half–burned, as black as coal, and his pain was unbearable. He begged: "Poison me, or shoot me." He suffered for three whole days and nights, and died in the evening of the third day. His sister Mani was murdered later, when a non–Jew turned her over to the Gestapo.

Feyge Chmelniker, her daughter Itta, and her son Khayim, were murdered. Her other two daughters and a son, who were not in Zinkov, survived.

Moyshe Fukelman hid with a non–Jewish family in Stanislavchik. At some point he heard that things were better in Transnistria (Romania) and paid a non–Jew to transport him. The non–Jew made a false bottom on his sledge. This caught the attention of a policeman, who thought the bottom was too thick. He stabbed into the bottom with his bayonet, and pierced Moyshe as he lay there. There was a gush of blood. The non–Jew was beaten almost to death; Moyshe was left to suffer. He was allowed to be taken out on the next day. He was dead by then.

Avrom Shpialtsh (Tsukernik) and his two sons survived.

Brayne Berzman, the *shammes's* daughter, survived.

Tsirl Rubinshteyn survived, but her entire family was murdered.

Rassi Kibrik was murdered. Her daughter Beyle and her brother survived.

The Margolios family was murdered.

The Rosens and the Strianiks (he was a dentist) were murdered.

Perl Tsufenis's son and his daughter Rokhl were murdered.

Yankev–Ber, the "Honey–Jew," apparently hoped to save himself by showing friendship; on the first day the German murderers entered the city, he walked out of his house with bread and salt – perhaps he did this out of fright. But an SS man yelled at him: "You are a Jew, a traitor to your country," and shot him on the threshold of his house.

Moyshe Itzi made candles for sale. He lived near the Vinkovitz *brum*, and was killed during the first *Aktion.*

[Page 191]

Itzik "the imp," as he was called, and his sister Ester were severely tortured and shot en route to where they were being taken to be murdered, together with all the others.

Rissiya (Gedalya–Hersh's daughter), was a pious, wonderful woman. She was, poor soul, old, and couldn't walk. She was forced to run, constantly begging, "Shoot me, shoot me, murderers!" while they continued pulling her by her gray hair. The murderer stabbed her with his bayonet; her children witnessed it all, unable to help their mother in any way.

Shimen Laskin and his family had had a very hard life; but recently, shortly before the disaster, his life had improved. The children were grown, and each of them was working. Then the murderer arrived. The father was beaten inside the house. One son yelled, "Murderer!" and was pummeled. The other son, Yankl, and the daughter, Sarah, had to witness it, poor things. They were allowed to live only until the fourth *Aktion*. They wanted to scream, but could not open their mouths out of terror.

The Lermans' daughter Gissiye witnessed the murder of her father. She herself hid, and survived; but was murdered during the final *Aktion*.

Yekhiel Tan'i and the fish–seller lived not far from the poorhouse. He had two daughters. One was a teacher. Her husband, Yisro'el Vaserman (Yekhiel the blacksmith's son) was also a schoolteacher. The female teacher was one of the last people murdered in the town. Her husband became a captain in the army and survived; he is now living in Kiev. He is the only survivor of five children. Their child and grandmother were murdered during the first *Aktion*.

The Shenker family was murdered. Their children are apparently alive.

Arn, the bathhouse attendant, his wife, and their four children, were murdered.

The Goldfinds and the Shvartzes (the watchmaker) were murdered.

As soon as Hitler came in, the Ukrainians (with some exceptions) collaborated in the bloodbath. Even Jews who lived in the villages, and by now did not even know (the younger generation) that they were Jews, were not respected and were handed over to the Gestapo

The family of Mendl Petreshier was the first to be slaughtered. The entire family was handed over to the Gestapo.

In Proskurow, I met my best friend Rokhl Finkel. She told me that she and her younger sister had been in the Greshtshanke labor camp, near Proskurow.[117] Rokhl was pleasant, smart, and well–brought–up. I remember well how elegant she was when came into class. Her mother sewed a red ribbon on the left side of her apron (which all the girl students wore), because traditionally a Jewish child should not wear black. And so the apron remained. One day she was careless, and left the house to go to work, wearing her apron. A policeman came into the barracks and noticed the apron. He decided that she was a communist, and took her out to be shot. Her sister happened to be in the barracks and went to the window to see what would happen to her sister. Rokhl asked the policeman, "I beg you, take me a bit further away, I am ashamed to let people see me. Take me to that tree, where it is quiet. Let the tree be my memorial."

[Page 192]

The Averbukh family: Zisye, Hodl, and Mendl

She made this request because she did not want her sister to see her being shot. She addressed the policeman again. After all, everyone has the right to ask for one last thing before they die. The policeman responded, *"Zhidovka*, you are still romantic" and told her to run. But he shot into the air. She fell to the ground out of fright, believing that she had been shot. She thought, "If only I could get up and tell everyone that death isn't that bad, and it's not worthwhile suffering so much to stay alive." Suddenly, she felt a poke in the ribs. The policeman stood next to her. *"Zhidovka*, get up!" But she, poor soul, stuck to her idea: "What do you want from me? After all, I am dead." The policeman burst out laughing, and took her back to the camp.

[Page 193]

It later emerged that Rokhl had been murdered on December 3, together with her sister."

* * *

For a while, Yehudis stopped sending letters with tragic content. She continued on May 9, 1965, saying that she had been very ill with a high fever and had been in hospital. Her fever continued unbroken for ten days, during which she could not recognize anyone. The doctors said that the fever was caused by extreme agitation, and termed it "nerve fever." Yet, as soon as she came to her senses, she once again continued "the holy work," as she called it. Her next letter only arrived on September 6, 1965. It contained a new list of names belonging to our murdered brothers and sisters of Zinkov. She remarks,

"It's too bad that there are no Zinkov natives here to help me remember all the names of the victims. I would, of course, prefer that our memorial book mention and memorialize all those of our town who were murdered.

Death was terrible. But nothing can kill the will to live. This cannot be explained! But the lives of the survivors are terrible enough. I, for instance, live in two worlds. By day, I am a person like all others, with my family, with my work. I have my worries and my joys, just like anyone else. But when night falls, the nightmares come. I'm at home again, and I suddenly sense that a pogrom is coming (an *Aktion*). I run, I scream. I wake up in a cold sweat. Only God knows how long this will go on. I will never be happy. It's been 24 years since I listened to music or went to a concert. I have not danced and will never dance again. When I pass by a place that is playing jazz music I run away, because it reminds me that the German murderers accompanied every *Aktion* by the sounds of wild jazz music and inhuman screaming.

[Page 194]

We have *sworn an oath that we will never forget this and never forgive it.*[18] I am sure that you too, our fellow natives of Zinkov, will join us in this oath... Every Jew there swore that anyone who survived should remember forever, and never forget, not only the disaster itself, but the disgrace of our murder as well. We cannot forget this, and will not forget it!"

Signed: **Yehudis Laufer**

Assembled from her letters: **Yisro'el Roytbord.**

* * *

Conclusion of the "Destruction" chapter

The tragic chapter of "Destruction" cannot end without a few concluding words.

The heartrending, tragic account in this chapter cannot fully convey the bloody events that actually took place. Who can recount the anxiety and agony of each victim, of the inconceivable and inexpressible murder of a people?! Who can express their boundless pain?!

What is left for us, the survivors, but to protest? We need, and must also seek and find, consolation, because the life of our people must go on. The ancient writers of our prayers and *piyyutim*, who were live witnesses – no less than we – of the evil edicts and torture that were the fate of our people, wrote, for example, in the Thirteen Attributes of God's Mercy, which we chant during the closing prayer of Yom Kippur:[19] "You have collected all our tears in a bottle to be stored." This short expression reveals an entire allegorical image: after the writer commands the holy city of Jerusalem, which lies in ruin and has reached the very depths, to beg for mercy, not for itself, but for its people ("beg for mercy for your people"), because every heart aches and every head is battered – he turns directly to God requesting that all the tears be collected in a flask for storage. In other words, let the tears not be lost, let them be collected for the ages and generations. What is the purpose? The only purpose is to awaken sympathy and understanding, and the conscience of mankind.

[Page 195]

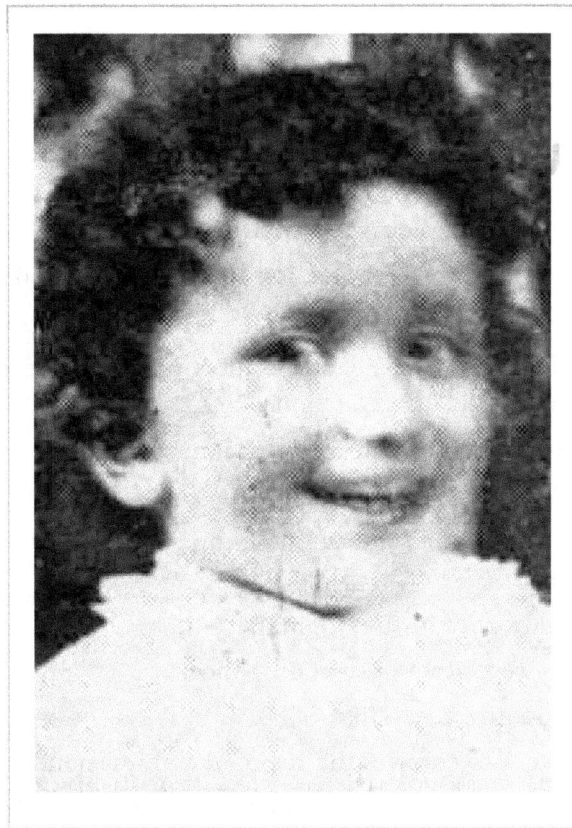

Luni (Lib), the son of Khayim and Sheyna Vayntroyb – the only survivor of his murdered family

Yes, dear sisters and brothers, many tears have collected in the flask. They are dripping down the sides; the flask is overflowing. We need to bring them before the court of the world, with admonitions, and demand justice and decency.

Remember well, you children of all nations, races, and continents. If you will be ruled by cruelty, it will destroy not only our people (God forbid), but will destroy you as well, all of you–because with today's means and technical possibilities, destruction will be total!

Therefore, let there be an end to the darkness, ignorance, cruelty, and moral corruption, and let justice and decency gain control over our world.

And I, who write these sentences with profound sorrow and grief, would like my bitter tears over the destruction of the daughter of my people to be added to the eternal flask of tears and serve as a witness and memorial to the destruction of my close friends and relatives.[20] *Yisgadal ve–yiskadash shme raba!*[21] May the great Name of God be exalted and sanctified!

———

Translator's Footnotes:

1. The heading is repeated in Hebrew and in Yiddish.
2. *Zhid* is a Slavic pejorative for Jews.
3. Khane may have worked in the post office.
4. *Yizkor* is the traditional exhortation to remember the deceased.
5. Isaiah 2, 4.
6. Accounts of large–scale disasters affecting Jews are often headed by the title of the biblical book of *Lamentations*.
7. The German term for roundup operations was *Aktion*.
8. I could not identify "Vikovits roar."
9. I could not identify the precise meaning of "field coat;" it may be a military issue garment.
10. The quote marks are in the original.
11. *Schutzpolizei* were state protection police.
12. I could not identify *sveytshke*.
13. The *Gebietskommissar* was the regional commissioner.
14. "Sage of Nehardea" and "Yantanikhe" seem to be local nicknames. Nehardea was the location of one of the major rabbinical academies in Babylonia, during the 3d–5th centuries.
15. In the story "Three Gifts" by the major Jewish cultural figure Yitzchok Leybush Peretz (1852–1915), 'Three Gifts' of martyred souls are delivered to heaven as the price of entry,

16. Accusations of this kind were made after the war.

17. I was not able to identify this camp.

18. The italics are in the original Yiddish.

19. The *piyyut* is a Jewish liturgical poem, usually sung, chanted, or recited.

20. "The destruction of the daughter of my people" is a quote from Lamentations 3, 48.

21. These are the opening words of the Mourner's Kaddish, said in all the mourning rituals.

———

[Page 196]

Regards from Postwar Zinkov
– from letters to Moyshe Grinman
by Leonid
Translated by Yael Chaver

August 8, 1945

Good morning, my dear ones!

I send you my warm regards and best wishes for your lives.

Dear Moyshe, I am immeasurably happy to learn about you. I wept constantly while I read your letter, because we two are the only ones left alive. We have no one else. Only you and I are left, of our large, beautiful family, It is extremely painful and distressing.

I know, my dear, that what I am about to write you will cause you much grief. But it cannot be concealed. You should know, and the American people must know, what this damned Fascism is. It means that wherever a German foot stepped, it obliterated the people, the culture, and all the good that was achieved by us over decades. I was on the front the whole time, and personally saw how the accursed Germans abused Jews, killing children and elderly people.

They killed 3200 souls in Zinkov, among them all our relatives. They were unable to flee, because Father and Mother were old, and our sisters were burdened with children; thus, they were all murdered. Our Solomon was in the army, where he fell; his family was shot by the Germans. It is hard to describe all the taunting that our people suffered at the hands of the beasts. During the pogrom in Zinkov, they collected the young children, set them on a wagon, and surrounded them with barbed wire. A child who jumped off to run to his mother – who was also being taken to her death – was immediately speared and thrown back on the wagon, where he died among the other children. In one house, they cut a living child into four pieces, before their parents' eyes, explaining, "We're leaving this meat for the Russians." Afterwards, they raped the young mother in front of her husband and parents, and later set fire to the house on all sides, burning them all alive inside the house.

When I was in Moscow, I met our relatives from Odessa and Medzhybizh. Everyone in Medzhybizh had also been killed. Grandmother in Medzhybizh had lived until the Germans arrived; they murdered her.

I can't describe everything; my nerves won't hold out.

Our country endured many horrible terrors, but we gritted our teeth and believed in our victory; now we are celebrating the holiday of victory… We must now work hard to rebuild the destroyed towns and villages, and need much strength and resources.

My dears, I embrace you all heartily, and kiss you.

Your brother, Leonid.

September 20, 1946

Good morning, my dear ones,

I want to report that I went to Zinkov and Proskurow a few days ago. Aunt Eyde and her son Boris are living in Proskurow. We have no one in Zinkov. I visited the graves on August 6, as it was the yortsayt of the pogrom.[1] The yortsayt was on the ninth day of Av.[2] There are a few graves in Zinkov, but it is impossible to know where someone was buried. The situation there is very bad. The entire town was destroyed; only 30 residents are left, of a population that numbered 3500. You cannot imagine how hard it was to stay there for a few days. I remembered everything and everyone from the days when I would come to visit this large, beautiful family! Now there is only me. It is so hard and miserable. You are my only consolation. Things are a bit easier when I think of you; I am happy to read your letters and look at your photographs. I really long to be with you, but that is impossible.

My life is not bad. I am busy rebuilding the destroyed economy. We were badly hurt during the German years, and now must do much work to heal all the wounds, and live even better than we did before the war...

Well, my dears, I will stop here. I wish you everything good and kiss you all.

Your Leonid.

Write me more often.

———

Translator's Footnotes:

1. The *yortsayt* (also known as *yahrzeit*) is the anniversary of a person's death, when it is customary to visit the grave. Jews often referred to German *Aktions* as pogroms.

2. In Jewish tradition, the ninth day of the month of Av is a fast day, which a number of disasters in Jewish history occurred (primarily the destruction of both Solomon's Temple by the Neo-Babylonian Empire and the Second Temple by the Roman Empire in Jerusalem). Other national tragedies are commemorated annually on this day as well. In 1946, the ninth of Av was on August 6.

———

[Page 198]

The Return to Zinkov
(excerpts from letters)
Translated by Yael Chaver

As soon as Zinkov was liberated by the Red Army, the leaders of the Zinkov Association and aid committees in America approached the Russian War Relief, and donated a whole ton of clothes for Zinkov. The Relief sent them immediately, and instructed the Zinkov Relief Committee to send all inquiries about their relatives and friends to the town's leader.[1] The Relief Committee did so, and some time later received news about the few remaining Jews of Zinkov, who had survived and returned to the town.

One letter, received by the Relief Committee, was from the 74–year–old Alter Pakhter, included the following: "I am the only survivor of a family of 36." He goes on to describe the remarkable miracle of his rescue:

"In Frampol, over 500 Jews were driven into a large cellar. The doors were bolted shut, and the Jews were left to die in terrible agony from hunger and lack of air. Crazed by terror and hunger, people flung themselves down to lick the damp earth, to delay the tragic moment of death a bit. A few days later, the dead bodies were thrown out into the street. As you can see, I was fated to live to witness the joyous days of liberation from the German murderers. A peasant named Semyon Vasilyevich Bazay from my village noticed me still breathing. Putting his life and the life of his family at risk, he sneaked me away and hid me for 23 months." The elderly Alter Pakhter asks the Zinkov Relief Committee to try to find his relatives in America, and provides their names.

Among the letters from Zinkov survivors who returned to their home town after Liberation was one from Sonia Kiper, Burd's niece. She recounts how she and others returned to Zinkov, and describes what they

[Page 199]

found there. "After the Red Army liberated Zinkov, I came home, where I found ruins instead of buildings, and barely 35 lonely, exhausted, unfortunate people, children with no parents and parents with no children. It is terrible to live in a wasteland that resembles a cemetery. Four of us are living in one house: I, Fishl's son Sonye, and my two girlfriends. Life here is difficult, materially and psychologically, but we must adjust to the situation, because we are happy to have survived and be free. There is no one to complain about, because the war is continuing, and, after all, we are not the only ones. But we hope the war will soon end, and everything will be better."

It is clear from these letters and others that the Jews of Zinkov, and even those from the surrounding villages, are returning home; and that the aid sent by the Zinkov Relief Committee is extremely important and crucial.

Translator's Footnote:

1. The reference to the "town leader" is unclear.

[Page 200]

The Scream

by Y. Ben-Shachar (Shvartsman), Haifa[1]

Translated by Yael Chaver

Arise, you gates! Lift up, you eternal doors,
Speak, Zinkovites, speak, heads held high,
Of your source – the town you cherished;
Of your home town–the glory of your past.

Raise your voice – sing out;
Old and young–all town natives.
You who were rescued – break your silence:
You who are free – express your joy...

The voices fall silent, there's no sound:
Throats are hoarse, no answer.
Hearts ache, tears flow
Over the mass grave of Zinkov!

Almighty God: give us strength and courage,
Turn away the sword, trouble and pain![2]

Translator's Footnotes:

1. I have not attempted to reproduce the rhyming schemes of the poems on pp. 200–203.

2. This poem, translated from Hebrew, includes tropes of Jewish mourning, some of which are biblical. Line 1 is a quote from Psalms 24,7.

[Page 201]

A "Lamentations" Poem on the Destruction of Zinkov

by Y. Ben–Shachar (Shvartsman)
Translated by Yael Chaver

Zinkov, Zinkov, sweet home town
All mothers are beautiful, none is ugly.
You were my cradle–
What has become of you now?!

Your beautiful hills and thick forests,
Springs, lakes, and wide fields,
Breweries, tanneries, and water–mills.
You were all my cozy home.

You were a Jewish soul,
You saw the Jewish future.
You raised us in the Jewish spirit,
With the finest Jewish traits and customs.

Wake up, Mother, cry your heart out

For your children's enormous disaster!

May God remember![1] May God remember

Your pure lambs, which were lost...

––

Translator's Footnote:

1. The poem's title refers to the biblical Book of Lamentations. This phrase is translated from the Hebrew in the original.

––

[Page 202]

The Cry for Help
Translated by Yael Chaver

Zinkovites, join forces,
Away with the borders, break the boundaries!
Rich and poor,
We're all equal.

Let each help as best he can;
If not now, when?![1]
Let this book be a memorial for all
To remember those unforgettable years.

In memory of sisters and brothers,
Flesh of our flesh, limb of our limbs,
They died for their Jewish souls.
Let us weep, and lament, never tiring.

They were taken to the slaughter in *tallis* and *tfillin*
By the Ukrainian murderers, under German rule.[2]
The German dogs despised babies in cradles,
They slaughtered Jewish women.

The day will yet come – the day of revenge!

That will be our great consolation.

They'll be cursed by God, shunned by men.

Reviled by all, blessed by none!

Zinkovite brothers, join forces,

Away with the borders, break the boundaries!

We're writing this book for future generations,

Not only for ourselves!

———

Translator's Footnotes:

1. This well–known phrase (*Ethics of the Fathers*, 1, 14) is attributed to the sage Hillel the Elder.

2. The *tallis* is the prayer shawl that men wear during communal prayer. *Tfillin* are the phylacteries worn by men for weekday morning prayers.

[Page 203]

On the Ocean Billows

by Chana

Translated by Yael Chaver

A fragment of a moody poem, written by a distinguished daughter of Zinkov, while on the ocean en route to America.

Billows stretch on your way,
You barely decided to find a shore.
You survived long battles
Until the word boomed out: Go,
But be whole, don't speak of sorrow!

Let your spirit no longer break
At every step, at every turn.
The dark ocean flows calm and quiet.
The night comes, dark and cool.

My ship floats over the waters
And my heart keeps rumbling:
You've left all your loved ones
Back in the land of your birth.

I knew God's bright world
At first sight:
Beautiful, blue, summer, fields,
Childhood, dreams, radiance, images

All engraved on my memory.

My town is turned to ruin and waste.

All that enchanted and astonished you

In those wonderful summer nights.

[Page 204]

Now the town stands cold and empty,
A different generation is coming.
On its own life's flow
To a new world, large cities,

A generation strange and alien...
And the buildings stand as before.
The peasant sows and reaps.
The old feeling awakens:

The trees sway in silence,
This is your
Good old home.
Your youthful dream comes awake.

All is as it was then.

Your home, your world, newly born...

[Page 205]
[blank page]

[Page 205]
[blank page]

[Page 206]

Eulogies[1]

Translated by Yael Chaver

Translator's Footnote:

1. Pp. 206–215 (except for the last section on p. 215) are translated from Hebrew.

[Page 207]

Beyle Yoshpeh

The widow of Yekhiel Yoshpeh (may his memory be for a blessing), wife and mother of a respected Zinkov family. The head of the family was member of the community council of the town, and active in all communal affairs, especially during the years of the civil war, when regimes would constantly change; the Petlyura army gangs would come to town and occasionally demand a ransom–money and food – and threaten the townspeople with slaughter and murder. More than once, he risked his life when meeting with the murderous *hetmans*.[1] Typhus was rampant in our region in 1919; he died of the disease, aged 49. His wife Beyle was then a young widow with five children, who worked hard to sustain the family. Her son Nachum was in the first group of pioneers that emigrated to *Eretz–Yisra'el* in 1920. She and her other sons emigrated in 1926, with the exception of Yosef, who stayed in Russia and secretly continued his Zionist work until the end of 1927. She was a devoted, dedicated mother, who loved to help her children – farmers and construction workers alike. She was bedridden in her last years, and left this life at age 77. May her memory be for a blessing.

Translator's Footnote:

1. *Hetman* was the title of Cossack commanders.

Beyle Yoshpeh,
may her memory be for a
blessing

[Page 208]

Yekhiel–David (Khilik),
son of Nakhum Yoshpeh
(may his memory be for a blessing)

Khilik Yoshpeh
(may his memory be for a blessing)

There is much to say about Khilik (may his memory be for a blessing), who had barely lived when he was killed.

The Israel Army Archive section that commemorates fallen soldiers contains a file with reminiscences about Khilik (may his memory be for a blessing) offered by his teachers, friends, and commanders. Below are extracts from the section about him in the Ministry of Defense's *Yizkor* book.

"Yekhiel–David (Khilik) Yoshpeh, son of Nakhum and Rivka, was born on May 1, 1930, in *moshav* Merhavya.[1] His two first names commemorate his grandfather Yekhiel (may his memory be for a blessing), a Zionist in his Ukrainian town, who died during the Petlyura period, and his uncle David, another fervent Zionist, who died en route to *Eretz Yisra'el*. He was the only son of a farming family, and hoped to continue this work. He started school in his small *moshav*, then transferred to the regional school where he graduated from 10th grade. He was a leader among his school friends, and though he was often mischievous, his teachers loved him and appreciated his gifts and thirst for knowledge. After he finished school, he developed a deep love of nature; he then enrolled in Mikve–Yisra'el, where he devoted himself to the study of agriculture.[2] He was the center of the student group; handsome, strong, cheerful, and inspiring.

"When Israel's War of Independence broke out, Khilik (as he was called) had to quickly end his studies. The core group planning a new agricultural settlement, of which he was a founder, was organized in Mikve–Yisrael and moved to Kibbutz Geva to serve in the Palmach.[3] He was released for a period in order to help on his parents' farm. He loved the work and planned far–reaching improvements for the farm, but had to leave a few days later, as he was called up for military duties. After the kibbutz settlements of Sha'ar HaGolan and Masada were abandoned due to the war, the Arabs started plundering their property and trucking it away.[4] Khilik and his comrades chased the robbers and caught a truck full of stolen property. However, the Arabs tracked them and they barely managed to escape. Khilik was wounded in the arm and leg, but was able to get away unaided. He was sent to the Tiberias hospital, but before he was sent home to complete his recovery, he went to see his injured friends at the Tsrifin base. He did not come home for the rest of his leave, feeling that his wound was not severe enough to keep him at home at a time when every fighter counted. His friends said that his presence gave them a sense of security and faith. He joined a unit with his friends from school and the kibbutz, and fought with them again. During the "Danny" operation, on the Ramallah–Latrun road, he was injured in the neck.[5] He refused water, asking that it be given to those more seriously wounded.

"As they were retreating, he and the two who were helping him were hit by a shell. All three were killed.

[Page 209]

All three were buried in a single grave at Mount Herzl in Jerusalem.[6] May his soul be bound up in the binding of life!"

We would like to add to the account of the Ministry of Defense:

When Khilik turned 13, he would sometimes come home and ask his mother: "Please give me a hat. I'd like to help the old folks to pray and join the *minyan*." Khilik (may his memory be for a blessing) grew up in an atmosphere of disturbances and war.[7] At age 14 he was active in the Palmach youth force. At 18, he continued his studies at Mikve Yisra'el, but his heart wasn't in his studies. He was one of those who demanded that the school year be shortened, due to the emergency. When he came home for Passover in 1948, he couldn't sit still. When his mother reasoned with him, saying that he was her only son, he said that each person was an only son in his own right, and no one would survive without defending others. When his mother pointed out that some people stayed home, or were able to avoid going into battle, he answered simply, "They are not models for me." Khilik was very close to his home and his beloved parents, but saw it as his duty to defend the homeland, realizing that he needed to defend his people, his land, his village, his farm, and his parents. A person must defend his homeland himself, not by way of delegates. He fulfilled this duty to the end. May his memory be blessed!

Translator's Footnotes:

1. A *moshav* is a cooperative farming community.

2. Mikve–Yisra'el was the first Jewish agricultural school in then Ottoman Palestine, established in 1870.

3. Members of the Palmach (the elite fighting force of the Haganah, the underground army of the Zionist Jewish community during the period of the British Mandate) combined military training, agricultural work, and Zionist education, in the framework of an existing kibbutz.

4. Sha'ar HaGolan and Masada were at the foot of the Golan Heights, in northern Israel. The defenders of both settlements retreated, due to lack of reinforcements, after attacks by Syrian forces in May, 1948.

5. The "Danny" operation took place in July 1948, with the intention of relieving the Jewish population and forces in Jerusalem, then under siege by Arab forces.

6. Mt. Herzl, on the western outskirts of Jerusalem, is a national memorial and educational site. It is the location of the main Israel Defense Forces cemetery.

7. Confrontations between Jewish and Arab groups in 1936–1939 are known in English as the Arab Revolt, and in Hebrew as the Events.

Eliezer Shvartsman
(may his memory be for a blessing)

He came to *Eretz–Yisra'el* in 1922 with his wife, in order to join his brother Yisra'el and help build the new Zionist community. He created a family here, and brought up his children with fine national and Zionist values. When his children grew up, they were a credit to our nation: during the early months of the State of Israel, his son was the first pilot to fly the planes from Czechoslovakia, and later became a flight instructor.[1] He is now a colonel in the Israel Air Force. Eliezer Shvartsman's daughters are married to high–ranking engineers and officials; one is a teacher. Throughout his life in Israel he did all he could to build up the community, and was a guard and defender. He fought in the defense of Haifa and witnessed the founding of the State of Israel and its development. A faithful provider, he secretly gave charity to those in need. During his final illness, he made sure that his wife would have a livelihood and not be dependent on her children, loving and devoted though they were. He died on the seventeenth day of Sivan, 5725 (June 17, 1965), at age 66. May his memory be blessed!

Translator's Footnotes:

1. In 1948, Czechoslovakia sold fighter planes to Israel, bypassing the U. S. arms embargo.

[Page 210]

Fanny Yoshpeh–Grabelski
(may her memory be for a blessing)

Fanny was the daughter of Yekhiel Yoshpeh (may his memory be for a blessing), who was known in the town as Yekhiel–Itzi, Manish's son. The family had lived in Zinkov for generations; Yekhiel was renowned for his lineage and learning; he was a long–standing Zionist and community member. He died unexpectedly in 1919, at age 49.

Fanny was born in 1901, the only daughter in the family and sister to four brothers. She grew up in comfortable circumstances and studied with excellent private tutors: Aharon Shenkelman taught her Hebrew, and Asher Alterman taught her Bible. She continued her studies in Proskurow, and twice avoided death during the pogrom that affected that city's Jews.[1] Fanny was not active in community matters in Zinkov, as she was too young to participate in the youth groups. But her education at home led to her desire to emigrate to *Eretz–Yisra'el*, which she did in 1921.

As is known, the British stopped all immigration to the country in May, 1921. When Fanny reached Kantara, on the Egyptian border, she was detained by the British authorities; it was only thanks to the intervention of Dr. Wallach, the director of Sha'are Tzedek hospital in Jerusalem, that she was allowed to enter the country for six weeks, as a tourist.[2] Of course, she stayed in the country, and worked to help all her family members to immigrate as well.

Fanny was one of the first students in the Henrietta Szold School of Nursing, but she preferred working in early childhood education. She completed her studies in the Kindergarten Teachers' College, and was very successful at this work during her first years in Jerusalem. She and her husband were among the first settlers in the Rechavya neighborhood in Jerusalem.[3] She was beautiful and gentle, modestly behaved, and always ready to help others. Her life was full of distress: she took care of her mother for many years, her husband was seriously wounded during the fighting in Jerusalem, and his health remained poor. Fanny devoted herself to his care to his last day. She was widowed at a young age, never complained, and found comfort in her work in the Organization of Working Mothers.[4] She died after a long, serious illness, and left one surviving son. May her memory be blessed!

———

Translator's Footnotes:

1. A deadly pogrom broke out in Proskurow in February, 1919, in which 1,500 Jews were massacred.

2. The British Mandate authorities restricted Jewish immigration to Palestine in March, 1921. Sha'are Tzedek hospital, founded in 1901 by Dr. Moshe Wallach, was the first modern hospital in the country.

3. The Rechavya neighborhood was built outside the walls of the Old City in the early 1920s.

4. This womens' organization was founded in 1921, and ran day–care centers, among other activities.

[Page 211]

Aharon and Necha Frenkel
(may their memory be for a blessing)

Aharon Frenkel (may his memory be for a blessing) immigrated to *Eretz–Yisra'el* in 1924, along with his son Netanel (may he live long). He settled in Rishon LeZion and started a small farm on the outskirts of the town. His wife Necha (may her memory be for a blessing) arrived in 1925 with their other three children (may they live long). The farm supplied them with a living for many years. They were overjoyed when the sons, daughters, and many pioneers from Zinkov would celebrate holidays in their home. Aharon died at age 72. His wife Necha died at a ripe old age, 14 years later. She witnessed the establishment of Israel, and was survived by sons and daughters, grandchildren and great–grandchildren. May their memory be blessed!

Yosef Vartsman
(may his memory be for a blessing)

He immigrated in 1924, worked for a time in construction, in Haifa, and switched to clerical work in Tel Aviv. He witnessed the establishment of Israel, and was survived by a daughter. May his memory be blessed!

Veli Zaltzman
the daughter of Yosl Arkis
(may her memory be for a blessing)

She immigrated in 1925, together with her daughter Yehudit and her son Ya'akov. They joined her sons Fishl and Moyshe (may they live long). She lived for several more years and died at a ripe old age. May her memory be blessed!

Aharon Shenkelman, his wife Yenta,
and their daughter Sarah
(may their memory be for a blessing)

They apparently immigrated in 1925, spent several years in Eretz Yisra'el, and suffered from illnesses that caused their untimely deaths. Aharon was learned, pleasant, and loved company; he was a scholar and an expert on Hebrew. All who knew him appreciated and valued him. See, in this book, the article "Aharon Shenkelman, My Master and Teacher," by Y. R. His wife, Yenta, was his faithful partner through good and bad during their lives. She ran the household efficiently and was a devoted caregiver to their ill daughter. May their memory be blessed!

[Page 212]

Aba (son of Moshe) Nesis
(may his memory be for a blessing)

He immigrated in 1923, worked in construction in Haifa, and traveled with the Frenkel family to Rishon LeZion for Pesach on 1925. After the holiday he was traveling to Haifa in a car driven by an Arab. The car overturned and killed him, at age 23. May his memory be blessed!

Zev Nesis
(may his memory be for a blessing)

Zev Nesis
(may his memory be for a blessing),
died in America

Polya Goldenberg, neé Fayerman
(may her memory be for a blessing)

Polya Goldenberg, née Fayerman
(may her memory be for a blessing)

She immigrated in 1924, with her husband Shlomo, and had a son and daughter whom she brought up to love the country. May they live long! Her son Ya'akov is a senior officer in the Israel Army. She witnessed the establishment of Israel, and died in December 1948. May her memory be blessed!

[Page 213]

Mendl Vaysman
(may his memory be for a blessing)

Mendl Vaysman
(may his memory be for a blessing)

Died in Israel in 1956

He immigrated in 1922, with the second group of pioneers from Zinkov, and worked at road–building and construction. Later, he joined transportation cooperative and eventually headed the organization. He witnessed the establishment of Israel. He died in 1956, following a brief illness. May his memory be blessed!

Moshe Gornik
(may his memory be for a blessing)

He was exiled from Zinkov to Siberia because of his Zionist activity, and emigrated from there in 1930. He worked in construction in Haifa, and later established a farm in the Bet She'arim *moshav*. He witnessed the establishment of Israel. He died after a long illness, survived by two sons and a daughter. May his memory be blessed!

Rachel Raydman (daughter of Moshe), Chaim's son and her son Ya'akov
(may their memory be for a blessing)

Her son, Ya'akov (may his memory be for a blessing), immigrated before she did and brought her over. She enjoyed her last years in his home. She died at a ripe old age and was survived by children, grandchildren, and great–grandchildren in Russia. Her son Ya'akov witnessed the establishment of Israel. He died several years after his mother and is survived by his wife Masha, who runs the household according to family tradition. May their memory be for a blessing!

[Page 214]

Mendl Kurtzman
(may his memory be for a blessing)

He immigrated with the first group of pioneers from Zinkov, on April 3, 1921. Upon his arrival he joined *Gedud Ha–Avoda*, founded, among others, by Yehuda Kopelevitch.[1]Shortly afterwards he was injured by a trolley while working at Nuris, near En Harod. The resulting infection caused his death a few days later. He was 20 years old. May his memory be blessed!

Translator's Footnotes:

1. *Gedud Ha–Avoda* ("Labor Battalion") was a Zionist–Socialist work group (1920–1927), with the goals of labor, settlement, and defense.

Shlomo (son of Yekhiel) Shapiro
(may his memory be for a blessing)

He immigrated in 1921 and worked at road building in Tzrifin. One day, at work, he started running a high fever, and was taken at the end of the day to the "Hadassah" hospital. His surgery revealed that he had a severe intestinal illness; he died the same day, because of faulty diagnosis and proper care in the hospital. He was 20 years old. May his memory be blessed!

David Feldman (the carpenter)
(may his memory be for a blessing)

He immigrated with his wife and children in 1921 and settled in Jaffa. His trade provided him and his family with a good living. He was an observant Jew, whose house always welcomed pioneers from Zinkov. He died only a few years after immigrating. His wife Pearl brought up the children according to her husband's wishes. May his memory be blessed!

Dov (Berl) Soliternik
(may his memory be for a blessing)

Dov (Berl) Soliternik
(may his memory be for a
blessing)

He immigrated with the second group of pioneers and was one of the first members of *Gedud Ha–Avoda*, with whom he worked building roads in the Jezreel Valley. After some time his leg was injured, and he had to find a different direction for his pioneering spirit.

[Page 215]

He joined the first class of the Hebrew University, completed his M.A. studies *cum laude* and carried out research on ancient Greek and Greece. He then was sent to Estonia, where he married, and later returned to *Eretz–Yisra'el*. As an educator, he served as the vice–principal of Bialik School, then considered the best school in Tel Aviv. He died in 1939, at age 36, and was survived by his wife and two children. May his memory be blessed!

Sonia Yoshpeh
(may her memory be for a blessing)

She was the daughter of Chaim–Baruch Vartsman, an important Zinkov family, and immigrated with her husband Menachem and their two–year–old daughter. They spent their first year at her brother–in–law, Nachum's, farm in Merhavya. Sonia was happy to do her part in the hard farm labor. They moved to Jerusalem in 1927. She soon became seriously ill, and died young. May her memory be blessed!

Shimon Saliternik
(may his memory be for a blessing)

He immigrated in 1921, with the first group of pioneers from Zinkov, immediately joined *Gedud Ha–Avoda* and was very active there. After many struggles, he was able in 1923 to bring over his parents, Ben–Tziyon and Yetta, as well as his sisters Etya and Bracha. In Eretz Yisra'el he was active in *Gedud Ha–Avoda*, the Ben–Shemen youth village, and the housing company. His 36 years of life in the country were marked by many community efforts. May his memory be blessed!

Malkaleh
(may her memory be for a blessing)

Malka, the youngest daughter of the cart-driver, was horribly murdered by the Nazi killers. Her husband, an official of the Soviet government who ran a pharmacy that the Nazis needed, was allowed to live. However, he could not continue living after Malkaleh's death. He committed suicide by setting fire to the pharmacy; he died in the flames.

Malkaleh
(may God avenge her blood)

[Page 216]

[blank page]

[Page 217]

Natives of Zinkov in America

[Page 218]
[blank page]

[Page 219][1]

Founding the Zinkov Society

Borech (Benny) Laskin,
former protocol–secretary of the Zinkov Society

Translated by Yael Chaver

During the first decade of the 20th century, after the failure of the first Russian revolution and the outbreak of terrible pogroms against Jews throughout Czarist Russia, many Russian Jews and their families emigrated to America.[2] Several families of our small town, Zinkov, also left for America. Their example was followed by many young people, who became convinced that there was no hope for them if they remained in Zinkov, as there was no work and it was impossible to earn a living. As for intellectuals, they were not allowed into the upper classes of the Russian *gymnaziya*. There was a quota for Jewish students; besides, Jews were forbidden to live in many large Russian cities where there were *gymnazyas*.

This was the state of emigration to America until 1914, when the First World War broke out.

New arrivals in New York often met with their townspeople in the 7th Street park on the East Side, and exchanged news of their home town, which had come through their families. This, as well as letters, was how our Zinkov natives maintained their links to our town. This continued for a long time, until the first Zinkov immigrants died, and there was need of material help, through a *Chesed shel Emes*, to help bury the deceased.[3] It was then that the natives of Zinkov first realized that they needed to establish a Zinkov Society.

Our fellow Zinkov native Morris Buchalter – then very young and energetic – devoted himself, with several other natives of Zinkov, to this important task. It did not take long before the organization was established. To this day, it bears the name "Zinkover–Podolier Benevolent Association." When I came to New York after the First World War, the society had about 120 members. They brought their families over from our home town; thanks to this, the Zinkover Ladies Auxiliary was created. Together, the organizations were busy helping the Jewish institutions: HIAS, the Denver Sanatorium, the Orphanage, *Maot Hittin*, as well as providing support to needy families.[4] They held a ball or a theater benefit nearly every year, raising money for the support of community institutions.

[Page 220]

Our esteemed friend Harry (Shabse) Zala (seated)

Standing behind him, from right to left: Moyshe Grinman, Zala's wife, Borech (Benny) Laskin, and Moyshe Garber

During the first years after the Russian revolution, news would come from Zinkov describing hunger and want; the Zinkov Society immediately created an aid fund. Members of our society visited all the Zinkov natives here in America, collected money, clothes, and shoes, and sent everything to Zinkov. Other packages with food or tools were sent to those who asked us for help. Those who had left Zinkov and were living in other Russian cities, such as Kiev, Odessa, or Moscow, also received aid in their new locations; our Society even contributed large sums of money to the Jewish colonies in Birobidzhan. But on a much larger scale, our Society helped to build up the Jewish homeland, the State of Israel. It began contributing this aid in the first days of the new state and is continuing to do so up to the present day. The thousands of dollars that the Society collected in the past were sent to the Histadrut and the United Jewish

Appeal in America.[5] Several projects were initiated. Money came from the Society's members, but most contributions were voluntary, from natives of Zinkov, including many who were not members. Our women's organization was also very active in the projects to benefit Israel, and earmarked some of its funds for this purpose.

[Page 221]

This is only a short glimpse of the activities of our Zinkov Society.

On March 10, 1956, the Society celebrated its fiftieth anniversary. This occasion marked the start of a campaign to attract young members. The children of members were granted special privileges. The campaign is still ongoing. We hope that this will help us attract new energy, and ensure the Society's existence for many years to come. Below is the list of old and new activists of the Zinkov Society:

Mordkhe Zaltzman	Idel Berger	Yisro'el Roytburd
Naftali Foyerl	Zissi Burd	Moyshe Garber
Yankev Rigard	Zissi Natenzon	Moyshe Grinman
Pini Saliternik	Moyshe Buchalter*	Max Frayfeld
Yeshaya Burdman	Shapse Zala**	Dovid Fuks
Nokhem Druker	Sam Greenberg	Avrom Rapoport
Jack Silverman	Levi Greenberg	Y. Hauptman
L. Bleker	Philip Rozenblat	B. Shiley
Noyekh Shpilerman	Shloyme Nesis	Benny Laskin[6]

—

Translator's Footnotes:

1. Pages 216 and 218 are blank in the book.
2. The first Russian revolution began in 1905.
3. *Chesed shel emes* ("Charity of Truth") is an organization in many Jewish communities with a mandate to prepare members of the Jewish community for burial according to Orthodox tradition.
4. HIAS (the Hebrew Immigrant Aid Society) was established in 1881. The Denver Sanatorium was founded 1904 by the Jewish Consumptive Relief Society. *Maot Hittin* is the custom of collecting money to help the local poor cover the cost of Passover supplies.

5. The Histadrut is the General Organization of Workers in Israel, which was one of the most powerful institutions in the country before Israel was founded.

6. The   asterisks   in   the   original   list   indicate   the   following: *Active participant in the founding of the Society; Chairman for thirty years ** Devoted financial secretary for many years.

———

[Page 222]

Erecting the Monument
Translated by Yael Chaver

The monument

[Page 223]

Below are the inscriptions carved into the monument:

Our martyrs, killed in the Holocaust –
Do not forget
Their blood, shed by murder –
Do not forgive
For them, the last of the community –
A memorial
Their murder as innocents –
A reminder for the generations

[Page 224]

The Erection of the Monument

The Monument

Borech Laskin
Former Secretary of the Zinkov Society
Translated by Yael Chaver

The Society's protocols for 1962–1963 detail how the decision was reached to erect a monument memorializing the martyrs of Zinkov, murdered so brutally by Hitler's killers. The special committee for this purpose that was set up started their work immediately. The task of the committee was not a simple one. A large sum of money needed to be raised in order to erect the monument, and the committee made every effort to this end. People were asked to donate according to their abilities. Large sums came in from Zinkov natives who were not members of the Zinkov Society but lived in New York, other locations in the United States, and even in Canada. Much time and work were invested until the committee was finally able to gather the means and set the monument up in the Zinkov Society's cemetery.

On the day the monument was unveiled, many Zinkov natives, and many members of the Zinkov Society, gathered in the cemetery. Natives of Zinkov came from outside New York, and even from Canada. I stood with my wife among fellow Zinkov natives, when the rabbi began the eulogy for our slaughtered brothers and sisters, our Zinkov martyrs. Suddenly the monument before me seemed to vanish, and my imagination transported me thousands of miles away, to my home town of Zinkov. I saw myself standing next to a great pit, into which the cursed murderers threw thousands of murdered men and women, elders and children of my home town, including my entire family. I saw many of my childhood friends whom I left behind forty years ago, when I parted from my home and went to America. A shudder went through my body. I stood there petrified, thinking for a minute that it might be a bad dream; unfortunately, it was a bitter reality.

[Page 225]

When I awoke from that terrible nightmare and saw that I was standing at the monument with my wife, and listened to the rabbi's eulogy, I posed myself the question: What is the purpose of erecting this monument? Is it possible that we built it only so that we, here in America, should remember the terrible catastrophe that happened in Zinkov twenty years ago? In an instant, I had the answer: No, that's not the only reason! The monument is mainly for our children and grandchildren, those born and brought up here, in America; when they come here to visit their ancestors in the future, let them see the monument and read the inscription. Let them grasp the disaster that overtook their people in Europe, during the period of Hitler (may his name be blotted out). It will help them remember what they read in books about this tragic era of the Jewish people and all of humanity. They will remember their murdered grandparents with respect and honor, the ancestors of their tribe, as well as the partisans and the ghetto fighters, who met the menacing vandals with weapons. Let them give the same respect and honor to the brave Jewish fighters who overcame all hardships and defeated their enemies, laying strong foundations for the State of Israel, the great world center of the Jewish people. May the monument we dedicate here remind our descendants in future generations of the bitter, tragic past, and strengthen their desire and determination to help build the State of Israel, and to support the builders in every possible way, so that we will no longer be at the mercy of murderers and vandals, and Israel will be the eternal home of the Jewish people.

This is the noble national project for which the Zinkov Society's committee has been admired and congratulated. It richly deserves everyone's acknowledgement of their work and care, which has preserved forever the memory of Zinkov, our town, where Jews lived for generations. By so doing, they have also preserved the eternal existence of our Jewish people.

[Page 226]

Our Memorial and Protest Meeting
(On the unveiling of the Monument to the martyrs of Zinkov, and the twentieth anniversary of their murder, 1943–1963)
by Moyshe Garber
Translated by Yael Chaver

The historic call to protest, by the famous French writer and humanitarian thinker, Emile Zola, against the libel trial of the time in France, brought against the Jewish Captain Alfred Dreyfus, of the French Army, opened with the following incendiary outcry: "I accuse!"[1] These two words shook the entire world and aroused the conscience of every decent person. We too shout it out to the whole world, in great sorrow and wrath: We accuse!

Every page of the centuries–old martyrology of Jews is dipped in seas of blood and tears, and throbs with pain to its foundations. But the murders and the brutal and terrible deeds carried out against our helpless people by the Nazi villains are unparalleled in all of human history, down the centuries and generations. They have outstripped by far all the mass murders in history, such as the massacres by Attila the Hun, Genghis Khan, the Crusades, and the Spanish Inquisition led by that pious mass murderer, Torquemada, may his name and memory be blotted out! Even the massacres perpetrated by Khmelnitski and Petlyura were child's play, compared with the sadistic, bloodthirsty deeds of the "civilized" German cannibals. And the so–called dignified, honorable, civilized world was silent, shut its eyes, blocked its ears, turned its face away, and did not want to hear the heart–rending cries coming from the dark slaughterhouses, from the murder and torture factories called concentration camps. They did not want to hear and see the outstretched, emaciated, twitching hands of millions of Jewish men, women, elders, and tiny innocent children, who begged in their last agonized moments, as they were taken en masse into the gas chambers and kilns, "Save us! Save us!"

[Page 227]

But no help was forthcoming. When it finally did arrive, it was too late. The wild animals in human guise had carried out their devilish mission. It was too late when people finally realized that their feigned ignorance and unwillingness to see, as well as their continued silence, helped the growth and empowerment of the disgusting, hateful, monstrous, sadistic Hitler–creature, the golem, who turned against its maker with its armored forces, its well–trained brown hordes, and with its bestial murderers and throat–slitters.[2]

There was a time when a single regiment would have been enough to clear out and destroy the murky den of the dangerous psychopaths, and do away with their devilish plans, but that wasn't done. The warnings and alarms sounded by Professor Feuchst – a German, actually – who was a bitter enemy of German Junker militarism and an even stronger enemy of the Hitler Nazi machine, were ineffectual.[3] Neither the French nor the British diplomats would listen to him. His final warning to them was: "If you do not use your eyes for seeing now, you will use them later for weeping." Sadly, his prophecy was fulfilled. It was not long before Churchill spoke to his people, and to the whole world, using the famous phrase "Blood, sweat, and tears." Alas, how much blood and how many tears could have been avoided!

Yes, the whole world wept and bled, and paid a horrible price for the negligence and shortsightedness of its leaders. But our unfortunate and helpless Jewish people paid a higher price in blood than anyone else. When the plans were laid out at Nuremberg for the complete eradication of the Jewish people, with all the particulars required by the cursed German attention to details, Chamberlain hastily flew to Munich, holding his umbrella, to sell off and betray England's best friend and ally, Czechoslovakia. Since then, Munich has become a byword and a synonym for shameful political and diplomatic treachery, and will remain so in history.

But the world has forgotten so quickly. The German wolves have decked themselves out in the pelt of innocent lambs, and have supposedly become a people like any other. Thousands of sadistic *übermenschen*, executioners, their hands still wet with spilled Jewish blood, live in luxury and pleasure and hold high government positions.[4] They remain unpunished for their fearful crimes. To our great sorrow, it seems that the world has still not learned from the immediate and distant past. We are told to forget: "Let bygones be bygones." But we cannot – and must not – forget. Is it possible to forget such horror? We will never, never forget, and never forgive! Let our curses, and God's wrath, follow them down all the generations!

[Page 228]

* * *

Far, far away across the sea, on Ukrainian soil, our impoverished Jewish town of Zinkov had stood for centuries. Dozens of generations came and went, and, like waves breaking on the shore, new generations came. Life was hard, with the Czarist pogroms and persecution. Earning a livelihood was not easy. And yet, Jewish mothers and fathers sacrificed, denied themselves food, so that their children would have a Jewish upbringing. Our town produced more and more fine, intelligent, idealistic young people, good merchants, teachers, and proud artisans. Life in the town was not always monotonous and harsh. There were moments of spiritual uplift and pleasure, such as on the quiet Shabbes days with their twilight walks; the joyful holidays; the peace and beauty of the magnificent natural surroundings, Jewish celebrations, weddings, etc. We continued our Jewish national, religious, and cultural life, until...

Until the coming of the greatest enemy of the Jews of all time, who with boundless brutality cut down this way of life, and uprooted all that was Jewish. The brown vandals turned you into a heap of ashes, ruins, and a wasteland–you poor, beloved, and unhappy town of ours. And you, dear, cherished, beloved old friends, what happened to you?! In which gas chamber did your holy souls rise up to heaven? In which crematorium were your emaciated, starved, tortured bodies burned and charred, and your bones turned into ash for fertilizing cursed German fields? Your bodies were not interred in a Jewish cemetery, and your souls are wandering in the abyss, seeking salvation. Your graves bear no markers; your names were not carved into stone.

Therefore we, the living remnants of Zinkov, have set up a monument to you. Today, on the twentieth anniversary of your death, we stand here with pained, suffering hearts and mourn your terrible murders, along with the slaughter of one-third of our Jewish people.

[Page 229]

No, this monument is not a lifeless stone, as some skeptical pessimists have tried to convince us. A stone is lifeless only when it lies within the mountain, before it is quarried. We, however, have seen to it that the stone is shaped and polished. We designed it according to our understanding, wishes, and feelings. We burnished it, and carved words and dates on it - words that give it meaning, content, purpose, and, most importantly, a soul. A melancholy Yiddish song describes a daughter standing at her mother's grave, weeping and mourning, and while sobbing tells the gravestone,

"Oh, stone, beloved stone, you were once a mother, after all." Can anyone say that such a stone is lifeless?! From now on, this monument is not just a piece of stone, but an eternal symbol of that which was so beloved and dear to us, and no longer exists, and will never exist. Let this monument stand here, on Zinkov ground, and remind our future generations of the terrible destruction of the Jewish people during the years of animal, black–brown brutality, the years in which the Hitlerite Nazis, the inhuman murderers danced their devilish dance. Let the stone ensure that nothing is forgotten, and serve as a warning and a reminder that we must always be on guard, and never allow a catastrophe such as this to happen again, God forbid. This is the monument for the four thousand Jews of Zinkov, who were murdered because of their faith during the Second World War, in 1942–1943, as part of the systematic extermination of six million Jews. Here, the souls of our martyrs will find salvation. Every year, we will gather here to mark the anniversary of their deaths, mourn and weep, and say Kaddish for them.

Yisgadal ve–yiskadash...[5]

Translator's Footnotes:

1. "J'accuse!" in the original French is here translated into Yiddish.

2. The golem in Jewish folklore is an animated anthropomorphic being that is created from inanimate matter. The most famous golem narrative involves Judah Loew ben Bezalel (in late 16th–century Prague).

3. I was not able to identify Professor Feuchst.

4. Nietszche's term *übermensch* (Superman) was used by Nazi ideologues to describe their idea of a biologically superior Germanic master race.

5. These are the opening words of the *Kaddish* prayer.

[Page 230]

Remember what the Amalekites did to you![1]

by Moyshe Grinman

Translated by Yael Chaver

Dear fellow natives of Zinkov, and distinguished Rabbi Shore!

For the past 21 years, we have mourned the terrible disaster. For the past 21 years, day in, day out, we have been unable to forget the great calamity that befell us, the Jews of Zinkov, along with the entire Jewish population of the world. Every year, we remember and retell what this new Amalek did to our brothers and sisters. Let the world not forget how gruesomely they exterminated six million Jews, among them 3,200 of our fathers, mothers, brothers, sisters, and innocent children. The 3,200 Jews of Zinkov are no more. They were annihilated by the Nazi murderers–who by water, who by fire, who by hunger, who by poison gas.[2] Our Zinkov people were killed by fire, on the ninth day of Av, 1943. The great synagogue with its magnificent eastern wall, is no more.[3] It was completely hand–carved. Such synagogues were rare, and it was a great source of pride to us...It is now overgrown with grass.

When we Jews of Zinkov mourn the terrible destruction of our town, we cry out, "Remember what the Amalekites did to you, do not forget!" Do not forget! They took away all our dearest ones. Where are our little Moyshes, our little Sarahs, our little Rivkas? Where are they?! On the day of our great and boundless sorrow, we must remember our murdered fathers, mothers, brothers, and sisters; and not only with tears. We must also remember them with the firm wish that such a great catastrophe will not recur, and that our people, along with all other peoples, shall be spared mass death and murder, and live in a world of peace and friendship.

Let this monument also be your gravestone, my dear parents, sisters, and brothers! I am the only surviving member of my entire family. Not one of you was buried in a Jewish cemetery. This is why I carry a world of sorrow and wrath in my heart.

Translator's Footnotes:

1. Translated from the Hebrew, this is a quote from Deuteronomy 25, 17. The people of Amalek are considered a hereditary enemy of the Israelites.

2. This is an expansion of the well-known Rosh HaShana and Yom Kippur prayer *Unetaneh tokef* ("Let us now relate the power of this day"), which includes the phrases "who by water, who by fire." According to tradition, it was composed in Mainz, Germany, in the 11th century. In 1943, the ninth day of Av was on August 10. The ninth day of Av is traditionally considered the day on which both the First and Second Jewish Temples were

destroyed; the date has come to represent a day of terrible national disaster.

3. The eastern wall of a synagogue, which Jews face while praying, contains the ark that holds the Torah scrolls, and is therefore the most beautifully decorated.

[Page 231]

My Outcry of Pain

by Avraham Rappaport

Translated by Yael Chaver

I want to speak in Yiddish, my mother–tongue, and hope everyone will understand me. I will speak as briefly as possible, clearly and plainly, because it is very important for our young people to gain an idea and knowledge of what is happening here.

Our Zinkov Society is in mourning. We mourn for our immense loss, for the tragic murder of the martyrs of Zinkov. Our heads bowed and our eyes filled with tears, we stand here before the monument that symbolizes their memory. It is true that "One generation goes and another generation comes, but the earth remains forever," meaning that people leave the world, people come into the world, and the earth is eternal.[1] But these martyrs, the martyrs of Zinkov, the men, women, and children, like all martyrs of our people – they had barely lived; they were torn away from us in the midst of their lives. Many were gruesomely murdered as they began to flourish.

We are persecuted and hounded in every generation. But who could believe that such a terrible catastrophe would occur in this century?!

Our pain is enormous.

Our sorrow is endless.

What comfort can we find in the unveiling of this monument? What consoling words can I say to the brothers and sisters of this Society on their great loss? What words of comfort can we say to all the natives of Zinkov, who have responded so warmly with their contributions and have made possible the unveiling of this monument? Consoling words can echo only weakly in all our hearts. There is no consolation at all for the immense loss of those nearest and dearest to our lives.

[Page 232]

I would like to say only that the martyrs are deeply rooted in our hearts. We will mention their names at every chance, and never forget them. It is impossible to explain their deaths cannot be explained, nor can they be erased from our memory. Each one of us is a living monument to these eternal martyrs. We therefore unveil this monument and gaze at the Hebrew, Yiddish, and English inscriptions carved in large letters; they will preserve for eternity the bright memory of our martyrs.

It is very possible that the letters on the monument will eventually disappear, washed away by rain and snow. It is also possible that, generations from now, the monument itself will be eroded by storm and wind and turn to dust, to be completely blown away. But we swear, brothers and sisters, we swear that our hearts, the hearts of our children and their children, and the hearts of future Jewish generations, will forever bear the indelible memory of the terrible catastrophe that overtook Europe during the Second World War, when the dark and fearsome Nazi murderers rampaged freely. The memory will remain carved in the hearts of the entire Jewish people, and in the hearts of the finest sons and daughters of all humanity.

We will never forget, we will never forgive!
I want to shout out, as loudly as possible:
It is a pity about those who have been lost and are no longer among us! Cries of pain for those who were murdered, but will never be forgotten!

———

Translator's Footnote:

1. The quote is from Ecclesiastes 1,4.

———

[Page 233]

Fence Dedication

Zinkov–Podolia Benevolent Association[1]

Translated by Yael Chaver

Dear friends, brothers and sisters, and friends from our home town!

As you all know, we decided to install a fence around our cemetery. We therefore wish to notify you, sisters and brothers, that we have achieved this, and the fence has been installed. God willing, on Sunday, October 22, all of us, sisters and brothers, need to be at the cemetery to celebrate this event, as done by every society, and we will have a fine time. Sisters and brothers, be at the cemetery no later than 10 a.m., please come on time, and bring along all your friends. We will eat and drink, and wish each other life and not death.

Every member that will not attend our celebration will be fined 2 dollars.

The leader of the celebration will be the householder Rabbi Alter Efrayim Orenshteyn. You are therefore asked to come on time. In case of rain, the event is postponed until the following Sunday.

For the Zinkov Benevolent Association's Arrangement Committee, Nathan Furel, Chairman
Khayim Levenshteyn, Secretary

Directions:

Take the Canarsie train from Delancey St. Change to City Line "L", go as far as the last stop. Then take the traction car to Springfield Ave., where the cemetery is located.[2] A truck will wait for you there and take you to the cemetery.

Zaltzman, Secretary

Translator's Footnotes:

1. The announcement is undated.
2. "Traction cars" were a kind of trolley.

[Page 234]

To All Natives of Zinkov![1]

Translated by Yael Chaver

Dear friends,

We are very happy to announce that the Monument Committee is planning to publish a Yizkor Book for our town. The book will be a living monument dedicated to the memory of the martyrs of Zinkov.

This Yizkor book will illustrate, in word and image, the Jewish life of our home town, from its earliest days to the last destruction by the Second World War. We will also describe the social, communal, religious, and political life of the town.

Also included will be the history and activity of our Society in New York over the past 55 years.

We are working together with *Yad VaShem* in Israel, which already has a picture of our Monument.

We are in need of various documents, stories, and pictures that are connected with the life of our home town, Zinkov, as well as of financial help.

We therefore appeal to you, our fellow townspeople, near and far, to participate in this project, *and send us materials for this purpose, as well as financial contributions.*[2]

We appeal to you: Fulfill your sacred obligation, and help us to attain our goal of publishing the Yizkor Book, just as you helped us to erect the beautiful, imposing monument.

For the Committee: Moyshe Grinman, Chairman

Secretaries: Yisro'el Roytburd and Moyshe Garber   .

Translator's Footnotes:

1. Page 234 contains a Yiddish text alongside an English translation. However, I am translating the Yiddish text.

2. Italics in the original.

——

[Page 235]

With Thanks and Acknowledgment
Translated by Yael Chaver

Below are the names of those who are now, and will in the future be, mentioned with praise, respect, and wonder, for their noble brotherliness and warm solidarity. These are Zinkov natives and non–natives, members and non–members, whose generous contributions have helped to forever preserve the particular memory of the four thousand martyrs of Zinkov, the bloody victims of the horrible, gruesome Nazi plague, as well as the memory of our beloved home town Zinkov, in general.

These are the names of those who, like us, understood the goal of the ethical and spiritual obligation that gave us no rest and finally urged us to erect the memorial monument. Thanks to their financial help, and their warm letters, they whole–heartedly joined in our thought, and efforts, and, as one, handed us the mandate. They motivated us to make every effort and continue regardless of any obstacle, until the monument project came to full fruition.

Now the monument stands tall and proud on our Zinkov soil, and Jews who pass by stop and look at it with wonder. They approach, and read the inscriptions, carved in three languages, which explain the reason, the purpose, and the creators of the imposing monument that stands here. More than one Jew wipes a tear away and leaves the memorial with aching heart and bowed head. We hope that, for many years to come, we will continue to gather every year at this memorial, the symbol of our great disaster, and pray *Kaddish* on the anniversaries of the deaths of our martyrs, mourning their tragic end. May this monument bring us all nearer to each other and inspire us to friendship and brotherliness, as well as to devotion to our Society and to ensuring its continued existence.

[Page 236]

This is the honor roll of those who contributed to the memorial:[1]

Zinkov Society	Pessie Burd, California
Sam Darman, Miami	Bob and Shirley Shpigel
Shloyme Hofrichter, Baltimore	Mr. and Mrs. Laskin
Ezra Gorenshteyn, Baltimore	Sadie Horovitz
Anna Kusher	Mr. and Mrs. Khayim Davidovich, Hazleton

Liza Zelikman

Mr. and Mrs. Pini Brill

Mrs. Akivis

H. Stoyr (or Stein)

Dr. Buchalter

Velvl Laskin

H. Toker

Shimen Rozental

Sam Hershman

Volf Brothers, Canada

Mr. and Mrs. Smith

Mrs. Celia Feld, Philadelphia

Elka Berger, may she rest in peace

Dovid–Johann Kirshners

Mr. and Mrs. Landau

(Cookie Gladshteyn)

Eva Nesis (wife of Velvl Nesis, Canada)

N. Taytlbaum, Canada

Gitl Buchalter

Abe and Rachel Rapoport

Mr. and Mrs. Ben Shilley

Moyshe Garber and wife

Sam Zaltzman

Meir Mandelblit, Philadelphia

Abe Schwartz

Irving Fink

Khane Heshl Levine, Reb Moyshele's daughter

Mrs. An. Vinakur

Mrs. Rose Silverman

Jack Hofman

Berish Vaysberg (may he rest in peace)

Pessie Saliternik

Yisro'el and Khane Roytburd and son Moyshe

Levi Greenberg

Irving Federman

Avrom Shenkman, Philadelphia

Helen Klesik

Frida Vaysberg

Marsitshizever, Baltimore

Hershl Vaserman

Hershl Rapoport

Melvin Gaferman

Becky Shapiro

[Page 237]

Yoysef Krantz

Sam Buchalter

Moyshe Grinman and son

Dovid Fuks

Sylvia Shafi (Polenski)

Benny Zaltzman

Dave Fisher

Gary Graferman

Max Frayfeld

Harry Diamond

Lyuba Dyechtayarova, California

Sam Volfbayn

Mrs. Ziman

Levi Berger, Canada

Fania Trachtenberg

Sam Greenberg

Sid Klurfeld

Philip Kestman

Sam Lesser

Esther Zayontshik, Philadelphia

Sonia Zem, Peretz Gelman's daughter

Louis Blecher (may he rest in peace)

Michael Katz

N. Pearl, sister of Rokhl Rapoport   Esther Yashever, Philadelphia

Weinstein Funeral, Director

President of the Zinkov Society: Dovid Fuks

Chairman of Memorial Committee: Moyshe Grinman

Secretaries of the Committee: Yisro'el Roytburd, Moyshe Garber

The Memorial was unveiled on the 20th anniversary memorial ceremony, June 23, 1964.

Translator's Footnote:

1. I have transliterated many of these names rather than attempting to reconstruct their English versions.

[Page 238]

List of Donors to the Zinkov Memorial Book
Translated by Yael Chaver

In Israel[1]

Moshe Averbukh, *moshav* Havatzelet

Amnon Ben David (Blinder), Netanya

Yosef Ben David (Blinder), Netanya

Shlomo Ben David (Blinder), Netanya

Yisra'el Ben Shacher (Shvartzman), Haifa

Shlomo Goldenberg, Haifa

Yekhiel Grabelski, son of Fanny Grabelski–Yoshpeh (may her memory be for a blessing), Jerusalem

Yisra'el and Khaya Vekselman, Tel Aviv

Ahuva Vartsman, wife of Zvi (Hershl) Vartsman

Henikh Vartsman, Tel Aviv

Batya Vartsman, wife of Yosef Vartsman (may his memory be for a blessing), Tel Aviv

Moshe Yoshpeh, *moshav* Kfar Hess

Nakhum Yoshpeh, Eilat

Khava Lakhterman, wife of Mati–Tsirls (may he rest in peace), Tel Aviv

Aharon Nesis, Haifa

Avraham Segal, *moshav* Kfar Hogla

Menachem Saliternik, Holon

Buni Federman, Tel Aviv

Pearl Feldman (may she rest in peace), wife of David the carpenter, Tel Aviv

Khanokh Frenkel, Tel Aviv

Yitzchak Frenkel, Haifa

Netanel Frenkel, Haifa

Shmuel Koren, *moshav* Neta'im

Zev and Mara Vartsman, Tel Aviv

Rachel Zelikman, Tel Aviv

Ya'akov Zaltzman, Haifa

Fishl Zaltzman, Haifa

Yosef Yoshpeh, Jerusalem

In the U.S. and Other Countries

Dr. Hayman Buchalter

Moyshe Buchalter

Polin Burd, Los Angeles

Pini Bril

Moyshe Garber

Ezra Gornshteyn, Baltimore

[Page 239]

Sam Darman, Miami

Sam Hauptman

Ezri Halen, Baltimore

Ya'akov Hofman

Paul Halen, Baltimore

Sadie Horovitz

Sam Hershman

D. A. Volf, Canada

Volf brothers, Canada

Sam Volfbayn

Volfshaut

Hershl Vaserman

Chapel, Vinsteyn

Shloyme Vaysberg, Los Angeles

Esther Zayentshik, Philadelphia

Lina Zelikman

H. Toker

N. Tenenboym, Canada

Rivka Katz, Philadelphia

Beni Laskin

Gitl Malin, Pittsburgh

Haskel, Monuments

Reuven Rozental, Haifa

Masha Raydman, wife of Ya'acov (may his memory be for a blessing), Tel Aviv

Tova Shtaynbas, kibbutz Tel–Yosef

Yeshaya Shtaynbas, *moshav* Kfar Vitkin

Brayne Shlayer–Segal, Hadera

Peysi Gorenshteyn, Baltimore

Dave Greenburg

Sam Greenberg

Yoysef Grinman

Moyshe Grinman

Davidovich family, Hazleton

Cantor Avrom Fligman

Cantor Benjamin Fligman

Izi Federman

Itsi Federman

Celia Feld, Philadelphia

Rivka Katz

Henny Kusher

Jack Kipnis

Khayele (Helen) Klasik

Sid Klurfeld

Kesman brothers

Vili Kesman

Krants

Dovid Kreytshmar

Shimen Rozental

Avrom Rapoport

Mrs. Rubinsteyn

Yisro'el Roytburd

Milton Roytburd

Sylvia Shapi

J. J. Shvarts, Philadelphia

Heyb Shvarts

Vayzner and Fefer, Monuments

Vays, Monuments

Sprang, Monuments

Chapel, Midwood

Phil Maidanik, Gravestones

Eva Nesis, Canada

Pessie Salant (Saliternik)

Esther Zayn (Zayontshik)

Esther Silver

Sarah Postel (Shpialter)

Dovid Fuks

Mrs. L. Shvarts

Ben Shiley

Avrom Shenkelman, Philadelphia

Ida Sherman, Los Angeles

Sore Shpialter

Sima Shraybman

"Haskel Monuments"

"Vays Monuments"

"West End Chapel"

"Sprang Monuments"

"Shvarts Real Estate"[2]

Translator's Footnotes:

1. These names have been translated from the Hebrew.

2. Many of the names in the list are duplicated or near–duplicated.

English Section
Transcribed by Genia Hollander

[Page 3]

Foreword
The Committee

We have written these chapters in English especially for our American children and grandchildren so that they too should know at least something about the horrible Holocaust in which a third of our people, (4 million) were systematically slaughtered in cold blood under the most gruesome and barbaric circumstances.

We also want our children to know that when our people, men, women and children were being annihilated in the thousands and millions, no one in the entire civilized world came out with a protest. No one raised a finger to do something about it.

We also want our children to know where their parents and grandparents came from and how they lived in their native hometowns and villages for many generations. We don't pretend to be literary experts; neither does this small memorial book claim any literary value.

We just tried to the best of our knowledge and ability to put in print our boundless sorrow and bereavement. This we did with every fibre of our hearts and souls.

We only hope that our effort will not be in vail – which our message will penetrate deep into the souls and hearts of our young generation, even to some older brothers and sisters who still do not grasp the full scope of the greatest tragedy that had ever befallen the martyred Jewish people.

———

[Page 4 - English] [Page 226 - Yiddish]

Protest and Condemnation
Written and delivered by Morris Garber

Eulogy at the unveiling of the Monument dedicated to the memory of our four thousand martyrs who were mercilessly massacred by the most vicious, brutal and beastly Nazi cannibals in the years of 1942-1943.

Every page of our long history of martyrdom is saturated with rivers of blood and oceans of tears.

For thousands of years, we have been the scapegoat for every ruling tyrant. We have always been the lightning rod to divert the wrath of the suffering people against their grafting, plundering, cruel rules who tried to cover up their infamous deeds by accusing the Jewish people of every crime imaginable and unimaginable.

Since the early medieval days and to this day, pogroms, frame-ups, and cruel persecution had all one pattern and one purpose – to use it as a smoke screen; to blind and enrage the ignorant masses with the venomous poison of Anti-Semitism and animal Jew-hating.

There were many cruel mass-murderers as far as history can record during which the Jewish people paid more than their share of blood and suffering.

There were Attila, Genghis Khan, the crusades, the Spanish inquisition with the insane and sadistic grand inquisitor – high priest Torquemada and many others.

Even the mass slaughters of our people by Chmelnitski and Petlura were mere child-play in comparison with the blood-chilling Holocaust of the "cultured" people. "Master Race" is what they called themselves – all doctors, crystal pure Arians, the top cream of the entire human race. Be damned forever and ever you devils-cutthroats, cold-blooded murdering demons.

And the entire civilized world, bragging so proudly of democracy, justice and human compassion, closed their eyes, stuffed up their ears, turned their faces to the wall and refused to hear the heart-tending cry that was coming from the vermin-infested slaughter houses – murder factories, better known as concentration camps!

[Page 5]

They refused to see the outstretched emaciated, convulsive hands of innocent Jewish men, women and children who, in their last agony were being driven to the gas chambers and crematories, pleading and begging: "Help! Please help us!!!"

But help did not come and when it did, it was too late – much too late The Hitler "supermen" had carried out their outrageous and atrocious assignment with great zeal and with accursed German accuracy – far more diligently than was expected even by their insane masters.

Too late – the world sobered up and realized that by being indifferent and pretending not to see and not to hear or care and, in some cases, even giving direct assistance, they were to blame for letting this Hitler monstrosity come into absolute and final power. This Frankenstein demon fell upon his creators with all the might of his mechanised panzer war machine and hordes of his well-trained and well-schooled obedient robots in the art of destruction and mass-murder. The "Blitz" was on.

The mask was off – the objectives of this horrible brown plague became clear to the panicked and bewildered world.

They set out to subjugate and enslave the entire world – to plunder and rob; to kill and kill and kill and above all to exterminate completely the entire Jewish race.

And how dangerously close they came to achieving this satanic plan of theirs? Just stop and think what hell on earth this world of ours would have been had they, God forbid, succeeded!

There was a time when this snake pit of dangerous Hitler gang of psychopaths could have been cleaned out with one army regiment and the allies still had the power to do it, but they didn't

We don't know whether it was just criminal negligence or a case of choosing the lesser evil. It was a boomerang that was aimed at the "worse" evil but it came back with a terrific impact and hit furiously those who hurled out this boomerang.

So the prophecy of Professor Firster (A German) came true after all. When this German pacifist warned the leading diplomats of the free world and proved to them with undeniable documentary, evidence that the worst Calamity the world had ever seen was imminent; when he pleaded with them to take action before it would be too late, they turned a deaf ear and ignored his warnings. He then told them: "If you refuse to use your eyes now and see, you will use them to weep". We all remember Churchill's famous words: "Blood, sweat, toll and tears".

Yes, the whole world bled, wept, and paid a horrible price for the near-sightedness and stupidity of their leaders and the Jewish people paid far, far more than anyone else.

[Page 6]

When the blueprint for the complete annihilation and obliteration of the Jewish people was already in the files of Nuremburg – waiting to be carried out – Chamberlain flew with his umbrella under his arm to appease the mad and arrogant leaders of the "Master Race".

There he sold out England's best friend and ally – Czechoslovakia – and when he returned he proudly waived his worthless piece of paper promising the world peace for a long time to come.

We all know how long this "peace" lasted.

Now the world "Munich" became a synonym to shameful political and diplomatic betrayal and will remain so forever for posterity to ponder.

What hurts the most is how fast the world had forgotten and what hurts more painfully is that a great many Jews do not want to remember; some even try under all kinds of pretences, to appear as apologists for the German blood orgies.

Yes! You rotten and ugly murderous hearts are still the same. Quite often, we are told to forgive and forget – "let bygones be bygones".

We can't stop others but how can we forgive and how can we forget? Is it possible to forget such a horrible nightmare? Is it possible to forgive such monstrous crimes by man against man?

Oh no! We will never forgive and never forget.

Instead of subduing, instead of keeping the mad dogs on chains for the safety of the rest of humanity, the Germans were put on their feet in a hurry and were being catered by the East and West alike.

Thousands of sadistic Nazi murderers are in high government positions, they are well paid and lead a luxurious and comfortable life and remain unpunished as though nothing happened.

Too often, we hear already alarming reports that here and there the hideous Nazi snake is raising its ugly head again and hissing with hate and poison like in the good old times.

Swastikas on the walls of Synagogues and bombs are a too frequent occurrence and the German scientists working feverishly to help Nasser realize his dream of destroying Israel; arrogant hoodlums parade openly in Nazi uniforms displaying the hated swastika spider on the streets of free America They even have already a Nazi fascist international and a world-wide secret underground too! They don't rest and never give up their dream of completing Hitler's satanic aspirations.

Therefore, we too must always be alert and on guard to see and watch that the evil dreams of the little yet dangerous Hitlers can never come to pass again.

What happened to you, dear old hometown of ours? What did the modern blond Huns do to you? A heap of rubble, charred ruins and complete devastation. That is how the crazed German vandals and their partners in crime – the local criminal Ukrainians, wiped you off the face of the earth.

[Page 7]

And you, dear beloved parents, sisters, brothers, aunts, uncles, cousins and other relatives? And you, dear neighbours and dear old friends of our younger years? Where are you and how did you meet your bitter end? In which gas chamber did the German barbarians rob you of your last breath of life? In which infernal crematorium did they burn and fry your starved, emaciated and tortured bodies?

Which of their cursed fields did they fertilize with the ashes of your bones? Or, did they cut you down with machinegun fire and dead or half-dead, you fell into the mass-graves, which they forced you to dig with your own hands? Perhaps there are no graves at all? Certainly, there are no tombstones on you graves as it is and was and will always be the custom and ritual of all humans.

Therefore, we – the Zinkover survivors, decided to erect a symbolic tombstone on this symbolic grave of yours. May your tortured souls find rest and peace right here on Zinkover soil among all the Zinkover who found their eternal home here.

Today, we stand here with heads bowed and aching hearts. We mourn your unnatural and inhuman tragic death. With your tears, we consecrate this holy piece of land and this monument, which we dedicate to your eternal memory.

From today on, this memorial will be the symbol of all that was so dear to our hearts and now it is no more and will never, ever be again.

May this monument stay here high and proud for many centuries. May it always remind us and our children and our children's children of the horrible slaughter, of the gruesome brown Nazi regime, in which six million of our innocent Jewish brothers and sisters, old and young were exterminated in cold blood, brutally and systematically, according to plan and pattern worked out and carried out thoroughly by the Germans and their eager partners in crime – the criminal elements among the Poles and Ukrainians.

Let us give our solemn promise that every year we will gather around this monument to observe the Yahrzeit of our holy martyrs, to mourn and to weep and to say Kaddish for their souls.

Sunday, June 23rd, 1963.

[Page 8]

Zinkov

Morris Garber

Far, far away across the ocean, somewhere in the Russian Ukraine stood our poor little native Jewish town – Zinkov.

Hundreds of years, it had stood there. Generation after generation came and passed on to make room for new generations, like waves after waves on the surfs of the ocean.

It was a hard life under the cruel despotic Czars and their almighty "tchinovnicks" (officials). Their humiliating, degrading laws and edicts of oppression and limitations weighted down heavily on our shoulders. We were reduced to the level of second-class citizens and as such, we could not move around freely in the country. A great number of areas and cities were completely taboo for us. We had to live where we were told to – not where we wanted. We always lived in fear of pogroms and persecutions.

Education in the broad sense of the word was denied to us (with some exceptions here and there). The means and ways of making a living were limited to petty trading and domestic artisanship such as; tailors, shoemakers, smiths, tinsmith, coopers, watchmakers, furniture makers and some other. We were completely excluded from agriculture and heavier industries. Under these oppressive conditions, making a living even a poor and modest living was an eternal hard and difficult struggle.

Yet, the Jewish parents saw to it that their children should get the traditional Jewish learning and upbringing even if it had to be at the expense of their daily piece of bread. Education of children, especially boys, was a must and above all other necessities of life.

Still, in some miraculous way, our small town managed to produce a fine intellectual, idealistic youth, great religious scholars and fine and honest workers and tradesmen.

The inherent hunger for knowledge and education was the driving force for self-education and then the hard-acquired, precious knowledge was passed on to

[Page 9]

others in the way of private tutoring. (A more detailed and vivid account of the hardships and obstacles that Jewish young people were confronted with in their quest for learning and acquiring a career, is in my chapter "Externs").

Life in these small communities was not always that monotonous and colourless. There were three times when rays of sunshine broke through the dark, dreary clouds and brought a little joy and spiritual uplifting.

There were the holy Sabbaths and gay and solemn holidays that brought peace and tranquillity into every Jewish home and relaxation into the heart and soul of every Jew.

Now and then, young people got married and every wedding was a special event for the entire village. The musicians walking ahead of the bride and groom with their parents and guests and almost the entire populace of the town following at a respectable distance. They all marched slowly over the streets under the sound of music until they came to the old and huge shul in front of which, under open sky, the ceremony was performed under a portable canopy called the "chupah".

Here I must stop and dedicate a few lines to the memory of this shul which I mentioned above.

It was a tremendous and massive structure of the very old school of architecture. The most amazing feature of it was the Holy Arc – "Aron-Kodesh". It extended from the floor to the ceiling at a height of at least three stories. The artistic work of the arc is hard to describe. The carving and gilding of all the symbolic birds and animals and other figures was just breath taking.

I always wondered as to how old this temple was; who were the people who financed such an expensive undertaking and who were the artists that had erected this phenomenal wonder. My curiosity was never satisfied because even the oldest people of our town did not know.

Once, on the evening of "Kol-Nidre", 32 women were trampled to death in this shul because of a false fire alarm.

Now there is not a trace left of this remarkable landmark. The barbaric German vandals razed it to the ground on which it stood from times unmemorable.

The youth of our town were organized in a number of political and cultural groups such as singing, dramatics and others. Traveling actors used to come in at times and put on shows. Acrobats used to perform on the streets with us kids following them around all day long. Our local dramatic club used to put on a play, once in a while, to ring a little light into the not very bright life of the Zinkover inhabitants.

The serene beauty of the landscapes surrounding our poor little town was somethings words fail to describe.

[Page 10]

On one side of our town there were green hills rolling down to a most beautiful and picturesque valley with a winding river in the centre of it. On both sides of the river and as far as the eye could see were scattered a number of peasant villages. The little colourful huts could hardly be seen in the setting of their orchards and gardens. Quite often, artist-painters would come to put this beauty of nature on to canvas.

On the other side of our town, endless stretch of wheat fields fringed on the far horizons with blue-green forests. When harvest time cane and the wheat was ready for reaping, the fields looked like a sea of gold waving under the touch of the slightest breeze.

Over these hills and fields, the Jewish families of Zinkov used to come out in the summer Saturdays at sundown dressed in their best fineries (as little as they had) to walk and promenade for show and pleasure, to breathe in the fresh aromatic air and to feast their eyes upon God's majestic world.

It was a real spiritual treat to watch the awe-inspiring beauty of the setting sun beyond those green hills, bidding farewell with the last reflection of a pinkish-golden horizon and spreading long shooting shadows of dusk. Slowly and gradually, as if reluctantly, the final reflection of the sun was disappearing beyond the hills on to the other side of the valley. It was getting dimmer and dimmer until the entire valley vanished in a shroud of darkness. Here and there, a flicker of a light from a peasant hut broke through the darkness and went out again.

A soothing and peaceful silence descended on earth as if Gold himself and all his creation retired to rest in peace. Only the tireless croaking of the frogs, the chirping of the crickets and the rhythmic rush of water over the milldam sounded like a symphonic accompaniment in harmony with this calm and tranquil evening.

The older people had left. Only we, a small group of boys and girls, (like todays' teenagers) lingered on. We stretched out on our backs feeling the cool fragrance of the grass. Up above, we could see the dark and almost black cupola of the sky densely studded with bright, shiny, blinking and winking stars.

At times, we would sit in a circle talking, joking and flirting with the girls. Then we would start to sing happy songs, sad songs, nostalgic songs of love and hope, songs of golden youth and dreams. It was almost blasphemy to break this magic silence with the dissonance of our singing.

In moments like these, we were completely oblivious of the trials and tribulations that most of our parents had to face in order to provide for their families even the most meagre necessities of life.

We refused to face the cold realistic facts that we were helpless and useless idlers – a heavy burden on the backs of our fathers and mothers. Although we were at the prime of our years and physical maturity, there was no prospect for us to do anything constructive to enable us to stand on our feet and on solid ground. Agriculture was forbidden; civil service was emphatically denied; there were no industries of any kind and even if there had been, Jewish workers would most certainly have been rejected. The future looked grim and hopeless but youth has a power and a charm of its own. It refuses to let you worry about problems such as these; it makes you drink in all the jo, the dreams, the bright hopes of golden mirages and utopian fantasies with no regard for practical reality.

[Page 11]

Little did we know that world-shaking events were around the corner; that threatening dark clouds were gathering on the far horizon; that these clouds would unleash a horrible storm, which would severely shake the foundation of the entire world. Little did we know that soon a horrible, cruel, bloody and devastating war would break out and would put an end to the old values of tradition and morality, to human honesty and compassion.

And so it was the beginning of World War I with all its cruelty, destruction, bloodshed, human suffering, revolutions, counter revolutions and anarchy.

Out of this nightmare emerged two political camps with opposing ideologies locked in a struggle of life and death and bent on destroying each other. There was an uneasy peace for a period of little over twenty years. The violent friction between these two political camps gave birth to the German Hitler-Nazi monstrosity. We will not go into detail about the carnage of the black-brown Nazi plague. I have done this in other chapters of this book

I only want to repeat that it was the most vicious and most brutal foe our people had ever fallen victim to in all our long history of persecution and martyrdom.

World War I was horrible and gruesome enough and the events that followed were still worse – much worse. But, after it had simmered down, we, the more fortunate, had a chance at least to run – to emigrate to all corners of the world. We managed to escape to the United States, Canada, Argentina, Brazil, Palestine and many other countries wherever we were given asylum.

Our poor and unfortunate dear ones who were left behind did not have that chance. When they had fallen into the vice of the beastly German murdering executioners, there was no way of escape, like the fly that had fallen into the web of the lurking spider.

With inhuman and merciless brutality, the bloodthirsty Nazi barbarians uprooted all that was Jewish, murdering, slaughtering, burning, ravaging and devastating the entire European Jewish community leaving death and ruin in their wake.

So lived and so died our holy martyrs. So lived and so died our dear old hometown of Zinkov.

[Page 12]

Externiks

Morris Garber

Our thorny path towards education and a career under the Tsarist regime in the years long gone by.

Dedicated especially to our children and grandchildren of school age.

In a previous chapter, I already gave a general picture of our burning hunger for learning and knowledge and the insurmountable hardships and obstacles that were put in our way. The policy of the Tsarist regime was to keep its vas masses in primitive darkness and ignorance. They were afraid to educate the people. An educated people might start seeing things in a different light and they might present a dangerous threat to their absolute rulers. That is why schools were so few and rare.

Our town of Zinkov was larger and more progressive than the other small Jewish communities nearby. Therefore, we were fortunate to have had a six-grade government school, which was named after its principal. It was known as "Sumnie-witche's School" (Shkola).

Not too many of our Jewish children were lucky enough to have become students of this school. The graduates of this "temple" of learning were treated like real cultured intellectuals, receiving their due respect amid people who, in their great majority, were ignorant and illiterate. In reality, these graduates knew much less than the children who came out of our elementary grammar schools. So goes the law of relativity. People and things can look different and have contradictory values in different times and places.

I also mentioned before that the task of Jewish religious education was taken care of by Rabbis (Melamdim) and their "Cheders", and a "Talmud Torah", if a community was lucky enough to have one, and by self-taught young scholars in the houses of prayer.

The crucial problem, however, had to be met by those Jewish youths who were striving for a higher, worldly education or those whose ambition it was to elevate themselves above the average level and to make a place for themselves in those few and limited professions to which only a couple of narrow avenues were still open.

The pharmaceutical and dental professions along with some less impressive and less inviting fields of endeavour were still open to the Jewish youths (because there were very few Gentile aspirants in this field).

[Page 13]

In order to be admitted into these professions, a certain degree of education was required: for druggists assistants, four years and for dentists, six years of High School. The Russian gymnasium was an eight-year or eight class-school. Of course, there were no gymnasiums in our small town. The only one that really counted was the one in the capital of our province – Kamenetz-Podolsk, 60 miles away from our Zinkov. So we had to study and study hard and then go to Kamenetz to take the exam. Because we were students outside of a school, we were called: "Externs or Externiki", which means outsiders, just as a medical student who is practicing his profession inside a hospital is called an "intern".

It took months and years of hard, nerve-wracking and backbreaking labour. We had to have the endurance, patience and calm of a saint in order to keep it up. The closer we came to the tests, the harder we worked, the less we slept giving up every little pleasure and every bit of freedom and relaxation which are a part of a growing adolescent.

We stayed up nights in groups of two and three making sure that each would keep the other from falling asleep. We kept washing our eyes with cold water to stay awake. Only when our brains became numb and refused to absorb any more cramming did we then stop for a couple of hours sleep.

We had to be in the city of Kamenetz at least six weeks prior to the date set for the exams. It was important to engage the help of a local and experienced teacher in order to make sure that we were ready to face the ordeal of the tests. Again, we studied day and night and lived on a starvation diet. Most of us came from not too wealthy families. The children of the richer families did not have to be "externs". They were inside the schools not outside.

Finally, the day came, or rather the week of judgement. Scared and with pounding hearts we entered the holy sanctuary of learning – the huge auditorium was brightly illuminated with row after row of separate tables. At each table were two or three teachers for every required subject the imposing uniforms of the teachers scared us and confused us even more.

It was a known fact that the teachers, those high priests of education, disliked us very much. Even Christian externs and more so the Jewish ones. It was their belief that no extern, however brilliant, could ever equal an inside student. Armed with this dogma and prejudice, it was no wonder that they hardly ever passed an extern the first time. Some of us got discouraged and gave up. But the more stubborn and persistent ones tried over and over again until they finally made it. These adolescents were like the salmon fish who, by some mystery of nature, work their way against the strong current of rivers (mostly Columbia River) towards a certain destination. They make attempt after attempt until they succeed or perish in their attempt. They never stop and never turn back. That is exactly how it was with our externs. Some did not have the will and stamina, or the financial means to continue. However, some were determined to reach their goal at all cost, even to the degree of giving up their faith in order to be admitted to the universities and medical or law schools. Some of these converts became famous doctors, lawyers, engineers and professors. However, at such a terrible price!

[Page 14]

That is why, dear children of ours, I have written this chapter especially for you so that you should draw a parallel and realize how lucky and how blessed you are to find at your disposal a network of fine schools and capable teachers where there are no "extern". Here you do not have to dream to be admitted to a school but it is the law of the land that you must attend a school and your parents are responsible if you do not. Here you do not have to sell your faith for a diploma of any profession. It is there, ready and waiting for you if only have the desire and the ambition and the will to reach out for it.

So let the picture of your parents and grandparents struggle for a bit of education always be engraved in your mind and in front of your eyes to stimulate you, to encourage you in your drive towards a profession of any kind or in industry or commerce.

This, I believe, is the finest legacy we have to leave you for now and after we will be gone into the far beyond.

[Page 15]

In Memoriam

Hyman Davidowitz

With heartfelt gratitude to Rose Davidowitz and her children for their most generous contribution towards the printing of this Memorial Book.

Brother Hyman Davidowitz was a good-standing member of our society for many years. Although he lived far away from New York, he was in close contact with our Fraternal Organization and generously contributed to every charitable cause that our society sponsored.

He carried in his heart an undying and nostalgic longing for his old hometown of Zinkov where a great number of his relatives and friends perished in the most vicious and most barbaric Nazi Holocaust.

In the city of Hazelton, Pa., where he lived with his family and carried on his prosperous business for more than two decades, he won for himself prominence, respect and admiration by his outstanding deeds of philanthropy.

To paraphrase the famous words of our late President J.F. Kennedy, he never asked what the society could do for him but he gladly and willingly did all he could for society and all of its activities. Hyman Davidowitz's deeds of charity and social activities are so many that it would take pages to tell all about them in detail. We will, therefore, limit ourselves to a few of the most important ones:

Our late brother Davidowitz and his family bought the site and contributed a great deal towards building a camp for children and adults. As a gesture of gratitude for their magnificent accomplishment, the people of Hazelton decided to name it "Camp Davidowitz".

The concluding words of the dedication speech were: "We are proud to fly the banner bearing the name of the camp that they have presented to our Centre. We hail Camp Davidowitz and salute our benefactors".

It was again our Hymie who broke the ground and helped erect the Jewish Community Centre of Hazelton, Pa., of which he remained President to his last day.

His generous support to the local hospital was well known.

[Page 16]

He never turned back anyone who came to him for help – Jew or Gentile.

Hyman was the regional director of the U.J.A.

Mr. Morris Rothenberg, the National Chairman of U.J.A. writes in a personal letter to Mr. Davidowitz, among other glowing words of praise, the following: "Your inspiring leadership was something that cannot be forgotten". (At the Reading, Pa. regional meeting alongside Eddie Cantor).

We are proud to recount all these wonderful achievements of a descendant from our old and little town of Zinkov.

Mrs. Davidowitz already continues the great work of her beloved husband. She is a tireless worker well known in her own right.

By starting this book with a considerably generous contribution, the Davidowitz family paid the highest tribute to the memory of their husband and father.

We honour his memory.

SURNAME INDEX

www.ingramcontent.com/pod-product-compliance
Lightning Source LLC
Chambersburg PA
CBHW050410110426
42812CB00006BA/1851